THE PROFESSIONALIZATION OF HISTORY
IN ENGLISH CANADA

DONALD WRIGHT

The Professionalization of History in English Canada

UNIVERSITY OF TORONTO PRESS
Toronto Buffalo London

ISBN 0-8020-3928-6

Printed on acid-free paper

Library and Archives Canada Cataloguing in Publication

Wright, Donald A., 1965–
The professionalization of history in English Canada / Donald Wright.

Includes bibliographical references and index.
ISBN 0-8020-3928-6

1. Historians – Canada – History – 20th century.   2. History – Study and
teaching (Higher) – Canada – History – 20th century.   3. Historiography –
Canada – History – 20th century.   I. Title.

EC149.W73 2005   907'.2'071   C2004-905980-7

University of Toronto Press acknowledges the financial assistance to
its publishing program of the Canada Council for the Arts and the
Ontario Arts Council.

University of Toronto Press acknowledges the financial support for
its publishing activities of the Government of Canada through the
Book Publishing Industry Development Program (BPIDP).

This book has been published with the help of a grant from the
Canadian Federation for the Humanities and Social Sciences, through the
Aid to Scholarly Publications Programme, using funds provided by the
Social Sciences and Humanities Research Council of Canada.

For Harriet and Frances

Contents

Acknowledgments

This book, which began as a thesis at the University of Ottawa, could not have been completed without the support of my supervisor, Dr Michael Behiels. It is to his patience, encouragement, and insights that I owe my greatest debt. I would like to thank Dr Donald Davis as well. His interest in the project from the beginning went beyond the call of duty. Dr Thomas Bender at New York University deserves thanks for supervising my research on American philanthropy and the development of the social sciences in Canada in the pre-Canada Council era.

Throughout the research stage, I was assisted by several archivists: Harold Averill, University of Toronto Archives; Cheryl Avery, Univer- sity of Saskatchewan Archives; Tina Bradford, Dalhousie University Archives; Betty Brock, Stanstead Historical Society Archives; Gordon Burr, McGill University Archives; Judith Colwell, Canadian Baptist Archives, McMaster Divinity College; Cheryl Ennals, Mount Allison University Archives; Mary Flagg, University of New Brunswick Archives; George Henderson, Queen's University Archives; John Lutman, J.J. Talman Regional Collection, University of Western Ontario; Pamela Miller, McCord Museum Archives; Sue Young Park, Columbia University, Rare Book and Manuscript Library; Carl Spadoni, William Ready Division, Archives and Research Collections, McMaster University; Lewis Stubbs, University of Manitoba Archives; Patricia Townsend, Acadia University Archives; Richard Virr, Department of Rare Books and Special Collections, McGill University; and Anke Voss Hubbard, Rockefeller Archives Center.

Of course, the research for this project would not have been possible without financial assistance in the form of graduate scholarships and research grants. These included: a Fulbright Scholarship (1998), a Rockefeller Archives Center Research Grant (1997), a Social Sciences and Humanities Research Council Doctoral Fellowship (1996–7), the Sir John A. Macdonald Graduate Fellowship in Canadian History (1994–6), a University of Ottawa Excellence Scholarship (1994–8), and a University of Ottawa Research Scholarship (1993–4).

Along the way, several individuals assisted me in the form of counsel, criticism, and, at one point, a UNB library card, despite my lack of a UNB affiliation. In alphabetical order, they are Sheila Andrew, Rusty Bittermann, Ramsay Cook, Eric Damer, Ramsay Derry, Ken Dewar, David Frank, Chad Gaffield, Ralph Guentzel, Ged Martin, Margaret McCallum, Brian McKillop, Duncan Meikle, Sergio Piccinin, Alison Prentice, Donald Smith, and Gillian Thompson.

At the University of Ottawa, I was fortunate to be surrounded by a supportive cast of fellow graduate students. Thanks to David Calverly, Steve High, Lise Legault, Jo-Anne McCutcheon, and David Moorman. A special thanks to David and Jennifer Hartman.

The following individuals generously allowed me to interview them: Margaret Banks, J.M.S. Careless, Jill Ker Conway, David Farr, Sylvia Van Kirk, Peter Waite, the late W.J. Eccles, the late James A. Gibson, and the late Irene Spry. On short notice and with good cheer, Dr Banks also read the final manuscript from beginning to end. Daniel Samson and David Bright read portions of the final manuscript.

I would like to thank the Canadian Historical Association for its permission to reprint in chapter 3 portions of my booklet *The Canadian Historical Association: A History* (Ottawa, 2003). Chapter 5 first appeared as 'Gender and the Professionalization of History in English Canada before 1960,' *Canadian Historical Review* 81, 1 (2000). It is reprinted by permission of University of Toronto Press Incorporated.

Len Husband, Canadian history editor at the University of Toronto Press, proved enormously helpful in transforming the dissertation into a manuscript and, in turn, guiding the manuscript through the review process. The anonymous reviewers were similarly helpful. Their criticisms and suggestions have made this a shorter and sharper book.

Finally, I want to acknowledge the moral and financial support of my parents, Jack Wright and Donnie Wright. If they have not always understood my choices, they have always supported them.

Joanne Wright deserves many thanks not only for enduring endless ramblings about the historical profession, but for adding many insights along the way.

Of course, no one listed above is responsible for any errors of fact and/or interpretation in what follows.

THE PROFESSIONALIZATION OF HISTORY
IN ENGLISH CANADA

Introduction

This book studies the professionalization of history in English Canada from the late nineteenth century to the mid-twentieth century.[1] During this period history became a profession, something one did for a living; in the 1880s and 1890s universities began to appoint men to teach history. In 1896 Toronto's George Wrong founded the *Review of Historical Publications Relating to Canada*, an annual publication that provided a forum for critical reviews. Following the First World War, the pace of change quickened: in 1920 the *Review of Historical Publications Relating to Canada* became the *Canadian Historical Review*; two years later, the Historic Landmarks Association, a group dedicated to the preservation of historic landmarks, became the Canadian Historical Association (CHA); and the Public Archives of Canada, located in Ottawa, became the site of annual summer pilgrimages for historians from across the country. With the assistance of American philanthropy, during the 1930s two multi-volume series, the Frontiers of Settlement Series and the Canadian-American relations series, were published. In addition to these tangible markers of history's professionalization – the appointment of professors and later the creation of history departments, the founding of the CHA, the publication of the Canadian-American relations series – in the first half of the twentieth century historians cultivated expertise, authority, and status and marked boundaries between who could and who could not be a historian.

Ironically, historians have shown little interest in the history of their profession. Carl Berger studied the writing of Canadian history, not the historical profession. William Duncan Meikle focused on one individual, George Wrong; Robert Bothwell wrote about the history of one department; and Paul Phillips examined the teaching and writing of

British history in English Canada.[2] In each work the professionalization of history is either assumed or plotted as an inevitable rise. Phillips, for example, referred to the 'birth of a discipline' and 'the rising profession.'

What does it mean to say that history professionalized? Two basic approaches dominate the study of professions and professionalization. In the first approach the characteristics that, taken together, constitute a profession are stressed, including prolonged training in a definable body of knowledge, a credential system, a code of ethics, self-government, and legislated access to a particular labour market. Professionalization, then, refers to the acquisition of these characteristics over time. The second approach does not deny or negate the first approach; rather, it stresses the power and control that professions possess and the monopolies that they enjoy. A profession promises privileged access to financial and social rewards for its members. Historically, professionalization has been 'a process by which producers of special services sought to constitute and control a market for their expertise'; it has been a 'collective assertion of upward social mobility.'[3] Stated crudely, professions have been seen as conspiracies to make more money. Feminist scholars would agree, but they would add that if professions were conspiracies to make more money, they were conspiracies to make more money for men. Gender was not incidental to professional projects; it was central. Drawing on gendered assumptions about authority and knowledge, professions garnered and defended economic and social privilege for men.[4]

This book draws on both approaches. In the last decade of the nineteenth century and the first five decades of the twentieth century, history acquired some of the key characteristics of a profession. Of course, the historical profession did not acquire the characteristics of, say, the medical profession; through an elaborate credential system and legislative protection, medical doctors created monopolies in highly defined sectors of the medical labour market. In other words, while only a licensed physician can practise medicine, anyone with an interest in the past can write history. Moreover, historians were never able to translate their expertise into money in the way that doctors proved able to do. Yet history became a profession, and professional historians were full-time experts with prolonged training in a particular body of knowledge. Like other professionals, historians developed a set of common assumptions, questions, methods, and values and built an association to articulate and defend their shared interests. Finally, in an attempt to enhance their status, historians also drew boundaries between what they did as historians and what amateurs did as historians. These boundaries were also gendered: the 'ideal' historian was male.

While drawing on the two basic approaches to the study of professions, I reject the narrative structure of onward and upward movement that characterizes so much of the literature on professions. Even authors who study a particular profession with a critical eye refer to that profession's rise.[5] History did not experience a rise from nothing to something, from darkness to light; rather, the study and practice of history changed. Thomas Bender cautions historians against Whiggism in the writing of intellectual history when he argues that an intellectual community is best studied on its own terms, not in relation to what succeeded it. 'One system, in this way of looking at things, would be replaced by another when the earlier could not work, whether not working was defined socially or intellectually. Instead of a study of a movement from nothing to something, the emergence of modern academic professions represented a reorganization of intellectual culture – from a civic foundation to a professional and academic one.'[6] From this viewpoint, the professionalization of history was not a rising curve but a flat line: one way of organizing intellectual life gave way to another way of organizing intellectual life. Conceiving of the professionalization of history as a flat line as opposed to a rising curve reminds us that what came before professional history was not weak and inferior but simply different. It also draws our attention to the costs, not only the benefits, of professionalization: these costs included the exclusion of women from the practice of professional history and the privatization of history, that is, the transformation of history – at least in its academic incarnation – into a private conversation between experts speaking a technical language.

Why did intellectual life in general and history in particular professionalize? As Canada became a modern, urban, and industrial society in the late nineteenth and early twentieth centuries and as the state expanded in size and function, a demand arose for a different kind of knowledge and the rational application of that knowledge to the intensified and seemingly intractable problems of, for example, poverty, unemployment, and dominion-provincial relations. Moral philosophy and religious knowledge were seen as increasingly irrelevant to the problems that confronted the country. Knowledge must be based on scientific principles and rigorous research, and above all, it must be practical.[7] In this process, universities assumed a leadership role; they would become less centres for the guardianship and transmission of religious values and more centres for the production of 'facts.'[8]

This is not to say that the professionalization of history was a product of modernization. That would be ahistorical. The historical profession unfolded in a particular historical context – the modernization of Canada – but it unfolded on its own terms and in its own ways. Its terms meant that, even as historians sought to make history into a social science, they did not sever history's roots in the older humanistic ideal of the liberal arts.

It is this question, the relationship between fact and value, that lies at centre of the historiographical debate on the emergence of the social sciences in English Canada. In their respective scholarship, S.E.D. Shortt, A.B. McKillop, Ramsay Cook, and Marlene Shore argue that in opposition to the philosophical idealism and theology in nineteenth-century intellectual life, twentieth-century intellectual life – increasingly located in the university – emphasized the empiricism of the new social sciences. Although uneven, this transformation was largely complete by 1920.[9] According to Ramsay Cook, 'The new social science, which gradually replaced the old religiously based moralism, overcame the nineteenth-century crisis of authority that accompanied the questioning of religious certitude. And with the new social science came a new professional leadership, replacing the older religious leadership.'[10] A.B. McKillop observes that between the 1870s and the onset of the Great War, 'the life of the mind shifted in major ways.' As he explains, 'Recognition of the complexity and interdependence of economic and social relations gave rise to questions about the nature and mechanisms of social causation for which traditional Christian teleology had, it seemed, no adequate answers.'[11]

According to Michael Gauvreau, however, social scientists did not operate in a value-free paradigm. Taking Harold Innis as a case study, Gauvreau demonstrates that Canada's leading social scientist between 1920 and 1950 maintained a consistent belief 'that social science was a single, unspecialized, philosophical perspective in which history could elucidate the creative interplay between the physical factors of the environment and the realm of human values and culture.'[12] In other words, there was no divorce between religion and the social sciences, between value and fact. Idealism and empiricism were not mutually exclusive, and facts collected by social scientific methods could be applied to moral ends. McKillop would agree. 'The writings of Harold Innis on the nature and implication of communications,' he wrote in 1979, 'bear the direct marks of their nineteenth-century cultural inheritance.' That inheritance was the moral imperative 'to reconcile inquiry with affirmation.'[13]

This book, therefore, studies the emergence of a historical profession committed to the research ideal embodied in the new social sciences and a historical profession equally committed to questions of human values. Professional historians were not somehow schizoid, nor was theirs a contradictory project. Rather, historians always understood their discipline to be both a social science and a humanity. The Canadian Historical Association was one of the four sponsoring bodies of the Canadian Social Science Research Council in 1940.[14] Three years later, in 1943, historians supported the establishment of the Humanities Research Council of Canada.[15] As A.L. Burt said in 1949, 'Personally, I am opposed to that distinction or that fixing of a gulf between the so-called social sciences and the humanities, and personally, I feel that rather strongly because my subject is always on both sides of the gulf, and in some places we have been cut in two as a result.'[16] As Frank Underhill once argued, those in the university must be prepared to make value judgments and to sound the alarm of moral indignation. After all, he wrote, 'it is hard to see where such public servants can come from except from the university.'[17] At times, one ideal could be stronger than the other – until 1920 history was primarily conceived of as one of the humanities, in the interwar years it was a social science, and in the 1940s it was one of the humanities again – but both visions were always present.

That both visions were present also explains what this book is not about: objectivity. Professions have claimed and will continue to claim objectivity in the attempt to root out and rise above quacks, incompetents, and other competitors. In this sense, objectivity is not only an ideal to be aimed at but also a strategy to be employed. In his monumental work on the American historical profession Peter Novick isolates the 'objectivity question' and studies it over time as both the animating ideal of the profession and as a means to discipline the heretics and keep out the fakes.[18] English-Canadian historians almost never spoke about objectivity, however, because they did not seek a sharp separation of fact and value. In this they were very much a part of the moral imperative running through English-Canadian intellectual life that stressed a balance between enquiry and affirmation, continuity and change, tradition and innovation, the community and the individual.[19]

CHAPTER 1

History as avocation

In the 1880s and 1890s history had a vital and vibrant existence outside the university and only a tentative one inside it. Scores of men and women across English Canada dedicated their leisure time – and in some cases their lives – to collecting, preserving, documenting, and writing the history of their country. By 1900 over twenty historical societies and associations had been founded. Within a decade close to ten more would be created.[1] Because these men and women did not have advanced research degrees and because they did not teach in university history departments, historians have labelled them amateurs.[2] But to qualify the word historian with 'amateur' is ahistorical. After all, according to the contemporary definition of the word historian, these men and women were historians. Scholarly publications, peer review, and careerism barely existed. Whatever else it was – an avocation, a pastime, a hobby, often a passion, sometimes even an obsession – history was not yet a profession. These men and women could not have been historians according to today's definition of the word historian, that is, someone who earns his or her living writing about the past usually, but not always, within the university.

The focus of this chapter is history and historians outside the university in late nineteenth- and early twentieth-century English Canada: William Douw Lighthall and David Ross McCord; the active part played by such women as Janet Carnochan and Jenny Simpson; the creation of a national history association, the Historic Landmarks Association; and the career of William Dawson LeSueur. At the end of the day, these men and women helped to lay the foundations for history's eventual professionalization and contributed to it.

I

W.D. Lighthall loved history. Born in 1857, he graduated from McGill University in 1879 with an honours degree in literature and history; at his convocation he carried away two prizes, the Shakespeare Gold Medal and the Dufferin Prize for Best Historical Essay. After a Grand Tour of Europe, he returned to the McGill law school. Bright, bilingual, and indefatigable, Lighthall became an important and well-known Montreal lawyer, and in 1906 he would be named King's Counsel. Yet his passions lay elsewhere, in poetry, novels, philosophy, and history. Meanwhile, the country confronted an uncertain future. In the 1880s people began to question the very survival of a separate British North America. The execution of Louis Riel, the election of Honoré Mercier, the Jesuit Estates Act, and the Equal Rights Association threatened the already tenuous French-English, Catholic-Protestant relationship. The economy sputtered, talk of annexation filled the air, and Goldwin Smith dared to ask the Canadian question. Fired by the desire to cultivate a Canadian identity, a generation of nationalists instinctively turned to history.[3] Out of the past they would fashion a Canadian nationalism – which for them meant imperialism and the imperial connection – because it was in the past that they would find the stuff of great nations, the stories of heroic men, glorious battles, and great explorations.

Typical of this generation of historians, Lighthall penned romantic, inspirational history, but his historical writing was based on research. His 1889 pamphlet, *An Account of the Battle of Châteauguay*, exemplifies that nineteenth-century approach to history as part romance, part research. In it Lighthall rejects the argument that Britain was to blame for the War of 1812. Rather, he claims, the war stemmed from America's lasting hatred of England, its 'envy of her commerce and prestige' and 'especially [its] scheme for the conquest of Canada.' Within this context, the Battle of Châteauguay was a battle of freedom against repression and a victory for righteousness over injustice. Leading the American charge was the repulsive Major General Wade Hampton: 'self-important, fiery and over-indulgent in drink ... he was one whose chief virtues were not patience and humility.' Leading the Canadian defence was Lieutenant Colonel Charles De Salaberry, 'a perfect type of old French-Canadian military gentry, a stock of man of whom very little remains.' Reflecting history's close relationship to literature, Lighthall fictionalized De Salaberry's reaction to the news of the American advance: '"D— it!" he exclaimed, jumping up from his seat, "Hampton is at Four Corners and I must go and fight him!" and mounting his fine white charger, he dashed away from the door.' Finally, the pamphlet presents a morality lesson. The Battle of Châteauguay tells us that 'we shall always be able to preserve ourselves free in our course of development towards our own idea of a nation.' Lighthall based his account on printed primary documents, secondary sources, and 'local tradition,' that is, the oral accounts that still existed in and around Châteauguay. He weighed evidence, and when he could not determine which fact was the correct fact, he acknowledged his inability 'to obtain the necessary verifications from Ottawa or elsewhere.'[4] Trained as a lawyer, he gathered evidence, marshalled the facts, and presented an argument.

History also underpinned Lighthall's novels.[5] In *The Young Seigneur,* for example, an English-Canadian member of Parliament visits Quebec, where he is to meet a French-Canadian counterpart who will act as his host and guide. Over the course of the novel the reader is introduced to the history of Quebec, the seigneural system, the role of the Catholic Church, and varieties of French-Canadian nationalism.[6] History similarly informed Lighthall's 1908 novel; as its subtitle suggests, *The Master of Life* is *A Romance of the Five Nations and of Prehistoric Montreal.* It is the story of Hochelaga, what Lighthall called 'one of the most fairy-like tales in history,' at the same time as it 'is an attempt to picture the strange ideas of the Red Man's mind, life, and melancholy.'[7]

The border between history and literature in the nineteenth century was an open one while the historical novel was literature's dominant genre.[8] Sir Walter Scott's 1814 novel, *Waverly,* was the first in a very long line of historical novels in the English-speaking world, including British North America and later English Canada. John Richardson's 1832 novel, *Wacousta; or The Prophecy,* deals with Pontiac's armed uprising against the British at Detroit and Michilimackinac. Richardson assures his readers, 'Ours is a tale of sad reality ... Within the bounds of probability have we, therefore, confined ourselves.' His 1840 sequel, *The Canadian Brothers; or The Prophecy Fulfilled,* centres on the War of 1812. William Kirby's *Le Chien d'Or (The Golden Dog): A Legend of Quebec* (1877) and Sir Gilbert Parker's *The Seats of the Mighty* (1896) were enormously popular historical novels, and both were set in French Canada. Historical novels were novels, but they communicated historical truths. They were also essential to articulating loyalism and Toryism, the twin currents of Upper Canadian identity. To a colony and later a young nation, the historical novel promised continuity between past and present.

Dennis Duffy calls this the 'greater truth' of the historical novel, 'that humans in the past had overcome daunting obstacles and that those in the present could do the same.'[9] This was very much Lighthall's project: history offered inspiration, direction, continuity. An unbroken line connected imperial Canada to New France to Hochelaga.

Lighthall's interest in the fate of Hochelaga points to another feature of nineteenth-century intellectual life in English Canada: the absence of hard lines within and between the still very embryonic disciplines. When four or five shallow graves were accidentally unearthed on the western slope of Mount Royal in 1898, Lighthall played the part of anthropologist.[10] He organized an expedition to excavate the site where he hoped to unlock the fate of Hochelaga and its 'mysterious people.' In the end, he discovered the skeletal remains of two others: a young man and a young woman. Over the course of the next thirty years, he would publish some six articles on Hochelaga, its people, and its history.[11] Their significance lies in what they reveal about intellectual life before its professionalization.[12] Disciplines and sub-fields and specialization did not yet exist. The military history of British North America and the history of pre-Contact aboriginal peoples, history and anthropology: Lighthall did not – indeed, could not – make such distinctions. They would occur later. Meanwhile, he ensured the preservation of the skeletal remains; after all, 'they will doubtless be regarded with interest by scholars.'[13]

The question of preservation was an important one to turn-of-the-twentieth-century historians. For David Ross McCord, it constituted an obsession. Born in 1844, McCord belonged to a prominent Anglo-Quebec family.[14] As his father had done, he studied the law and was called to the bar in 1868. For the next fifteen years or so he practised law in Montreal; he also dabbled in municipal politics, serving as an alderman from 1874 to 1883. However, the 1880s signalled a dramatic change – McCord began to collect. From Temple Grove, the family's Mount Royal estate, he cast his collector's net far and wide in an obsessive attempt to build a national museum. Like Lighthall, he was an ardent imperialist and committed romantic. Wolfe, Montcalm, Brock, and Tecumseh: to him all were heroic, galvanic, and inspirational. Yet McCord also displayed a commitment to research and accuracy. In her study of his ethnographic collection, Moira McCaffrey notes that 'McCord sought to document, research and display his collection according to the most advanced scientific guidelines.' He also 'initiated research projects as varied as the determination of geological sources of stone used to make hunting weapons and pipes; the identification of feathers in headdresses; the chemical analysis of glass beads; the meaning of wampum belts; and the interpretation of design elements.'[15] In addition, McCord was a voracious and critical reader of history. He understood that the 'Archives' were essential.[16]

As a result of his reading and his research, his collection showed a detailed knowledge of Canadian history. Although he did not write history, he did posit an interpretation of Canadian history through a deliberate museum arrangement. Arranged chronologically by room, the early museum outlined North America's Native origins, the French Regime, the Plains of Abraham, and British North America. Themes of nobility, military accomplishment, French-English cooperation, pioneer endurance, constitutional progress, and national destiny dominated.[17] To be sure, McCord's 'narrative' was not particularly original; it fit the pattern of imperialism. Originality, however, is not the point; rather, as a historian, McCord was reflective and thoughtful and careful.

Lighthall and McCord were like other turn-of-the-twentieth-century historians in that history was not something they did for a living. Lighthall's legal career was one thing, history quite another; McCord was a man of inherited means, history a means to a nation-building end. Trained as an engineer, William Kingsford did not begin writing history until he 'secured absolute leisure' at age 65.[18] John G. Bourinot's career as the Clerk of House of Commons and his pioneering work in constitutional history were complementary.[19] By day, James Coyne worked as the registrar of deeds and titles for Elgin County; by night, he studied the history of southwestern Ontario.[20] William Canniff was a medical doctor as well as the author of two books dealing with the early history of Ontario.[21] Brigadier General E.A. Cruikshank served in the active militia at the same time as he dedicated every spare moment to studying the War of 1812 and the Niagara Peninsula.[22] Similarly, William Wood was commissioned in the 8th Royal Rifles in 1887 and eventually promoted to colonel. His military career, however, did not preclude a prodigious publishing record in Canada's military history and in the history of Quebec.

II

Women also were active in the turn-of-the-twentieth-century historical community as writers, organizers, collectors, and patriots. Agnes Maule Machar, Sarah Curzon, Elizabeth Murdoch Frame, Mary FitzGibbon,

Clementina Fessenden, Janet Carnochan, Matilda Edgar, and Isabel Skelton were as well known as their male counterparts.[23] Women formed their own historical societies (the Women's Canadian Historical Society of Toronto, the Women's Canadian Historical Society of Ottawa, the Women's Wentworth Historical Society, the Women's Historical Society of Bowmanville, and the Women's Literary Club of St Catharines), they participated in several other societies (the Ontario Historical Society, the Niagara Historical Society, the Manitoba Historical and Scientific Society, the Nova Scotia Historical Society after 1892, and the Huron Institute), and at least one woman (Jenny Simpson) took on a leadership position in the Historic Landmarks Association, forerunner to the Canadian Historical Association.

Invited to address the Wentworth Historical Society in 1891, Sarah Curzon spoke directly to the issue of her sex and the writing of history. At first, she explained, 'I felt compelled to decline your courteous invitation.' After all, one of her sex had 'never been recognized as in its right place when found upon a platform, even the very modest platform of the essayist.' However, she decided to accept the invitation. By opening its membership roll to women, and by extending to her an invitation to speak, the Wentworth Historical Society had upheld, in her words, 'the doctrine of the equal rights of woman as a human being.' The historical project as it was then understood was one for both sexes. As Curzon argued, 'Together, men and women built up this noble country by whose name we call ourselves; together they must preserve and develop it; and together they will stand or fall by it.'[24]

A few years later, Curzon proved the driving force behind the creation in 1895 of the Women's Canadian Historical Society of Toronto (WCHST). Its stated objectives were to encourage the study of Canadian history, to preserve historical records and relics, and to promote patriotism.[25] To these ends, the society published an *Annual Report* and the occasional *Transaction* (or occasional paper). In addition, it organized regular Saturday afternoon meetings, where members read papers on a variety of topics, at the same time as it participated in various efforts to promote history more generally. For example, in 1899 the WCHST organized a history exhibition at Victoria University, and in 1905 it joined the fight to save Fort York from a projected streetcar line.[26]

The early success of the WCHST encouraged Matilda Edgar to institute a similar society in Ottawa. In June 1898 'Thirty-one ladies assembled in [her] drawing room' and the Women's Canadian Historical Society of Ottawa (WCHSO) was born. Like its counterpart in Toronto, this society would create a space for women to study history and promote patriotism. Although the WCHSO did not neglect the larger history of Canada, it focused on the history of the Ottawa area. Titles of papers read before the meeting include 'Lumbermen of the Ottawa Valley' and the 'The History of the Ottawa General Hospital.' Like every other historical society at this time, the WCHSO took a keen interest in preservation and commemoration. Among other things, it arranged in 1914 for a portrait of Colonel By, Ottawa's founder, to hang in the council chamber of city hall, and in 1917 it founded the Bytown Museum in the Old Registry Office in Ottawa.[27]

Why did women create historical societies of their own? Both Sarah Curzon, who founded the WCHST, and Matilda Edgar, who founded the WCHSO, were early feminists and active in the National Council of Women. They deliberately founded these societies to advance a particular agenda: through the study of women in history, they wanted to promote contemporary women's rights. According to Beverly Boutilier, Curzon turned to history 'in order to further the cause of women's rights, and thus to redefine the parameters of female citizenship.'[28] Furthermore, women created their own societies because they were either altogether unwelcome or cast in auxiliary roles within some historical societies in Ontario. For example, the Lundy's Lane Historical Society did not permit women members, while the Elgin Historical and Scientific Institute and the Wentworth Historical Society (WHS) created women's auxiliaries.[29] By 1900 the women's auxiliary of the WHS had become the Women's Wentworth Historical Society. Boutilier suggests that the WHS was 'perhaps typical.'[30]

The creation of separate historical societies was, in part, an expression of early feminism and of exclusion, but to stop here is to miss how much men and women worked together in a shared historical project. For example, women continued to serve on both the executive and the council of the WHS throughout the 1900s and 1910s.[31] In other words, the existence of a ladies auxiliary and then a separate women's society did not preclude the participation of women in the WHS. The same pattern can be seen in the Elgin Historical and Scientific Institute (EHSI), founded by James Coyne in 1891. In 1896 the EHSI expanded to include a ladies auxiliary, or women's branch as it was sometimes called. Within a few years this branch became the Women's Historical Society of the County of Elgin. However, women continued to sit on the executive and council of the EHSI and to give papers at its regular meetings.

In 1900 there was a woman vice-president, a woman secretary-treasurer and a woman councillor. In some years, women made up nearly half of the council in addition to holding two and sometimes three executive positions.[32]

Men did not see the creation of the women's historical societies as a threat. W.D. Lighthall was very pleased to have been named an honorary member of the WCHST; in his own words, he was in 'deep sympathy' with the society's objects. 'The founding of Woman's Can. Hist. Society is a noble idea,' he declared. 'I pressed [two Montreal women] to found one here the other day.'[33] James Coyne was similarly positive. Although unable to accept its invitation, he hoped that the 1896 event at Fort York hosted by the WCHST would provide a 'great impetus' to all historical societies.[34] Charles Mair, one of Canada's leading poets, who used historical themes in his writing, welcomed the WCHST as a positive force for Canadian womanhood and Canadian nationhood: 'The sacred domestic instincts of Canadian womanhood will not suffer in the least degree, but will rather be refreshed and strengthened by [that] which I trust your society proposes to do not only in searching for fresh materials for our public history but, more important still, in rescuing from destruction the scattered and perishable records of Ontario's old, and, in many respects, romantic home life.'[35] William Kirby, author of *The Golden Dog*, commended the Women's Literary Club of St Catharines in 1904: 'It is the women who like the Vestal Virgins of Rome keep alive the perpetual fire of love and devotion to this country. I hail wherever they are found those historical and literary societies like yours which devote such time to noble purposes.'[36]

It is clear that women were welcome allies in the cause of history and that Boutilier's characterization of the historical movement in turn-of-the-twentieth-century Ontario as 'male dominated' was premature.[37] As Boutilier herself observes, the indefatigable Janet Carnochan founded the Niagara Historical Society (NHS) in 1895 and served as its president until 1922.[38] Born in 1839, Carnochan became a high school teacher, eventually retiring in 1900. Her one great love, however, was history. As president of the NHS, Carnochan wrote over two dozen essays and pamphlets on the history of the Niagara region, published one book, raised the $5,000 needed to restore Niagara Memorial Hall into a local museum, and arranged for commemorative stone markers at various historical sites related to the War of 1812. At the same time she handled extensive administrative duties; in one year alone she counted 240 letters sent to people who had requested either a publication or some information on a variety of topics.[39] Moreover, Carnochan was not the only woman active in the NHS; at any given time, there were two or three other women on the executive and council.

Not all women achieved the prominence of Carnochan, but many took an active part in other historical societies. For example, in its 1900 report to the Royal Society of Canada the Peterborough Historical Society listed a woman on the executive and on the council; in addition, the society reported that another woman proved instrumental in raising the funds for a suitable monument to Peterborough poet, Isabella Valancey Crawford.[40] Meanwhile, a Mrs W.N. Ponton served as president of the Belleville and Bay of Quinte Historical Society from 1899 to 1901.[41] Founded in 1904 to further the causes of history, zoology, geology, botany, and civic improvement, the Huron Institute of Collingwood consistently listed women members, executives, and directors.[42] Indeed, the list goes on. The Thorold and Beaverdams Historical Society, the Halton Historical Society, the Victoria County Historical Society, the Perth Historical Society, the London and Middlesex Historical Society, the Lennox and Addington Historical Society, the Kingston Historical Society, the St Catharines Historical Society, and the Amherstburg Historical Society all welcomed the participation of women as members and officers.[43] Even the Lundy's Lane Historical Society, which Boutilier characterizes as a men-only group, had women on its executive by 1910.

From its beginnings in 1898 the Ontario Historical Society opened its doors to women. In point of fact, it was a Miss Sarah Mickle who moved that the newly created society be called the Ontario Historical Society rather than the proposed Ontario Pioneer and Historical Association.[44] Men clearly outnumbered women in the OHS, but women played a 'prominent role.'[45] They sat on the executive and the council, they presented papers at the annual meeting, they published essays and notes in the OHS journal,[46] and in one year a woman received first prize in the OHS History Essay Competition.[47] Clementina Fessenden used the OHS as 'her base' from which to agitate 'for a flag to spread the gospel of imperialistic patriotism. Eventually, the letters she wrote, the articles she composed, and the speeches that she gave resulted at the end of the nineteenth century in the creation of Empire Day.'[48] In addition to the eight papers she published in *Papers and Records,*[49] Janet Carnochan served as vice-president in 1915.

As historians, women writers echoed many of the themes of their male counterparts. Some women, it is true, deliberately broadened the scope of history to include the history of women in an effort to advance women's rights, but the vast majority of history written by women centred on the Loyalists, the War of 1812, military heroes, and colonial governors. Of the thirty-two papers written by women in the OHS *Papers and Records* between 1899 and 1922 only two were on the subject of women. For its part, the WCHSO concentrated on the same historical topics as Lighthall, McCord, Cruikshank, and Coyne had done. In the same year as it heard a paper on the women workers of Ottawa, it initiated a series of papers on 'Canadian Men of Note.'[50] Even the early feminist and founder of the WCHSO, Matilda Edgar, published three books on traditional subjects: the War of 1812, General Brock, and Horatio Sharpe, a colonial governor of Maryland.[51] Clementina Fessenden may have been a busy historical activist, but she did not believe in the parliamentary franchise for women.[52] Despite Sarah Curzon's personal commitment, the WCHST was never a women's rights organization per se.[53] Women historians imagined the Canadian nation along the same imperial lines as their male counterparts did. Canada's past was an imperial past and its history a romantic narrative of exploration, warfare, and settlement. 'In the historical societies of these decades,' Cecilia Morgan concludes, 'women and men often shared conceptions of gender, nation and empire.'[54]

By the turn of the twentieth century, then, scores of men and women were busying themselves with writing, collecting, and preserving the past. Numerous local and even some provincial historical societies existed, yet there was no national organization, no coordinating body capable of acting as an information centre. Never one to sit back and let things take care of themselves, W.D. Lighthall set his sights on the creation of a national historical association in the early 1900s. Owing to a pervasive neglect, he believed, Canadians had allowed their physical and architectural heritage to fall into disrepair. Dilapidated buildings that once had housed an important person and decrepit forts once the sites of key confrontations did not speak well of Canadian patriotism. In August 1905 he learned that the dominion government intended to sell as so many lots the old military common adjoining the fort and barracks in Chambly, Quebec. First, he wrote to the mayor suggesting that the city council issue a bond series in order to purchase and thus save the site from development.[55] Next, he contacted his old friend and comrade in things historical, William Wood of Quebec City, who was an active member of the Literary and Historical Society of Quebec. The Chambly Common, he explained, 'has many memories and should be left alone.' Now, more than ever, the time was right 'to begin the Historic Landmark Association.' Objects must be defined, a circular printed, and a petition to save the common started. Presidents, vice-presidents, secretaries, and a treasurer needed to be named, and because he 'shows such hearty and sincere interest,' they must seek the governor general as the 'Patron' (although 'I detest the word'). In any event, he declared, 'the important thing is action.'[56] A few weeks later, Lighthall received the go-ahead from Samuel Dawson, the honorary secretary of the Royal Society of Canada, to organize the association under the auspices of the RSC.

That the Historic Landmarks Association emerged out of the Royal Society is not at all surprising. Founded in 1882, the RSC quickly established itself as the country's chief organizational vehicle for intellectual life by providing a home to individuals and scholars across the country. Divided into four sections (I. Littérature Français, Histoire, Archéologie; II. English Literature, History, Archaeology; III. Mathematical, Physical and Chemical Sciences; IV. Geological and Biological Sciences), membership was by election only. Although its principal mandate comprised the organization of an annual meeting (always in the third week of May) and the publication of its *Proceedings and Transactions* (which ate up most of its annual $5,000 government grant), from time to time the RSC also lent its weight to historical causes. In 1891 the Royal Society assisted the Antiquarian and Numismatic Society of Montreal in 'its successful efforts to preserve the Château de Ramezay, built in 1705 and later used as a residence for British governors, from the prevalent "spirit of vandalism."' As well, the RSC 'actively promoted commemoration of the 400th anniversary of the voyages in 1497 and 1498 of the Cabots.'[57] When Lighthall and Wood, through the Literary and Historical Society of Quebec, urged the RSC to create a Canadian Landmark Association, they were not turned down.[58] After a flurry of letters and appeals and pitches for support from local historical societies, Lighthall and Wood settled on the 1907 annual meeting of the Royal Society of Canada as the inaugural meeting of the Historic Landmarks Association (HLA).[59] According to its founders, the HLA would act as 'an intelligence department' and lobbying group; it would keep an ongoing list of the country's physical heritage and, where and when appropriate, it would 'concentrate effective influence' for its preservation.[60]

In his article on the disciplinization of history in Quebec, Patrice Régimbald examines the role played by the RSC; its most important initiative, he asserts, was the creation of the HLA in 1907. His mangled history of the HLA notwithstanding, to call it the Royal Society's most important initiative is surely an overstatement.[61] After all, throughout the HLA's fifteen-year existence it remained thoroughly outside the university and the changes taking place within the study and practice of history. Although the University of Toronto historians George Wrong and W.S. Wallace joined the association there is no indication that they even indirectly, let alone directly, participated in its various activities. The executive consisted of men for whom history was a pastime, albeit a passionate one, rather than a career. The HLA did not define history in scientific terms; its first mission statement was rich in romance and full of energetic optimism. Although the author is not identified, it was almost certainly Lighthall. In the opening paragraph the word 'exultant' was used three times to describe Canada's heritage, its natural riches, and its pioneers. Of the self-governing dominions, Canada's history and its 'moving incidents' remain 'the most romantic of them all.' Soldiers, poets, priests, explorers, Norsemen, and Indians 'left landmarks to tell their story to all who listen understandingly.' Using a broad definition of landmark, the HLA cast a wide net: 'It may be a monument set up by pious hands; a building, a ruin, or a site; a battlefield or fort; a rostrum or a poet's walk; any natural object; any handiwork of man; or even the mere local habitation of a legend or a name. But, whatever the form, its spirit makes every true landmark a talismanic heirloom, only to be lost to our peril and shame.' These monuments and sites and landmarks would be neither the 'constricting grip' of a dead hand nor a bar 'to real progress.' Rather, they would carry a living message, a reminder of our greatness and an inspiration, 'lest, seeking the whole mere world of riches, [Canada] loses her own soul.'[62]

For fifteen years the HLA organized an annual meeting in conjunction with the Royal Society, published an *Annual Report*, and created a national registry of historic sites and important landmarks. It also provided a forum for women historians and women interested in history. Although the RSC remained in effect a male institution – section II did not elect a woman until 1951 – the HLA proved open to both women's membership and their participation. Admittedly, women never constituted more than a minority, but the fact of their participation is clearly evident in the minutes.[63] Moreover, that the association survived was largely due to Jenny Simpson.

Secured in 1914 as the general secretary, Jenny Simpson breathed new life into the association. It was in that year that the treasurer, George Durnford, presented a bleak report: 'annual receipts are dwindling' and membership was declining. In 1908 the HLA could count fifty-two individual members and six affiliated societies; by 1914 it counted only twenty-eight individual members and three affiliated societies.[64] It was decided to employ the services of a general secretary, someone who would undertake the day-to-day administrative work. Carrying a small stipend of $50 in 1914, Jenny Simpson's was the only paid position in the association. In his 1915 president's address, Pemberton Smith remarked that Simpson had 'devoted all her time to the work of the Association.'[65] In 1916 Simpson's stipend was raised to $125. It was money well spent. By 1918 the membership had increased to 131 individual members and eleven affiliated societies. In 1920 Simpson's stipend was again raised, this time to $200. In that year Lighthall moved that 'Mrs. Simpson's valued services & untiring devotion to the work' of the HLA be recognized; she was summarily presented with a set of the *Chronicles of Canada*.[66] When Simpson resigned her position in 1921, Lawrence Burpee, as president, spoke of her 'enthusiasm and untiring energy' to which 'the Association owes so much of its success.' More specifically, 'through the efforts of Mrs. Simpson, we are able to announce a substantial addition to the membership of the Association.'[67] In 1921 there were 136 individual members and twenty-two affiliated societies.

Lighthall, McCord, Carnochan, Simpson, the Bytown Museum, the McCord National Museum, and the Historic Landmarks Association: the many men and women who wrote history, founded associations, created museums, and erected monuments were historians. They were not historians according to today's definition – someone who has advanced training in the study of the past and earns a living writing about the past – but to expect that they could meet this definition would be ahistorical. Moreover, some of these men and women exhibited those traits associated with modern scholarship: ability in primary research, a sceptical approach, and a critical faculty. Lady Edgar gathered, annotated, and published a collection of letters, because she recognized the importance of primary sources to historical writing.[68] John G. Bourinot sounded not unlike a modern historian when he accepted the difficulty of writing contemporary history and thus avoided those topics 'too near to us to admit of a cool and purely historical treatment.'[69] William Kingsford opened his multi–volume history of Canada with a declaration of his commitment to the truth: 'The first duty of the historian is skeptically to weigh facts and to divest himself of all sentiment dictated by faith or nationality: otherwise he is nothing more than the mere partisan chronicler.'[70] Janet Carnochan referred to the 'great care' and 'close scrutiny' historians must exercise in their research.[71] E.A. Cruikshank defined the historian's 'scientific conscience' as 'the habit of accuracy, open-mindedness, impartiality of judgment and the love of the truth.'[72] As well, these men and women assisted in laying the foundation for history's eventual professionalization. They preserved, documented, and recorded the past; they published valuable primary document collections; in the HLA they created a national historical association; and some demonstrated what we now understand to be a modern approach to the writing of history. Take William Dawson LeSueur, for example.

III

Born in 1840 and educated at the University of Toronto and the Law School of Osgoode Hall, LeSueur worked as a civil servant with the Post Office in Ottawa. Although he would eventually be made chief of the money order system, his primary interests lay outside the civil service. Working for the Post Office provided the income necessary to his intellectual pursuits; in the evening and on weekends, LeSueur read widely and voraciously, trying to keep abreast of current debates in science, philosophy, and religion. Science and the scientific spirit, he argued, must be cultivated and advanced: 'if a spirit of rational enquiry can be awakened, if the work of science can be nobly conceived by us,' he wrote in 1879, 'then we shall be sure in due time to do our part faithfully and well in building up that structure of scientific knowledge which, in the years to come, shall be, as it were, the common home and shelter of humanity.'[73] In this sense, LeSueur was a modern.[74]

Following his retirement from the civil service in 1902, LeSueur dedicated himself to the study of history. The shift from philosophy to history was neither sudden nor enormous; after all, his writings 'had always shown a historical perspective,' particularly his essays on politics and morality written in the 1890s.[75] Moreover, he brought to the study of history the same critical spirit he had demonstrated as a philosopher. As events unfolded over the course of the next fifteen years, LeSueur's critical spirit landed him in legal hot water, cost him time and money to fight five court cases, and caused him no end of grief. At issue was his biography of William Lyon Mackenzie, the leader of the 1837 Rebellion in Upper Canada.[76]

In the early 1900s the publisher George Morang initiated a twenty-volume series on great Canadians. Called the *Makers of Canada,* it included biographies of Lord Sydenham, Joseph Howe, George-Étienne Cartier, and John A. Macdonald. As its title suggests, the series adopted a decidedly Whiggish, sometimes hagiographic approach. LeSueur contributed a volume on Frontenac.[77] In addition, he agreed to serve as an editor, and it was in this capacity that he read a manuscript on the life of William Lyon Mackenzie. According to LeSueur, the manuscript did not meet the standards of historical criticism. 'Declamation much more than historical analysis or careful research is [the manuscript's] forte,' he told Morang.[78] Based on LeSueur's recommendation, Morang rejected the manuscript. He then invited LeSueur to write a Mackenzie biography, but LeSueur baulked – he seemed an inappropriate choice, since his evaluation had led to the rejection of the original manuscript. Morang next approached George Wrong, who initially agreed but then quickly declined. Morang went back to LeSueur, and this time he consented. According to LeSueur, Wrong 'had been dissuaded by friends from entering on a subject which he could hardly hope to treat quite independently without exciting partisan feeling and criticism, which might be hurtful to his influence as a teacher.'[79] As a retired civil servant, LeSueur had more intellectual freedom than Wrong did as a university professor, but as events unfolded, LeSueur's freedom proved more illusory than real.

With access to Mackenzie papers in the possession of Charles Lindsey, the rebellion leader's son-in-law, LeSueur submitted the completed manuscript in April 1908. Instead of marking an end to his research, however, it marked the start of his troubles. Just one month later Morang rejected the manuscript on the grounds that it would only ignite controversy and thus injure the series.[80] Not only did LeSueur criticize Mackenzie, he dared to question the achievement of responsible government. LeSueur did not object to responsible government in principle; rather, he objected to what it meant in practice: party politics, corruption, and the abdication of moral responsibility on the grounds of political expediency.[81] LeSueur protested both Morang's reading of his manuscript and his disregard for intellectual independence: 'The demand is more and more being made that works pretending to be historical shall be based on independent research, and what on earth is the use of independent research if you are predestined to arrive at the conclusions of the multitude every time?'[82] Although not a professional historian, he articulated the quest for independence that would animate the professionalization of history.

For the next five years LeSueur found himself in and out of court. First, he fought for the return of the only manuscript copy of his biography so that he might seek an alternative publisher. This round he won. Next, he fought against the efforts of Mackenzie's heirs to secure an injunction prohibiting his use of any material gathered from the Mackenzie papers in their possession. This round he lost. The whole ordeal cost LeSueur both physically and financially. As he confided to his sister in January 1913, the doctor had prescribed a week of 'absolute rest.'[83] Although he rewrote his manuscript in accordance with the legal decision, it remained unpublished at the time of his death in 1917.

It was during his legal battles that LeSueur delivered a thoughtful, erudite, and, most important, modern treatise on the nature of history. His 1912 presidential address to the Royal Society of Canada remains a clear statement on history as an idea and as a practice. In it he betrays his keen intelligence and understanding of trends taking place in modern historical scholarship. He acknowledges the importance of the archives – after all, history must be based on original sources – but he cautions against the uncritical acceptance of facts. Not all facts are facts. For example, did not Frontenac in a dispatch to France deliberately exaggerate the number killed at Lachine in an effort to secure more 'men, money and material' for the fledgling colony? To rely on Frontenac's official dispatch, to accept it as fact, would be to distort the past. Therefore, documents must not be accepted at face value but rather must be subjected to criticism. However, LeSueur does not attempt to lay down a science of history: as human beings we are bound by human limitations and subject to human biases, he explains. History can never claim finality: 'Let two men work independently on the same period of history; give them access to the same documents and other sources of information, let them agree as to general methods, and let them be as free from prejudice as is possible for poor humanity, yet they will not tell you exactly the same tale.' Moreover, not only will two historians give different versions of the same event, but there is considerable risk involved for the historian who offers a new and different interpretation. Here, he spoke from painful experience. Myth and legend were powerful forces; to debunk myths and question legends was to court trouble: 'An original historian is an object of universal distrust, scorn and disgust.' In the end, the Victorian LeSueur left his audience with a modern approach to history: thorough research, judicious selection, honest citation, and a commitment not to grind any axes. Although imperfect because human beings are imperfect, history must strive to tell the truth as 'honestly and humanly' as possible.[84]

What is LeSueur's significance? A.B. McKillop ranked him as his generation's most wide-ranging intellectual and credited him with introducing 'a critical spirit' into Canadian intellectual life. But LeSueur is also important for what he can tell us about the professionalization of history in English Canada. He did not have a university career, yet he wrote history according to critical standards that were taking root in the university. He was not a professional historian, but he articulated some of the defining features of the professional historian. In other words, the impetus for history's professionalization came simultaneously from those outside the university and those inside the university; it came both from those men and women that historians today call amateurs and from those identified as the founders of professional history.

Yet even at the peak of their activity, the Lighthalls and McCords, the Carnochans and the Simpsons, and even LeSueur himself were being surpassed. Overlapping history's vibrant existence outside the university was its emergence within the university.

IV

As the nineteenth century gave way to the twentieth century, Canada experienced what has been called a great transformation. The transcontinental railway had been completed and it now carried tens of thousands of immigrants into western Canada each year; the industrial economy of central Canada expanded quickly, drawing more and more people to the cities. At long last, it seemed, the promise of John A. Macdonald's National Policy had been realized. The twentieth century, Wilfrid Laurier pronounced, would be Canada's century. Yet Canada's long-awaited economic boom generated as much unease and uncertainty as it did optimism. Immigration, industrialization, and urbanization produced new social problems. Canadians anxiously wondered how the country could possibly assimilate so many foreigners, while newspapers featured stories about loose women, abandoned children, filthy living conditions, horrific rates of alcohol consumption, and organized crime. Materialism, greed, and self-interest, it seemed, had replaced the Father, the Son, and the Holy Ghost. As Doug Owram demonstrates, Canada's economic and social transformation precipitated a transformation in the intellectual community: 'Canadian society was changing so rapidly by the early twentieth century that the tenets of idealism seemed less and less plausible as an answer to the problems confronting man.'[85] The intellectual community, increasingly centred in the university, began to turn away from moral philosophy and metaphysical speculation and turn towards empiricism and the social sciences. The university, like the rest of the country, itself was transformed.

The origins of higher education in Canada lay in organized religion. Beginning in the late eighteenth century and continuing throughout the nineteenth century, each denomination founded its own university: Laval and Saint Francis Xavier were Roman Catholic, Acadia and McMaster Baptist; Mount Allison was Methodist and Queen's Presbyterian. The university's mandate was broadly conceived in terms of moral instruction, religious knowledge, and education in the classics. Yet by the late nineteenth century this mandate seemed anachronistic at best, as a rapidly changing society demanded relevance from its universities.

James Loudon, president of the University of Toronto, captured this sentiment in his 1902 presidential address to the Royal Society of Canada. The 'provision of adequate facilities for research,' he began, 'is one of the prime necessities of university education in Canada.' Loudon did not limit his definition of research to the physical and natural sciences; indeed, he deliberately defined research to include all branches of knowledge. This was the function of the German university, where research had been made the 'fundamental principle.' Twenty-five years ago, he claimed, American universities began to follow the German lead by creating graduate programs leading to the PhD degree. Canadian universities, however, had fallen behind. Emulating the British example, which was marked by utter 'indifference towards organized research,' Canadian universities had limited their function to imparting 'a general and liberal education.' Not only was it out of date, it was irresponsible: 'To hold up before the student, either by theory or practice, solely the ideal of acquiring what has already been learned is medievalism pure and simple.' Fortunately, he added, some Canadian scholars, influenced by the German and American examples, were taking research seriously. In the final analysis, he concluded, 'the research university must be regarded as the only university.'[86]

In 1905 the Ontario government appointed a royal commission to investigate the future of the University of Toronto. The commission quickly tabled its report.[87] Taking its cue from American state universities, it recommended that new professional faculties be established; that an annual provincial grant be made to stabilize university financing; that academic and financial matters be separated by the creation of a senate and a board of governors; and that, while the denominational colleges could continue to teach, only the University of Toronto could confer degrees. The ideas contained in the report served as a model for new universities, particularly in western Canada. The University of Manitoba told a cautionary tale: one university in name, but three denominational colleges duking it out in fact.[88] Wanting to avoid such debilitating and time-consuming sectarianism, Henry Marshall Tory, the first president of the University of Alberta, charted a different course. In a long letter marked 'Private and Confidential,' written to the premier of Alberta, Marshall outlined his vision: 'one of the greatest dangers to good educational work is the denominational spirit.' Institutions in Nova Scotia, New Brunswick, Ontario, and Manitoba illustrated this point; the new provinces should not, in this instance, follow the lead of the older provinces. Alberta must create a state university, one capable of transcending particular loyalties in the interests of the general community.[89] This was also Walter Murray's hope for the University of Saskatchewan.[90] Like his counterpart in Alberta, he intended to build a state university that owed nothing to a particular group but everything to the larger community. Only a state university could provide the research facilities, professional schools, and expert knowledge now required by society. Meanwhile, those universities with 'grand ambitions' responded in similar fashion to the 'utilitarian demands of an industrial age.' McGill, Queen's, and Dalhousie 'widened their student constituencies by broadening their programs to include extensive professional training.'[91]

Against this backdrop, history's transition from a part-time activity for men and women outside the university to a full-time career for men and, on occasion, women inside the university was perceptible – but far from complete – by 1900. In his book on nineteenth-century English-Canadian historiography, Brook Taylor concludes that 'By the turn of the century Canada's amateur historians – for such they now were – had lost their sense of purpose. No longer able to look forward, they had no reason to look back.'[92] As an example, Taylor points to the string of very negative reviews William Kingsford received in the *Review of Historical Publications Relating to Canada,* the forerunner to the *Canadian Historical Review.* But Taylor overstates his case; there never was a malaise infecting 'Canada's amateur historians.' W.D. Lighthall's decision to create the Historic Landmarks Association was the incarnation of his energetic optimism and his sense of place within the historical community. Besides, it was E.A. Cruikshank, not a professional historian, who wrote the largely negative reviews of Kingsford's multi–volume history of Canada.

It is true that those turn-of-the-twentieth-century historians would become amateur historians as history professionalized, but they did not roll over and disappear. Local and provincial historical societies continued to flourish. Moreover, the new professional historians continued to consult the men and women who became amateur historians well into the century. George Wrong looked to Lighthall for information on Quebec history; in the early 1930s a young Alfred Bailey likewise looked to Lighthall for his extensive knowledge of Hochelaga.[93] Wrong also relied on non-professional historians to edit volumes for the Champlain Society.[94] Adam Shortt turned to Janet Carnochan for her newspaper collections.[95] Leon Harvey, who taught English and modern history at the University of New Brunswick in the 1920s, asked William Wood for advice on using a 'Movie Machine' to teach Canadian history.[96] The two University of Western Ontario historians, Fred Landon and J.J. Talman, regularly consulted James Coyne.[97] At the University of Saskatchewan in the 1920s, A.S. Morton and Frank Underhill initiated a document collection project that relied on the efforts of local historians to gather, preserve, and make available for research primary documents relating to the history of Saskatchewan.[98] Meanwhile, the editors of the *Canadian Historical Review* from the 1920s through to the 1940s regularly invited William Wood, E.A Cruikshank, and Judge Frederic Howay to review books.[99] In the 1930s Canadian historians working on the Carnegie Endowment's Canadian-American relations series insisted that Howay participate in the volume on British Columbia.[100]

Nonetheless, by 1900 the tide was beginning to turn: the historian would become someone who had specialized training, taught at a university, and earned his – and only rarely her – livelihood from the study of the past. The professionalization of history was not a single event or an overnight phenomenon; rather, it was a transition – and a slow and uneven one at that.

CHAPTER 2

From avocation to vocation:
the beginnings

In 1905 Oxford announced a new chair, the Beit Professorship of Colonial History. David Ross McCord duly applied. After all, he considered himself a historian, a man of 'special knowledge' of Canadian and colonial history.[1] However, his greatest qualification, he believed, remained the McCord family name, and it was this attribute – the prominence of the McCord family in Quebec history – that his letters of support stressed. Attached to his application, McCord included twenty-two testimonials from prominent English-speaking and French-speaking Quebeckers. Everyone wrote in approving terms, and each letter emphasized the McCord family and David Ross's connection to it. 'No one is your equal in such a sphere, acquired not only by study, but by the opportunities you have inherited and worthily taken advantage of – opportunities which carry you back to the Colonial days prior to the American Revolution,' the Hon. Mr Justice Loranger observed; 'Your family has taken part in the making of Colonial history.'[2] The Montreal journalist and writer George Murray followed suit. Indeed, McCord carefully underlined a portion of Murray's letter to draw its contents to the committee's attention: *'Mr. McCord's great grand-father was the father of the Parliament of Canada. The family [has] furnished the leading judicial record, six judges who sat, and a seventh, a member of the bar, who declined the honour. Mr. McCord has followed in the footsteps of his distinguished relatives.'*[3] Although the twenty-two letters were solid, they also struck a pathetic note. No one referred to McCord's scholarly activities, his publications, or his teaching experience, precisely because no one could. To have come from an eminent family did not qualify him, or anyone, for the position of professor of colonial history. However, another Canadian with more hope of success also set his sights on the Beit Professorship:

his name was George McKinnon Wrong, the first professor of history at the University of Toronto.

This chapter examines the beginnings of history's transition from an avocation to a vocation from the 1890s to the conclusion of the Great War. It opens with an examination of George Wrong and his early efforts to professionalize the study of history through the creation of the *Review of Historical Publications Relating to Canada*. It is here, in the pages of the *Review,* that the professionalization of history as a process of differentiation between professional and amateur and as a gendered process that posited men as the ideal historian can be seen. The Oxford-inspired department Wrong built at Toronto and the origins of history departments across English Canada are also studied. In addition to the creation of history professorships and separate university departments, there were other signs of history's early – but incomplete – professionalization. They included the development of the Public Archives of Canada in Ottawa and the publication of the multi-volume series, *Canada and Its Provinces.* Although prizing scholarly research and writing, the first generation of professional historians deliberately maintained a connection to history as a moral and patriotic project.

I

Born in 1860 in southwestern Ontario, George Wrong grew up in 'genteel poverty.'[4] His father was both a failed farmer and a failed inventor. 'He was always on the eve of making some invention that might lead to fortune,' Wrong recalled. He never did. As a result, 'I sing no praises of poverty, whose pangs I know.'[5] Nevertheless, the Wrong family valued education, and after a short stint as a clerk in a Toronto mercantile house, the Methodist Wrong converted to Anglicanism and in 1879 enrolled at both Wycliffe College as a theology student and at the University of Toronto. He graduated from Toronto in 1883 with a BA in mental and moral philosophy and civil polity. Although ordained an Anglican minister, he never assumed a parish. Instead, he returned to Wycliffe, where, for the next nine years, he lectured in ecclesiastical history and apologetics. In the summer of 1890 he went to Berlin to study history; two years later, in the summer of 1892, he entered Oxford. While there, Wrong learned of the death of Sir Daniel Wilson.

Born in Edinburgh, Daniel Wilson had been appointed professor of history and English literature at University College, University of Toronto, in 1853, where he established himself as a man of learning and accomplishment. When he applied for the position at Toronto he had already written two books, but he should not be thought of as a professional historian. He was interested in history, but his interests ranged widely, from English literature to archaeology, ethnology, and anthropology.[6] A polymath in every sense of the word, Wilson read widely and published even more widely at a time when the disciplines still met and mingled, before boundaries were marked and specialization became a reality. In 1873 he published a book-length study on Shakespeare and the supernatural; three years later he was asked by the attorney general of Ontario to inspect what was rumoured to be the grave of Tecumseh (he concluded that the remains were not those of the great Shawnee chief but a collection of bones, some human, others animal, including the leg of a deer and the rib of a dog).[7] Wilson also carried a heavy administrative load and in 1890 was appointed president of the University of Toronto. He died two years later.

When news of Wilson's death reached him, George Wrong prayed. 'Tonight,' he wrote in his diary, 'I have spent some time on my knees asking God's guidance ... I ask God to give what is best. I bow to his will and He seems to tell me that it is right to try to make this change.' With this sense of mission, Wrong applied to the University of Toronto.[8] Owing to financial difficulties, the university offered him a lectureship, not a professorship. Taking a cut in pay, Wrong accepted and thus began his thirty-five-year tenure at Varsity. In 1894 Wrong applied for the position of professor of history and ethnology. In his letter of application he referred to his qualifications: eleven years of 'collegiate work' at Wycliffe, Toronto, Berlin, and Oxford; a commitment to 'learning the art of teaching'; a book on Medieval history 'based upon the original authorities'; and a book in progress on the history of Canada under French rule. Although he could not claim a higher degree, he was well qualified for the position. He also was determined. 'In these days of historical interest,' he explained, 'I want to enlarge the course of the study of history.' His fourteen letters of support attested to his capacity as a teacher and a scholar. Rev. Nathaniel Burwash referred to his 'patient industry which is required for historical work.' W.J. Ashley, then professor of history at Harvard but formerly professor of political economy and constitutional history at Toronto, commended Wrong's capacity for original, independent research in addition to his ability to 'handle large masses of evidence'; 'I have seldom known a man who so quickly acquired the art of profitably dealing with original authorities.'[9] In the end, Wrong received the appointment.

Although it provoked charges of nepotism – Wrong was the son-in-law of Edward Blake, chancellor of the university – precipitated a students' strike, and led to a provincial investigation, no wrongdoing or undue influence was ever uncovered.[10]

Following his appointment, Wrong delivered an inaugural address. In paying customary tribute to his predecessor, Sir Daniel Wilson, he noted that as professor of history, English literature, and ethnology, Wilson had carried a 'huge burden.' Each subject required 'copious and varied reading,' and no single professor could keep on top of developments in so many fields; as a result, he said, it proved necessary to create separate chairs. 'This division of labor has come none too soon,' Wrong observed. Still, there were those who considered history to be a rather simple, matter-of-fact undertaking. Unlike chemistry or biology which had 'a technical language intelligible only to a special student,' 'any untrained reader can enjoy his Macaulay or his Froude, lounging on a sofa, or toasting his knees before the fire.' Indeed, there were few people 'so ignorant that they do not know something about History.' As a result, Wrong cautioned, 'men who have not given an hour's serious study to historical questions will assume the tone of experts and critics with a lightheartedness that is amazing.' The meaning of the past, after all, was 'only to be grasped when the insight and discrimination of a trained student are brought to the task.'

However, Wrong carefully steered away from the opposite extreme: clothing learning in 'superstition' and 'hidden methods,' thus placing it beyond the reach of a layman. Between these two extremes – that anyone could do it on the one hand and that only experts could do it on the other – Wrong sought a middle ground. Of course, history must be based on primary documents: 'I have little doubt that the increasing rigor of historical study will make it necessary for any great historian in the future to use manuscript as well as printed material.' But history must be accessible as well, not mysterious; it must be readable, even entertaining.

Finally, Wrong used his inaugural address as an opportunity to outline his philosophy of teaching. 'Students of History,' he explained, 'ought to become something more than passive receivers of other men's opinions, and earn the right to do their own thinking upon historical questions. The first axiom of sound historical study is that it involves some, if necessarily a very limited, dealing with original authorities.' In other words, teach students how to handle the very stuff of history. Here, they will learn important skills of criticism; they will learn that even primary documents contain 'mistakes' and that primary documents must be checked against other primary documents.[11]

Wrong's inaugural address reflected important changes that were taking place in the practice of history, not only in Canada but in Germany, England, and the United States. The nineteenth-century German historian Leopold von Ranke is credited as the father of modern history. In his history seminars at the University of Berlin, Ranke taught students the techniques of internal and external criticism of documents, and he instilled in them a commitment to studying the past on its own terms. His famous formulation, to study the past as it actually was (*wie es eigentlich gewesen*), constituted history's declaration of academic independence. The Rankean model soon migrated to England and the United States.[12] Herbert Baxter Adams founded the first history seminar at Johns Hopkins University in 1876, and the American Historical Association named Ranke its first honorary member at its founding meeting in 1884. Although there were important distinctions between history as taught in Germany, England, and the United States, there existed a shared commitment to the use of primary documents, to university training in how to properly handle those documents, to an emphasis on causation, and to the emergence of learned journals and national historical associations.

Between 1895 and 1905 Wrong attempted to realize the intentions he outlined in his inaugural address. In 1896 he founded the awkwardly named *Review of Historical Publications Relating to Canada*. As he recounted some forty years later, he had been influenced by developments in historical scholarship in Germany, England, and the United States: the German seminar, the American Historical Association, the *English Historical Review*, and the *American Historical Review*. Within this context, he sensed 'the need for some organ in Canada that should bring adequate criticism to publications related to its history.' The *Review of Historical Publications* did not publish original articles; rather, it was a place for 'searching and technical criticism of books on history.' Moreover, the authors of reviews were granted anonymity. Wrong believed that in a small country like Canada such anonymity was necessary to honest criticism.[13]

The *Review of Historical Publications* served its immediate objective, but it also served a related purpose. At times explicitly, at times implicitly, it carried on a conversation about what was and what was not history and who could be and who could not be a historian. It was women historians who endured the most 'honest criticism.' As argued in chapter 1, women were active participants in the turn-of-the-twentieth-century historical community. Agnes Maule Machar, Sarah Curzon, Elizabeth Murdoch Frame, Mary FitzGibbon, Clementina Fessenden, Janet Carnochan, and Matilda Edgar created historical associations; preserved and published primary documents; and wrote articles, pamphlets, and, in some cases, books. As history professionalized, however, women's participation grew more circumscribed. When the Women's Canadian Historical Society of Toronto (WCHST) was founded in 1895 and incorporated in 1896, the *Review of Historical Publications* extended an ambivalent welcome, which reflected the tension within the early historical profession. On the one hand, its welcome was warm: 'The Women's Canadian Historical Society of Toronto is now definitely under way, and has a wide field before it. There will be, perhaps, a stimulating rivalry between the sexes in historical work.' In other words, the appearance of a women's historical society did not constitute a threat to history understood as a pastime. On the other hand, the *Review*'s welcome was cold. Marking a boundary between amateur and professional history, the *Review* disciplined one woman in particular and cautioned the group as a whole. According to the *Review*, Mary FitzGibbon's paper on the discovery of a banner from the War of 1812 in a Toronto school attic, was 'too emotional' in its narrative style. Similarly, the *Review* warned, 'Some similar societies in the United States have, in their patriotic fervour, become more hysterical than historical.'[14] The boundary between amateur and professional was clearly gendered, since hysteria and the inability to transcend the emotional were understood to be specifically female characteristics. The appearance of a women's historical society constituted at least a potential threat to history understood as a profession.

The Women's Canadian Historical Society of Ottawa (WCHSO) offers a case in point. Founded in 1898, the WCHSO was dedicated to 'the encouragement of a study of Canadian loyalty and patriotism.'[15] However, the WCHSO was neither oblivious nor indifferent to the shift taking place within the discipline of history. For example, in both 1909 and 1911 it sent a delegate to the annual meeting of the American Historical Association, the professional association of American historians. In her delegate's report to the WCHSO, Jenny Simpson recounted Albert Bushnell Hart's presidential address and his insistence that 'scientific principles' be introduced to the study of history.[16] Elizabeth Bayly, in her delegate's report, similarly emphasized William Sloane's presidential address and his plea for strict attention to primary documents in the writing of history.[17] In the 1914–15 *Annual Report* it was recorded that, together with the Ontario Historical Society, the WCHSO had invited the American Historical Association to hold its 1916 meeting in Ottawa.[18]

Yet over a period of about two decades, those responsible for the *Review of Historical Publications* looked more and more unfavourably upon the WCHSO. In a 1902 comment on *Transactions of the Women's Canadian Historical Society of Ottawa*, Vol. 1, it was noted that, while the society was to be commended for its efforts, it was nevertheless the case that 'most of the papers are compiled from books which are more or less within reach.' What was needed was more attention to the preservation of local history, not the '"frequently rehearsed" story of Canadian "valour" and "endurance."'[19] Some nine years later, it was asserted in the *Review* that most of the papers in the WCHSO's *Transactions* were 'of a somewhat light description.'[20] In 1914 the WCHSO received another tepid review: 'Some of the papers ... show signs of independent research in the Archives; but it cannot be said that the Women's Canadian Historical Society of Ottawa is making full use of its opportunities in connection with the material at its hand in the Archives Department.'[21] Two years later the assessment was blunter: 'These papers, which are interesting and well written, are in most cases, however, not the work of experts; and they do not add much to the sum of human knowledge.'[22] Finally, in 1919 the most damning commentary was tendered: 'The *Transactions* of the Woman's Canadian Historical Society ... contains nothing of which attention needs to be called. Most of the papers appear to be compilations from well known and often unreliable secondary sources.'[23]

The WCHST earned a similar, and arguably more revealing, treatment. In their 1914–15 *Annual Report and Transactions*, the WCHST reprinted a primary document: an 1816 letter from a Mrs R. Hazen of Saint John. It was argued in the *Review* that the letter was 'full of information on the fashions in dress and furniture of the period, but not especially significant to the student of Canadian history.'[24] Because the professionalization of history involved the distinction of serious from frivolous or significant from insignificant areas of research, it was effectively argued that the domestic sphere was an insignificant topic for investigation. Since the domestic sphere was also the women's sphere, it followed that women's experiences were not 'especially significant to the student of Canadian history.' The interests of the WCHST were relegated to the frivolous (and feminine), outside the boundaries of serious (and masculine) historical enquiry.[25]

True, the *Review* writers criticized the WCHSO and the WCHST as unscholarly – their work was not scholarly according to emerging professional standards – but they also criticized them as women. No other local historical society endured such harsh criticism. Taking the Ontario Historical Society (OHS) as a comparative example, we see nothing but compliments in the *Review*. In 1900 it was announced that the *Papers and Records* of the OHS constituted 'excellent work,' while the president, James Coyne, had delivered a 'scholarly address.'[26] In 1901, 1904, 1905, 1906, and 1910 *Review* contributors heaped praise on the OHS: for example, 'The Ninth volume of the Papers and Records of the Ontario Historical Society is, like its predecessors, a credit to the Society.'[27] Although enthusiasm was tempered in 1913 and 1914, the high level of appreciation was resumed for the OHS's 'excellent' work in 1915, 1916, and 1917–18.[28] While the work of the OHS was not qualitatively different from the work of the WCHSO – both men and women historians embraced themes of Loyalism, heroism, and imperialism – in the *Review of Historical Publications*, the nucleus of an embryonic but growing historical profession, women's historical societies were singled out for 'searching and technical criticism,' to quote George Wrong. This marked the beginning of a strategy in the professionalization of history to equate history as a discipline with the perceived qualities of men – rationality, objectivity – and to make history as a profession a profession for men. Unlike W.D. Lighthall and William Kirby, for example, who welcomed women's participation, George Wrong took a dimmer view, as expressed in an 1899 letter. Referring to the Ontario Historical Society, he wrote, 'Women are in the ascendancy there and they will run the society into the ground.'[29]

Meanwhile, when Wrong learned of Oxford's newly endowed Beit Professorship of Colonial History, he considered submitting his name. The prominent Canadian imperialist and secretary of the Rhodes Scholarship Trust, George Parkin, encouraged him to apply: 'To me the post appears an important one, with large possibilities.'[30] Wrong agreed: 'The thought of Oxford is, of course, a delight. I love the place and when I heard that [a good friend] was going to Oxford I thought him a lucky dog and came as near as envying him as the law permits.' In addition to having founded the *Review of Historical Publications*, Wrong had undertaken a vigorous program of research and writing. Since his appointment, he had translated and annotated an eighteenth-century manuscript letter about Louisbourg, published a school textbook, and completed a biography of the Earl of Elgin.[31] In other words, he was qualified for the position in a way that David Ross McCord could never be. 'The distinction of a Professorship at Oxford is not to be regarded lightly,' Wrong declared; 'it is a great sphere.' But there were other factors to consider. The cost of education in England was prohibitive for a man of Wrong's means, especially when he had five children to put through school. Moreover, his appointment at Toronto was permanent, whereas the Beit Professorship was not. Finally, he added, 'I am not sure that I should not ... have a more effective influence here where we have a great nation in the making.'[32] If Wrong could not go to Oxford, he would have to bring Oxford to Toronto.

II

Wrong deliberately designed the University of Toronto's Department of History on the Oxford model. 'Oxford was much in my mind,' he later wrote, 'and my plans for a graduating department were largely shaped by the Oxford tradition.'[33] Between 1904 and 1918 he made fifteen appointments. Although some appointments were temporary, and not all those appointed to permanent positions stayed, twelve of the fifteen had completed at least one degree at Oxford.[34] No one had a doctorate and only two had an MA at the time of their appointment. The primary qualification for a position in Wrong's department was an Oxford BA. As he admitted in 1921, Wrong hired his staff on the basis of 'character, good manners, forcefulness as well as learning.'[35] In addition to seeking out Oxford graduates, Wrong introduced the Oxford tutorial method to Toronto. Because Toronto lacked the resources, tutorials did not replace the lecture, but they did bring students and instructors into closer contact.[36] Taking another page from the Oxford playbook, Wrong founded the Historical Club in 1904. Highly selective, the Historical Club held fortnightly meetings in the homes of wealthy Toronto citizens and organized debates on topics of timely interest.[37] However, Wrong excluded women. One of his early Oxford appointments, Keith Feiling, urged him to hold fast on 'the great Woman question.' By all means give them a degree, even give them the vote, 'but keep, oh keep them, out of our seminars of learning.'[38] This pattern – the exclusion of women from the discipline of history – would become more pronounced in the decades after the Great War.

Wrong emulated the Oxford model because, he believed, Oxford prepared young men for their future roles as national leaders. At Oxford in 1892 Wrong had been moved by the gilt letters over the gateway to the gardens of New College: 'Manners makyth man.'[39] The Oxford model did not emphasize training in original research so much as it emphasized finishing the man. Nation, duty, character, and confidence: this was the essence of history at Oxford.[40] Through history one learned important lessons of obligation and service. To these ends, Wrong sent his young protégés to Oxford for refinement, including Edward Kylie, Vincent Massey, A.G. Brown, G.M. Smith, Carleton Stanley, A.L. Burt, Frank Underhill, Charles Cochrane, and Donald Creighton. When appointing Kylie in 1904, Wrong conceded that he had not engaged in specialized research, but that he was 'especially valuable to us for Oxford leads the English speaking world in History just now.'[41] When Underhill complained about Oxford (he found it was cut off from 'real life' and a place where truth did not count nearly as much as a 'flippant tone' and 'the ability to make epigrammatic remarks'[42]), Wrong responded with a gentle rebuke. 'Luxury shocks me as I see it shocks you,' he told Underhill,

> Yet it may be that a year or two of luxury will do a Canadian youth no harm. I doubt whether the soul is after all much injured by the luxury of good pictures, carved furniture, comfortable easy chairs and beautiful rooms. Some of these things are more dependent upon taste than upon money and a large number of people in Canada could have them if they only had the good taste to desire them. Even Oxford luxury if it does not lead to indolence and arrogance may serve a useful educative purpose in leading to a desire for ease and beauty.[43]

For Wrong, it was the man, not the research. That could wait.

Of course, Toronto was not the only university in English Canada. At Acadia University John Freeman Tufts introduced modern history to the curriculum in 1875. Having earned his BA and MA at Harvard, Tufts had been influenced by new trends in historical scholarship. From Henry Adams, who was then at Harvard, he learned that history was not something to be memorized; rather, it was something to be interpreted.[44] The president of Acadia hired Tufts in a deliberate effort to modernize the curriculum. 'In making the appointment, [the president] made it clear that the former Classical system of education was no longer adequate, and that attention must now be given to such subjects as the Sciences, Modern Languages, Education, and History.'[45] In point of fact, the distinction of being English Canada's first professor of history belongs to Tufts. However, at a time when universities were very small – in the 1870s Acadia had a faculty of eight – Tufts quickly found himself the professor of history, logic and political economy.[46] According to one of his students – who himself became a historian – Tufts used his honours course to introduce students to different approaches to the study of the past and to different philosophies of history.[47]

Dalhousie University followed a path similar to Acadia's. It first offered instruction in history in 1865 when James De Mille was named professor of rhetoric and history. When he died suddenly in 1880, the university could not afford to replace him. Indeed, rumours circulated that Dalhousie might shut down altogether. It was at this point that George Munro, a wealthy businessman, offered to endow two chairs, one in physics and the other in history. The chair in history came with the stipulation that his brother-in-law, also a member of the Dalhousie board of governors, should receive the appointment. On the ides of March 1881 John Forrest became Dalhousie's first professor of history, and four years later he was appointed president and professor of history and political economy.[48] (George Wrong would later refer to Forrest as 'old' and 'ineffective.'[49]) History and political economy would remain attached for no reason other than penury; as Stanley Mackenzie, president of the university, explained in 1913, it was 'on account of poverty' that they were not separated.[50] Seeking a replacement for Forrest in 1913, Mackenzie selected James Todd. Having studied at Oxford, Todd had the right background. Mackenzie liked the 'Oxbridge' type: 'It may have its limitations and drawbacks but it is a very characteristic product.' To 'modernize' or 'bring up to date' these two institutions (Oxford and Cambridge) would be a great mistake.[51] When Todd left Dalhousie in 1916 to serve in the war, Mackenzie anxiously searched for another Oxford-trained historian: 'I tried particularly to get track of those who had been Rhodes Scholars as more likely to appreciate somewhat the Oxford tradition and methods and the British standpoint.'[52] In the end, he secured a Rhodes Scholar, albeit an American. In addition to an Oxford BA, Carroll Wooddy had a Princeton PhD. When he enlisted with the American military in 1918, Dalhousie did not offer history and political economy for the 1918–19 academic year.

McGill University created a distinct professorship of history in 1895. To this point history had been taught as part of English literature. Moreover, there is no evidence that C.E. Moyse, McGill's professor of English literature and history from 1878 to 1895, gave serious attention to history. As his University of London mentor said of him, Moyse intended 'to give his life to the study of English.'[53] However, in 1894 Charles

Colby joined the faculty as a lecturer in English and history, and in the following year, he was appointed professor of history. An alumnus of McGill, Colby had completed a Harvard PhD in 1890. In 1906 McGill's history department expanded with the addition of C.E. Fryer, also a Harvard PhD.

Appointed in 1869, Queen's University's first professor of history was Rev. George Ferguson; like those of his counterparts at other universities, his was, to borrow Hilda Neatby's phrase, a rather 'ample' chair.[54] For the princely salary of $1,400 per annum, he was professor of history, English and modern languages. Ferguson remained at Queen's for over thirty years. According to W.B. Munro, a senior Harvard historian, it was Ferguson who first taught him 'the habit of going to the fundamental sources of historical information.'[55] Following his retirement in 1907, Ferguson was replaced by a young Englishman, J.L. Morison. Whereas Ferguson had been responsible for both English literature and modern languages, Morison was responsible only for history. Two years later, W.L. Grant joined Morison, when he accepted an appointment to the newly endowed Douglas Chair of Colonial and Canadian History. Like their counterparts in Toronto, Morison and Grant could trace their academic training to Oxford.

At the University of Manitoba, history was initially taught with philosophy in the denominational colleges that constituted the university; moreover, it was taught not by trained historians but by priests and ministers. Although the University Act of 1877 had been amended in 1892 to allow the University of Manitoba to assume teaching responsibilities – as opposed to simply examining students and conferring degrees – it was not until 1904 that the university appointed professors in the natural sciences, fields that the denominational colleges could not cover. Of course, if the university could teach the natural sciences, should it not also assume responsibility for the humanities and the social sciences, thus leaving theology to the colleges? An acrimonious debate ensued, pitting the traditionalists (those who favoured denominational instruction) against the secularists (those who wanted to modernize the university and create a non-denominational, state-supported institution). When all was said and done, the University of Manitoba appointed three new chairs in English, political economy, and history in 1909, and Chester Martin became Manitoba's first professor of history.[56] A graduate of the University of New Brunswick and a Rhodes scholar from Oxford, he remained at Manitoba until 1929. Ralph Flenley, an Englishman and also an Oxford graduate, joined Martin in 1913.

Appointed in 1909, the University of Saskatchewan's first professor of history was E.H. Oliver.[57] Actually, he was expected to teach economics as well. He bristled at the prospect, and he let the president, Walter Murray, know that he was first and foremost 'a History man.'[58] This self-conscious identification as a historian is not surprising: Oliver had done his graduate work at Columbia University with James Harvey Robinson, one of America's most prominent historians. Building a veritable dynasty at Columbia, Robinson was a key figure in the professionalization of history in the United States. He himself had studied in Germany and returned with the obsession that history must be based on original source material. Another Canadian who had studied at Columbia was James Shotwell. As he recalled, 'There was no one in the academic world who had a stricter sense of the obligations of scholarship than James Harvey Robinson. While we had to read secondary works to get the general bearing of the details we worked on, they never were to be cited in class – only the original sources.'[59] Upon taking up the position at Saskatchewan, Oliver wrote to his former professor, asking for guidance. Robinson responded that what one teaches is really a personal matter, a matter of one's own 'tastes' and 'enthusiasms.' Nonetheless, he continued,

> let us deal with things worth while and not with the past in which we really have no natural interest. I feel now that little is worth while studying in the past – or better, presenting to students, which does not have some assignable relation to their own present or future. So I am partial to the explanations of our own plight, especially our intellectual prejudices. [Charles] Beard and I have struggled to give a basis for a more rational dealing with our own time. How far we have succeeded it is for you and others to determine.[60]

Advice in hand, Oliver proceeded to make the history of western Canada the focus of his research, and he did include it in the curriculum. Although the calendar did not list western Canadian history as such, Oliver nevertheless taught it as part of History 4, the British Empire. As he reported in 1914, 'The Christmas term is given over to a study of the History of Western Canada.'[61] Oliver dedicated more time to western Canada than he did to Canada, and when Canadian History was made a separate course in the following year, the calendar description noted that the course would treat the history of the west with 'special attention.'[62] Clearly, he wanted to present his students with a usable past, one that had some 'assignable relation' to their experience as western Canadians. After a meeting with his former student while on a tour of western Canadian universities, George Wrong concluded: 'like so many, [Oliver] would not willingly live in the East again.'[63]

Founded in 1908, the University of Alberta's first president and a physicist by training, Dr Henry Marshall Tory, assumed responsibility for lecturing in history. Indeed, he would remain head of the department until 1921. When E.H. Oliver learned that Tory was to teach history in addition to his duties as president, he could not contain his scepticism: 'I insisted that Tory's cause was ridiculous, that he was a man in Mathematics and had never done any work in history.'[64] History, Oliver believed, was not something that someone could simply do; it required training. In any event, Tory appointed Alfred Leroy Burt and Stanley Gordon Fife as lecturers in 1913. Both had been Rhodes scholars at Oxford. Educated at Toronto and Oxford, Burt created a Historical Club at Alberta along lines similar to those of the one he had belonged to at Toronto, including the provision that women could not be members. 'Altogether Toronto has helped to shape this place,' George Wrong concluded after his tour of the university.[65] On the other side of the Rockies was the University of British Columbia. Although created by the University Act of 1908, it did not open its doors until 1915. That year, S. Mack Eastman, with a PhD from Columbia, was appointed UBC's first professor of history.

Professorships in history, separate departments, a new journal, an incomplete but growing commitment to archival research: history in English Canada was slowly migrating to the university and taking on the trappings of a profession. In 1909 the time seemed right for a multi-volume history of Canada.

III

First conceived in 1909 by an American publisher who wanted to create something similar to the *Encyclopedia Americana*, a multi-volume history of Canada would prove a huge undertaking. After some preliminary investigations in Toronto, the publisher's representatives learned that if they could draft Adam Shortt and Arthur Doughty, the venture would be a success.[66] These two men were a logical choice. Knowledgeable, well connected, and highly regarded, Shortt and Doughty could give the project not only their knowledge but their network of contacts and the authority of their names. Shortt began his university career at Queen's in 1886, where initially he taught philosophy, chemistry, and botany and in 1891 was named the John A. Macdonald Professor of Political Science. Shortt took a decidedly historical approach to the discipline of political economy. In point of fact, he quickly emerged as one of Canada's most prominent historians, publishing some thirty articles on Canada's banking history and in 1908 a biography of Lord Sydenham.[67]

Meanwhile, Arthur Doughty was the dominion archivist; appointed in 1904, the former drama critic and librarian launched an ambitious archival program. He had observed historical methodology in Europe and the United States and was eager to replicate it in Canada.[68] In just a few years, Doughty oversaw the move to the Archives' first permanent home on Sussex Drive; he secured a substantial increase in the Archives' annual appropriation; he instituted three new specialized divisions within the Archives; and in 1907 he convinced the government to create the Historical Manuscripts Commission. Charged with the responsibility of advising the government on archival policy and of undertaking a program of document publication, the commission consisted of Doughty and five historians: George Wrong, Charles Colby, A.H. Gosselin, Joseph Roy, and, of course, Adam Shortt.[69]

In any event, when the publishers first approached Shortt and Doughty, the two men expressed reluctance. True, they had edited a collection of documents relating to the constitutional history of Canada in 1907, but the proposed multi-volume history of Canada represented a much more daunting task. After the initial meeting in May 1909 Shortt recorded in his diary that he did not think the scheme 'very feasible'; nevertheless, the publisher 'stuck to it' and arranged for a future meeting. In June the three men met again. This time Shortt and Doughty agreed. As they knew it would be, the project proved an enormous undertaking. Shortt's diary contains reference after reference to the long hours, the many meetings, and the numerous headaches he endured over the course of coordinating ninety authors writing 153 separate essays.[70] *Canada and Its Provinces* occupied the better part of seven years from its inception in 1909 to its conclusion in 1917, when the twenty-third and final volume appeared at long last. W.A. Mackintosh thought that it marked 'a definite point in the development of Canadian historical writing.'[71] Arthur Lower believed that it 'set a new standard in Canadian historiography.'[72] Donald Creighton referred to it as 'that vast Domesday inquiry.'[73] Danielle Lacasse and Antonio Lechasseur assert that the series 'still stands as a fundamental work for understanding pre-1918 Canada.'[74]

There is no question that *Canada and Its Provinces* constitutes an important landmark in English-Canadian historiography. Both *The Makers of Canada* and the *Chronicles of Canada* were more popular than academic in orientation.[75] As Shortt and Doughty explained in their introduction, in adopting the cooperative method they had followed 'the practice of modern historians in other and older countries.' In this way, they continued, a single topic would be covered from more than one angle. For example, a specific matter of public finance could be dealt with from financial, political, and historical perspectives: 'From each of the three standpoints new light is given, and a comprehensive view of the whole matter is thus afforded.' Besides, 'The range of facts is so wide and the topics so various and complex that no one author could possibly compass them.'[76] According to Carl Berger, the series testified 'to the need for specialization.'[77]

It was in this context that Shortt and Doughty enlisted E.H. Oliver to work on the history of the west. Within a week of arriving at Saskatchewan, Oliver began a project to collect, preserve, and publish a collection of primary documents relating to the history of western Canada. In a 1911 letter to Wrong, he outlined his historical research: 'Shortt and Doughty have induced me to contribute to the History of the N.W.T. for their History of Canada, and most of my time is being spent in Journals, Sessional Papers, etc. I am attempting in a humble way to collect documents, papers, etc. as Archives of the Province. When I was in Lloydminster in January lecturing I secured a couple of diaries of the Barr Colonists. I think I shall devote my spare time to such work for Saskatchewan.'[78] Walter Murray, of course, encouraged Oliver's research. It conformed perfectly to his vision of a state university as servant to that state. Excited by the possibilities in what was known as the Wisconsin idea, Murray reported in 1910 that the University of Wisconsin had enjoyed 'excellent results' from the 'prominence given to History, Economics, Political Science, and allied subjects.' He believed it to be 'a duty of the State University to provide special facilities for the study of social conditions and the problems of government.' Because 'important questions in transportation, trade, education and government' have already arisen, the 'growth of all these departments must be rapid.' Finally, in a statement remarkable for its clarity, Murray concluded, 'Public opinion requires the guidance of the expert. It is the duty of the University to provide it.'[79] The generalist, the man of letters, and the moral philosopher were fading beneath the rise of the university-trained, university-based expert who sought to apply new research and new methods to social problems.[80] By 1914 Oliver had managed to complete a two-volume collection of primary documents in addition to a general history of Saskatchewan and Alberta for *Canada and Its Provinces*.[81]

Although the series represents a landmark in English Canadian historical writing, it also betrays a continuity with earlier historians and earlier historical writing. Of the ninety authors, only a small minority were professional historians. The vast majority were civil servants, journalists, priests, or, in a word, amateurs. W.D. Lighthall contributed two articles. Although he went to the Public Archives for the specific purpose of undertaking original research on his assigned topic,[82] his article on the history of English settlement in Quebec is framed by a romantic narrative: 'The seeds of [English Canada's] progress were deliberately sown by strong and intelligent men, who brought with them those principles and customs, acquired through centuries by their island forefathers, that their descendants still cherish as their most precious heritage.'[83] It is noteworthy that the editors did not object.

While they wanted to present Canadians with an up-to-date and factual account of Canada's past, Shortt and Doughty intended the series to mould national character, to counter, in their words, the 'destructive tendency' of sectionalism 'by the positive and constructive idea of the Nation.' 'To the end that a broad national spirit should prevail in all parts of the Dominion, it is desirable that a sound knowledge of Canada as a whole, of its history, traditions and standards of life, should be diffused among its citizens, and especially among the immigrants who are peopling the new lands ... Good citizenship grows out of a patriotic interest in the institutions of one's country and a sympathy with the people who dwell there.'[84] To ensure that the series presented a unified interpretation of Canada, the two editors carefully selected their Quebec contributors. In his diary Shortt speculated that 'There will be difficulty in getting suitable contributions from Que. as the liberal and conservative elements are so radically opposed in their interpretation of historic events.' A few months later he recorded their hope 'to secure Mr. Chapais to supervise and largely contribute to the volume on Quebec.'[85] To promote unity over sectionalism, Thomas Chapais was the logical choice. He interpreted the conquest 'as a providential event that saved French Canadians from the Revolution of 1789' and he 'stressed the liberality and the conciliatory character of British policy.'[86] Although it was nearly sixteen months later, Chapais eventually agreed. In the end it was Chapais along with 'Father Drummond and

Abbé Gosselin, head of Laval, and Abbé Scott' who wrote the history of Quebec for the series.[87]

The use of history to promote national unity did not disappear with history's transition from avocation to vocation. To plot a rise in the transition from amateurs to professional historians is to obscure this underlying continuity. W.D. Lighthall and Janet Carnochan would have agreed with Shortt and Doughty that 'Good citizenship grows out of a patriotic interest in the institutions of one's country and a sympathy with the people who dwell there.' *Canada and Its Provinces,* therefore, embodied a conception of history that included both a commitment to critical enquiry and a commitment to patriotism. Canada's first generation of professional historians subscribed to archival research, but they did not embrace the notion of value-free research.

IV

George Wrong did not believe that history could be a science. In two public talks, both delivered late in his career, he reflected on the nature of history and the duty of the historian. For his 1927 presidential address to the Canadian Historical Association, Wrong tackled what he termed 'the historian's absorbing problem.' Given man's fickle nature, his immaturity, and his irrationality, given that there was 'no uniformity in his actions ... no single motive [and] no law of reason to which he is always obedient,' and given that he was 'so often false to himself and so false to others that perhaps more than half of his written testimony about them is untrue,' how was the historian to find the truth? Wrong argued that there never would be a science of history, that history would 'never be finally written.' Nevertheless, the historian had definite obligations: 'The first is making sure of the facts.' Facts were the necessary foundation of all history, he added. But facts alone did not make history. Indeed, the historian must pass to the second stage – interpretation. At this stage, the historian must exercise his imagination, he must be willing to discriminate, and he must be prepared to pass judgment.[88] It was this duty that Wrong took most seriously. As he explained in a 1932 address to the American Historical Association, the historian had a fundamental duty to pass moral judgment: 'The historian is the guardian of truth, truth not merely as to specific fact, but truth as expressing constructive standards of conduct.'[89]

Is Wrong the accidental father of professional history in English Canada? Carl Berger describes him as an 'ambiguous figure,' because he founded 'the [*Review of Historical Publications Relating to Canada*] and other agencies associated with the new "scientific" history, but he never accepted the nostrums of historical science.'[90] Looked at in another way, this ambiguity is actually clarity. Wrong remained clear in his conception of history and consistent in his commitment to it. He believed in the unity of historical truth. Historical truth, as he conceived it, comprised both the factual record and the moral good. History must be scientific in that it must be based on archival research. But archival research did not preclude the historian from making moral pronouncements. Wrong saw no contradiction between his commitment to research on the one hand and his commitment to moral judgment on the other. The two were perfectly compatible, because the truth, as he understood it, encompassed fact and morality. There is a clarity in his 1932 statement: 'The historian is the guardian of truth, truth not merely as to specific fact, but truth as expressing constructive standards of conduct.'

That history should be based on archival research, that it should not lose its capacity to judge, and that it ought to inspire formed the dominant approach to the study of the past among the first generation of professional historians. When Albert Henry Newman arrived at the Toronto Baptist College in 1881 as professor of biblical introduction, Old Testament exegesis and Church history, he sensed his was a divine calling. As he explained in a letter, 'It really seemed to me that I had been set apart as it were by Divine Providence for the work of writing an exhaustive history of the Baptists.'[91] Nine years later, the Toronto Baptist College became McMaster University and Newman became its first professor of history and civil polity.[92] Trained as a theologian, Newman nevertheless exhibited those traits associated with professional history (a commitment to the sources, a critical disposition, etc.). As well, he articulated a clear definition of history: 'the setting forth in literary or oral form of the development in time of the divine plan of the universe, in so far as this development has become an object of human knowledge.' Church history, meanwhile, was 'the narration of all that is known of the founding and the development of the kingdom of Christ on earth.'[93] Although a church historian, Newman echoed his counterparts in modern history in his adherence to original research and impartiality. The church historian, he explained, must 'represent the exact facts in their relations to each other and to the times and circumstances concerned in each case.' Moreover, 'he should deal as impartially with his materials as does the chemist with his specimens.' In his final three annual reports (1899–1901) Newman stated his intention to introduce the seminar method to teaching: 'I have often called your attention to the desirability of having a single class-room for all the work of my department to be used for other purposes as little as possible,' he reminded the chancellor; 'This would enable me to have maps, pictures, and books for use in the work of the department always accessible ... History to be taught effectively requires apparatus just as really as does Science or Physics.'[94] At first glance, Newman's references to chemistry and physics appear to be a straightforward effort to create a science out of history. In a sense it was. But Newman never attempted to separate the true and the good. He did not subscribe to value-free research. Although the researcher must subject documents to internal and external criticism, and although the researcher must exhibit impartiality, 'it is neither practicable nor desirable that the church historian should be indifferent to the subject-matter of his science or that he should be so destitute of convictions as to form no moral judgments on the opinions and acts of parties and individuals whose history he studies and seeks to expound.'[95] The true and the good, he believed, constituted an essential unity.

McGill's first professor of history similarly believed that history was about more than research, that it was about instruction as well. In a 1905 address to the Canadian Club of Toronto Charles Colby acknowledged that 'the historian should have, so far as is humanly possible, the disinterestedness of the dead; that he should not set forth the results of his researches with a view to justifying any special cause, or even to vindicate the record of his own ancestors.' In addition, however, the historian should do something for his country; he must write 'the great national history,' a script of citizenship that would explain, yes, but also instruct and inspire.[96] Or, as Colby wrote in an unpublished address, 'The scientific impulse has done much for historical scholarship, but man shall not live by bread alone.'[97]

Colby attempted his own great history in his 1908 book, *Canadian Types of the Old Régime*. Canadians now 'live in a generation which demands reasons, craves to know the cause of things, and which will not be put off with rhetoric, however glib, or rhapsody, however eloquent,' he stated. But if history offered 'the cause of things,' it must also offer instruction and guidance. Through his study of representative types in New France, Colby wanted to instruct English Canadians in the ways of French Canadians and guide them towards recognition and tolerance. 'It seems to me,' he commented, 'a thousand pities that of English

Canadians not one in ten understands the sentiments and aspirations of French Canada.' English Canada ought to understand 'why the habitant thinks, feels, and acts as he does.' Likewise, French Canada ought to appreciate the benefits of British political institutions and English criminal law, for example.[98] History, he once explained, introduced us 'to the supreme art, the art of living. The teacher [of history] who, having himself been stimulated by man's best achievement, can fill the souls of his pupils with the splendour of the same spectacle is helping them in no slight degree to raise themselves above the level of the corrupting and commonplace.'[99]

Queen's historian J.L. Morison agreed. In a revealing review article, Morison presented an unambiguous statement on the nature of history and the obligation of the historian. He opened his article with a snide description of the new scientific history, with its emphasis on the minute study of ever-multiplying documents and its 'conscientious elaboration of even unimportant detail.' The arrogant proponents of the new history, with their penchant for bibliography and their refusal to make moral judgments, threatened a revolution. Literary style had become the victim of 'increased attention to Archives and Record offices.' Morison did not object to research. 'No one doubts the place of scientific method in research, or the need for the strictest attention to minute detail; treatises, let us say, on medieval constitutional history call for a scientific apparatus at least as elaborate as that required in any of the exacter sciences.' But science did not mean value-free scholarship; it meant scholarship tested by original authorities. The difference was enormous. Morison wanted to retain the capacity to judge. That historians should refrain from moral judgment was little more than an 'intellectual fad.' 'As if history, in its more inspired moments, has not always been a recognized court of moral appeal, where men usurp, for a little, the office of the final judge.'[100]

Morison's colleague, W.L. Grant, likewise expressed his disdain for the mere fact chaser and chronicler. As he explained, the fact chaser would 'proceed to his work of "Chronological Classification," being careful first to provide himself with a cabinet full of small drawers in which to systematize his notes.' The problem, he argued, was that facts were infinite in number: 'Can we investigate them all? On what string are we to arrange our scattered pearls? The Chronological? How, then, are we to get perspective?' Grant concluded that historians ought to articulate some ideal and place it before their fellow citizens. In schools and in universities students ought to be presented with a lofty ideal to which they could aspire.[101] What might that ideal look like? Grant answered this question when, a few years later, he likened the study of colonial history in general and Canadian history in particular to a moral force in its capacity 'to advance the great spiritual drawing together of the Anglo-Celtic race which, were it to come, would be strong enough to guard the peace of the world.'[102]

Saskatchewan's first professor of history did not see a contradiction between fact and value, or between the true and the good: at the same time as E.H. Oliver defined himself as 'a History man,' he was studying for the ministry. He completed his bachelor of divinity at Toronto's Knox College in 1910 and, three years later, was ordained a Presbyterian minister. Although he deliberately incorporated the history of western Canada into the curriculum, that curriculum still emphasized the history of western civilization through courses in ancient history, modern European history, medieval history, and the British Empire. Although the ancient Greeks and Romans were far removed from contemporary life in Saskatchewan, Oliver saw in history an essential civilizing mission. In his diary he wondered if he could be both practical and 'an influence for good' like W.S. Milner, his classics professor at Toronto.[103] In other words, Oliver did not look upon history as something that was simply practical. For all the perspective and context history offered to contemporary social problems, it also taught moral lessons of duty and obligation.

Oliver's commitment to history as something both practical and moral, as both true and good was not contradictory. He thought the university, even the officially non-denominational University of Saskatchewan, should be Christian in orientation. He wanted voluntary chapel for the university community (although some faculty members felt it contravened the University Act) and he encouraged students to form organizations for Christian fellowship. To this end, he requested information from the head office of the YMCA in New York. In an address before the Presbyterian synodical banquet, Oliver stated that the university and the Church were 'both attempting to do the same work in working for a Kingdom of Enlightenment.' For Oliver, history must be based on the concrete findings of painstaking research but it need not be empty of moral purpose. In short, history did not preclude morality. It was the professor's job to inspire students to 'effort and noble endeavour.'[104] Oliver deliberately linked Christian morality and history, the good and the true.

Oliver left the University of Saskatchewan in 1914 to serve as principal of Saskatoon's newly created Presbyterian Theological College.[105] He believed that he could best execute his duty to the people of Saskatchewan as a minister, not as a professor of history. Clues to his departure from the department that he founded can be located in his diary. On his first night in Saskatoon Oliver prayed as he did every night: 'My evening prayer is that I may be here in Saskatchewan a workman that needeth not be ashamed.' This is a direct reference to Paul's second epistle to Timothy, in which Paul exhorts Timothy to present himself to God as 'a workman that needeth not be ashamed,' so that he might carry the word of God and the salvation that is in Jesus Christ (2 Timothy 2:15). Three years later, in 1912 Oliver noted that he seemed to be doing much more preaching and bible study than he had done in the past.[106] Eventually, the call of God proved greater than the call of Clio, and Oliver exchanged the gown for the cloth.

Wrong, Shortt, Newman, Colby, Morison, Grant, and Oliver: these historians embodied a larger transition animating English Canada's academic community. On the one hand, they were committed to facts generated by research. Since the turn of the century, English-Canadian academics had embraced research, what James Loudon, president of the University of Toronto, identified as 'the fundamental principle.'[107] On the other hand, they remained committed to the good. Truth comprised both fact and value.

The First World War, however, had an enormous impact. As several scholars have noted, the war accelerated that movement already present in academic life towards the research ideal as embodied in the new social sciences. Disillusioned by the moral calamity of the Western Front and terrified by the prospects of Bolshevism, the academic community shifted Canada's reform movement away from its social gospel roots and towards what they believed to be a sounder foundation in the social sciences. Social scientists, armed with a scientific understanding of society, could best provide expert direction on state policy.[108] Indeed, there was a general belief that a scientific understanding of society, its past and its present, would assist the immediate task of post-war reconstruction, provide the stability necessary to liberal democracy, and prevent a repetition of the war. A.B. McKillop argues that science filled the vacuum created by the general crisis of authority precipitated by the war:

> Until the Great War ... the proponents of the Ontario university's role as agent of a social and intellectual transformation firmly rooted in the industrial order had been on the defensive, for the authority of the past, rooted

in the biblical record, remained the fundamental basis of moral force in higher education. At the Armistice of 11 November 1918, much of that authority was gone, and professional apostles of the new academic order were readying themselves for the brave new post-war world.[109]

The University of Saskatchewan's Walter Murray captured this sentiment in his 1916–17 'President's Report,' when he emphasized history as a social science. From the premise that 'racial animosities, deep seated in history,' had set 'the world on fire,' Murray called for a deeper understanding of the historical origins of 'racial ambitions' and for a rethinking of 'those fundamental principles and laws which should regulate the conduct of nations no less than of individuals.' In doing so we would avoid another war. He then predicted a place in the sun for the social sciences: 'History, Law, Economics – the sciences of human society – will be appealed to as never before.'[110] In her study of the undergraduate arts curriculum in English Canada, Patricia Jasen argues that the interwar era was 'the most utilitarian of all eras in the history of the arts curriculum.'[111]

None of this is to suggest that historians functioned in some kind of moral vacuum or that they embraced the ideal of value-free research. What McKillop identifies as a moral imperative – an imperative that stressed a balance between enquiry and affirmation – continued to animate the social science project into the second half of the twentieth century.[112] Still, there were ongoing attempts to make history a social science, to make it more immediately useful. The question of values, if not abandoned, was submerged. Against this backdrop, the interwar decades were key years in the professionalization of history. As Queen's historian Reginald Trotter remarked in 1943, 'It was a period when history was rapidly coming into its own as a profession in Canada.'[113] The *Canadian Historical Review* replaced the *Review of Historical Publications Relating to Canada*; the Canadian Historical Association emerged out of the Historic Landmarks Association; and a new generation of historians – A.L. Burt, Frank Underhill, Chester New, Arthur Lower, Harold Innis, Donald Creighton, George Brown, Reginald Trotter, Duncan McArthur, Mack Eastman, W.N. Sage, Arthur Morton, and D.C. Harvey – exhibited a heightened self-consciousness as professionals.

CHAPTER 3

'The post-1918 generation': professionalization continued

Alfred Leroy Burt made the Public Archives his summer home in the 1920s. When classes ended in the spring, he boarded the train for the long trip from Edmonton to Ottawa. A historian of Canada with a special interest in the French-English relationship, Burt had discovered that the secondary literature was wholly inadequate. As he would note a few years later, it was this inadequacy that 'drove me to the Public Archives of Canada.'[1] Moreover, he was never alone. Beginning in the early 1920s, the Public Archives became the gathering place for historians from across the country. In numerous letters to his wife, Burt offered a running commentary on who was at the Archives and what they were doing. Harold Innis, Duncan McArthur, Frank Underhill, Chester New, Reginald Trotter, A.S. Morton, Bartlet Brebner, George Brown, W.N. Sage: everyone, it seemed, made repeated summer trips to the Archives.[2] 'It is quite interesting to see the actual renaissance of Canadian history in course of preparation,' he wrote in 1926. 'Certainly all the professional historians in Canada are turning their eyes on the Archives during the summer & a revolution is bound to come about as the result.'[3]

During the 1920s a rapid expansion in historical research occurred. Although there were notable exceptions – McGill's E.R. Adair, Manitoba's Noel Fieldhouse, and McMaster's Chester New, for example – most historians focused their attention on the writing of Canadian history.[4] A.S. Morton began his study of western exploration and early settlement. Harold Innis studied the Canadian Pacific Railway before turning his attention to the history of the fur trade. Arthur Lower examined the history of Canada's lumber economy. Chester Martin researched imperial relations and western settlement. Frank Underhill focused his energy on Canadian political history, Confederation in particular. Fred Landon began his research on the history of southwestern Ontario. W.N. Sage studied the history of British Columbia in both his Toronto dissertation and throughout his UBC career. George Brown conducted an investigation of British North America's trade with Great Britain and the United States. Having to abandon his interest in the French Revolution, Donald Creighton turned to the history of Canadian commerce. Burt, of course, studied the French-English relationship in the immediate aftermath of the conquest.

Burt's many letters to his wife capture the energy and excitement in the historical profession as a new generation of historians, what he would later refer to as 'the post-1918 generation,' came to maturity in the interwar years.[5] If the foundations of a historical profession had been laid in the 1890s and early 1900s, the profession emerged more fully and completely after the Great War. The revitalization of history departments, the emphasis on scholarly publication, the institutionalization of graduate studies, the development of undergraduate courses in methodology and historiography, the creation of the *Canadian Historical Review*, and the founding of the Canadian Historical Association were but different aspects of the same project: to professionalize the study of history in English Canada.

I

When the University of British Columbia's Mack Eastman enlisted in 1917, he was the Department of History; the university duly suspended instruction. When A.L Burt enlisted in the First Tanks Battalion in 1918, the dean of arts reported that the Department of History was now 'completely cleaned out.'[6] The war not only claimed the services of Dalhousie's professor of history and political economy, it claimed the services of his wartime replacement as well. Queen's University and the Universities of Manitoba and Saskatchewan relied on part-time instructors throughout the war. When hostilities finally ended, history departments across the country were revitalized as veterans returned and new members were added.[7]

By today's standards, departments were small: most had only two or three permanent members. Because of budget constraints, Mount Allison University and the University of New Brunswick did not have separate departments of history until the late 1930s. Yet there was an air of energetic optimism from Dalhousie in the east to UBC in the west. At any given time there were thirty-five to forty historians teaching at English-Canadian universities. Together they constituted a critical mass of men – the first woman appointed to a permanent position was Hilda Neatby in 1936 at Regina College, then part of the University of Saskatchewan – who identified themselves as professional historians and who embraced research and scholarly publication. The threat to publish or perish had yet to be uttered in the interwar years,[8] but there was a new and palpable pressure to produce.

When Arthur Currie, Principal of McGill University, hired Basil Williams, he made it clear that he expected him to research and write: 'I am indeed anxious that you shall keep up your writing and research work. For although you have been engaged primarily to teach, I realize that the more you write the better it will be for the University and for yourself. I am anxious to encourage you in that in every way I can, and I quite realize that I must give you every opportunity for production.'[9] A senior scholar from England with an Oxford MA and a strong record of publications, Williams agreed.[10] Within a few months of his arrival he complained that his overworked staff did not have the time 'to keep up with the constantly increasing literature of their subjects' or 'to do any original work.' He added, 'Some people hold that it is not the business of a professor to publish original work: but in the first place a university is more likely to attract good teachers if they feel they have the time to pursue their own work, & secondly there is little doubt that students are attracted to a university of which the teachers have a public reputation.'[11] In 1924 Williams requested a fourth appointment. The current staff is spread too thin, he explained in a letter to Currie: 'If the History work is to be good, the professor must be constantly keeping ahead of research and recasting his lectures ... The proverbial professor of old times who made a set of lectures & went on delivering them from father to son is gone for ever.'[12] Aspiring scholars could read the writing on the wall. Before beginning doctoral work, Arthur Lower published a handful of articles, including one in the *Canadian Historical Review*. These, he believed, contributed something to his 'professional reputation.'[13] Toronto's Ralph Flenley advised a young C.P. Stacey – who in 1929 had set his sights on an academic career – to 'get something in print' if he wanted to work at one of the better universities.[14]

Even George Wrong began to stress research and publication. Whereas in the 1900s and 1910s Wrong did not pressure his staff to undertake research projects, he placed a new emphasis on scholarship at Toronto in the 1920s. Hired in 1923, Lester Pearson had a Toronto

BA and an Oxford BA. As he recalled in his memoirs, 'It was never even suggested to me that I must get a PhD quickly or depart.' The 'age of research and scholarly production as the first requirement for prestige and promotion,' he said, 'had not descended on us.' If a junior member of Wrong's department happened to publish, that would be fine: 'But we were not plagued by this necessity.'[15] As his biographer made clear, however, Pearson's account of his brief tenure as a history professor was 'misleading.'[16] Wrong did not expect Pearson to get a PhD – his fetishization of the Oxford BA never waned – but he did expect him to undertake a large research project on the United Empire Loyalists. In a 1923 letter to Frank Underhill, Wrong emphasized the importance of research and the pressure he was now putting on his staff: 'As you know I have long had my eye on you in respect to University work and I have urged you to get a book with your name on the title-page. I quite understand the difficulties for a man in active academic life to get himself free for writing. I do hope, however, that you will manage this in the course of the next year or two ... *At the moment I am putting pressure on members of my own staff to do this,* and there are a dozen topics relating to Canada alone on which books are urgently needed.'[17] Making his way to the Public Archives in the summer of 1926, Pearson began a research project on Loyalist settlement. A.L. Burt reported that he rather enjoyed the research; Pearson, he said, 'is quite intoxicated by his study of the Loyalist settlement in Upper Canada'; he 'is as happy as a lark digging up materials.'[18] But Pearson's enthusiasm for the project waned. In his memoirs C.P. Stacey remembered Pearson as an amiable fellow, not as 'a massive scholar.'[19] According to John English, Pearson's sympathies lay with an older conception of history as moral instruction, which in the 1920s was increasingly incompatible with specialization, sustained archival research, and scholarly writing.[20] It was against this backdrop that Pearson left the academy for the civil service.

The transition to a newer conception of history also found concrete expression in more systematic graduate and undergraduate training.

II

'Prolonged specialized training in a body of abstract knowledge,' according to W.J. Goode, constitutes a core characteristic of a profession.[21] Although every school offered an MA program, only Toronto, McGill, and Queen's offered a PhD program.[22] At the University of Toronto George Wrong had supervised MA theses since 1893. Throughout the first two decades of the twentieth century, however, the MA program 'was little more than a BA plus an essay'[23] – and that essay could be as short as twelve pages.[24] References, when provided, were not formalized and bibliographies were irregular. In other words, the *apparatus criticus* of modern scholarship was either absent or inconsistent. Although the university had established 'the Degree of Doctor of Philosophy ... for the purpose of encouraging research' in 1897,[25] the history department itself did not offer a PhD until 1915 and had no doctoral students until the early 1920s. The department was too small and too focused on undergraduate instruction.[26] But in the early 1920s the university as a whole began to take its graduate program more seriously. In his 1922 report to the president, the chairman of the Board of Graduate Studies, J. Playfair McMurrich, noted that 'the organization of graduate studies under the direction of the Board of Graduate Studies did not sufficiently emphasize the importance of these studies in the work of the University.' As a result, 'Graduate work seemed to be an addendum to the undergraduate work, rather than a logical sequence.'[27] In order to organize graduate studies more efficiently and to raise its status in the university, McMurrich recommended a School of Graduate Studies. In 1922 the University of Toronto acted on McMurrich's recommendation.

It was in this context that the Department of History attempted to raise the status of its graduate program. In 1922 Wrong indicated that he wanted to increase the research component of the MA. For more convenient access to sources students ought to be pointed in the direction of local history, since there were 'a good many subjects which could be treated here.' Of course, any gaps could be filled in by a visit to Ottawa.[28] Yet it was possible for a student never to set foot on the campus and still receive an MA. Arthur Lower completed his Toronto MA in 1923 but did not physically attend the university. Employed at the Public Archives, he arranged to work under Adam Shortt's supervision, writing his thesis in the evenings and on weekends.[29] In 1924, however, Toronto instituted a series of changes. First, there would be a mandatory course for MA students in historical method, bibliography, and the development of English historical writing. Second, a distinction was made between MA by course and MA by thesis, with requirements – including residency requirements – for each option clearly listed in the calendar. Third, students who undertook a Canadian topic were 'expected to avail themselves of the facilities for research in the Dominion Archives at Ottawa.'[30] Also in 1924, Wrong organized mandatory group work for all graduate students in the first two months of their program. Under this scheme graduate students met with the various members of the department for about four hours of group discussion per week on subjects not necessarily related to their theses. 'We find that they are apt to feel rather at loose ends here until they settle down into this environment, and henceforth we shall keep them pretty busy doing work for us ... until they have settled into our conditions.' He later noted: 'We must also do more for them by way of social entertainment until they feel at home.'[31] To what extent Wrong realized his intentions is not known; nonetheless, his letters indicate a growing awareness of and interest in Toronto's graduate program in the early 1920s. By 1928 all MA students were required to have a language skill – either French or German – while those MA students presenting a thesis had to take both a written and an oral exam.

Toronto's PhD program underwent similar changes. Since its creation in 1915 PhD candidates had been required to take one major subject and two minor subjects in addition to demonstrating 'an adequate knowledge of French and German.' The thesis, moreover, had to be 'of such a character as to constitute an addition to the literature.'[32] Yet there were very few doctoral students: in 1919 there was one; in 1920 there were none; in 1921 there were two. The president, Sir Robert Falconer, could 'not understand how it has arisen that it has not been the custom of the department of History in the University of Toronto to grant a degree of Doctor of Philosophy.'[33] For his part, Wrong was sceptical of the degree. Speaking of Harold Innis's history of the Canadian Pacific Railway, he observed: 'It is a sound piece of research but it is almost formless in respect to literary quality and the text is overburdened by footnotes to an absurd extent. And this excess of method is what the American School of History glories in.'[34] Despite his misgivings, Wrong attempted to make the PhD program more systematic in 1924 by making the course in historical methods mandatory for doctoral candidates. In 1925 two candidates completed their doctorates: W.N. Sage and W.B. Kerr. A few years later, in 1928, the calendar outlined the department's increased expectations for the thesis: 'The thesis must be a work of original research. It must be worthy of publication.' The calendar also stated that doctoral students 'must be in attendance save when engaged in research in the Archives at Ottawa or elsewhere for the purpose of the thesis.'[35]

McGill also offered a graduate program. Although the university had conferred many MAs and the occasional PhD since the turn of the century, its graduate work was clearly subordinate to its undergraduate work. But as active research became more important to a university's mandate in the early decades of the twentieth century, McGill created a Faculty of Graduate Studies and Research in 1922.[36] True, the Department of History had admitted MA candidates since 1910, but the standards were low and the results uneven. When Basil Williams arrived in 1921, he intended to improve McGill's graduate program. After surveying the lay of the land at McGill, Queen's, Toronto, and the Public Archives, Williams submitted a detailed report. Among other things, he drew Principal Arthur Currie's attention to the quite inadequate provision for graduate students; as it was, the staff was overstretched by its responsibilities to undergraduate students. Ideally, the department would offer a distinct graduate program.[37] When W.T. Waugh joined the department in 1922 as its third member, Williams implemented a distinct MA program. In addition to graduate-level courses in British and European history, it included a mandatory course in historical method and criticism. Two years later the calendar listed a graduate course in Canadian history, 1840–67. Williams stressed the direct relationship between the department's graduate program and its reputation. 'On [graduate students] and on the work they produce will largely depend the reputation of McGill for original work in History.'[38] To protect McGill's reputation Williams and Waugh failed an MA thesis in 1923 because it did not meet the standards set by the 'best of the American universities.' According to Waugh, the thesis failed 'to show a grasp of the elementary principles of historical criticism.' Asked to review the thesis, Charles Colby agreed: it 'would not be accepted at Harvard, Yale or Princeton.'[39] In 1934 McGill accepted its first PhD students; ostensibly a three-year program, in practice it took four years to complete.[40] The first year involved course work, including the methodology course. Doctoral candidates, moreover, had to demonstrate proficiency in two foreign languages. The remainder of the program, of course, involved thesis research and preparation. According to the calendar, the thesis 'must represent a genuine contribution to historical scholarship.'[41]

In theory, Queen's University first initiated its doctoral program in 1889, when 'the Senate established in the humanities and sciences formal courses leading to the PhD in humanities and the DSc in the sciences.'[42] In practice, however, a Queen's doctorate was extremely rare. Meanwhile, its MA degree was not a research degree; according to Frederick Gibson, it would not be until 1917 that the university transformed its MA 'into a true graduate degree instead of a recognition of high standing in an honours course.' This increased 'emphasis on graduate studies was an essential element in the concept of a research-oriented university advanced by [political economist] O.D. Skelton and [physicist] Arthur Clark at the end of World War I.' Yet the PhD remained rare. Throughout the interwar years, 'Queen's honours graduates seeking to prepare for the doctorate were encouraged to go elsewhere.'[43] In the interwar years, very few outside doctoral students were admitted, although exceptions were made for students who wanted to work with a particular professor. Thus, the department of history had only two doctoral candidates in the interwar years; one failed to complete her thesis following her marriage, and the other graduated in 1931.[44]

In addition to its graduate program, Queen's introduced a special course in historical research. Initiated by J.L. Morison in 1922 and held at the Public Archives in Ottawa, the Summer School of Historical Research in Canadian History became an annual event. Open to students from any university who either intended to pursue postgraduate studies or who were already engaged in postgraduate studies, the five-week course emphasized instruction in the use of manuscript sources. According to one advertising brochure, the course would 'be conducted in daily seminars, attention being given to the problem of historical method and to the bibliography of Canadian history for the period studied.' Students would also be expected to present reports 'on special topics based upon intensive use of the first-hand materials in the Canadian Archives.'[45]

Although most historians teaching in the university did not have a PhD, the degree became increasingly common throughout the 1920s and 1930s. W.N. Sage took a purely pragmatic approach. Already teaching at the University of British Columbia, he decided that since he would be 'working at B.C. history anyway,' he 'might as well get some academic credit' for it. 'This is rather a utilitarian way of looking at it,' he told W.L. Grant, 'but the Canadian West is not exempt from the American worship of the PhD.' Besides, he continued, the UBC department was in an 'unsettled condition'; it was very important, therefore, to secure 'this PhD degree in as short a time as possible.'[46] In the mid-1920s Arthur Lower decided that he wanted to be a professor of history. Knowing that a Toronto MA would not be an adequate qualification, he looked south: 'I thought if I could get leave [from the Archives] for a term, I might go to some great American university and begin my training for a PhD.'[47] It was at Harvard that he finally became a historian. Although he called it a 'knowledge factory,' Lower admitted that it trained him in the discipline of history: 'Knowledge factory or not, Harvard turned me decisively away from amateurism. If one were to stay in its graduate school, one had to become a professional.'[48] Gerald Graham went from Queen's to Harvard in 1926, where he was overwhelmed by 'the American system of post-graduate education – which means grinding hard work, as part of the constant policy – "Thorough."'[49] At one point he referred to America's fetishization of the PhD. Nevertheless, he knew which way the wind was blowing: fetishized or not, the PhD was fast becoming the minimum requirement for historians.[50] Because of his interest in British history, and with a Parkin Travelling Scholarship, Graham left Harvard for Cambridge in 1927, where he enrolled in a doctoral program. As W.L. Grant stated, 'I quite agree that you are right in bowing the knee to Baal, and in doing research work for your PhD rather than BA work.'[51] When in 1929 C.P. Stacey realized that he wanted to be a historian, he decided at the same time to do a doctorate at Princeton: 'it occurred to me that if, in addition to my Toronto and Oxford experience, I acquired a Doctor of Philosophy degree in history from a good American graduate school my qualifications would be so impressive that job offers could not fail to flow in upon me.'[52]

In a 1926 article entitled 'Some Vices of Clio,' Toronto's W.S. Wallace accepted the reality of postgraduate studies, but at the same time he urged students to remember history's roots in literature. He acknowledged that the PhD had not yet become the *sine qua non* for academic appointments; yet 'there appears to be almost everywhere a tendency to regard this degree as a desideratum, and in many [North American] universities to regard it frankly as an essential.' This was not necessarily bad; after all, the PhD did represent two or three years of solid primary research: 'That this is a gain, no one who is conversant with the work of historians of the seventeenth, eighteenth, and even nineteenth centuries can deny.' Still, something had been lost. There was not one PhD thesis that even approximated 'a "great book,"' Wallace observed. Furthermore, the topics themselves were tragic in their narrowness. Looking at the list of dissertations prepared by the Carnegie Institute, he declared, 'one is filled with a sense of futility, the unreality, the misdirection of much in higher education in America today. That a student should spend two or three years in the heyday of life exploring the history of "Higher Education for Women in Missouri" or even "The Status of the American College Professor in the Nineteenth Century" ... can only be described as a tragedy.' If the PhD had become a reality, Wallace concluded, it should not mean the end of readable, literary history. Students must not forget their obligation to the art of history.[53]

In this brief article Wallace articulated the abiding contradiction of the profession: the need for specialization versus the need for generalization. Although clearly uncomfortable with the direction in which history was moving in the 1920s, Wallace was powerless to stop it. In 1928 he cautioned President Falconer against appointing someone 'simply because he knows how to read medieval charters. I see, from the standpoint of the library, so much of what appears to me undue specialization within the departments of the University, that I should be sorry to see the history department, which has always stood out against undue specialization, afflicted with the same disease.' By his own admission, however, he tended to be old fashioned: 'I, like Professor Wrong, belong to an era in which a professor of history "professed" all periods, and perhaps my views are antiquated.'[54]

Not only did graduate school train students in historiography and in historical methods – Wallace's misgivings notwithstanding – it also socialized students. As W.J. Goode observed: 'The student professional goes through a more far-reaching adult socialization experience than the learner in other occupations.'[55] In other words, graduate school instilled in students proper professional behaviour. Burton Bledstein went even further: graduate school 'indoctrinated the select participants' in the culture of professionalism.[56] Unfortunately, it is difficult to recount the graduate school experience; although mentoring relationships between professors and students certainly existed, they are difficult to locate. The supervisor-student relationship, after all, was an informal one. Surviving in the personal papers of Reginald Trotter, however, is a continuous correspondence with his doctoral student, John P. Pritchett.[57]

When teaching at Stanford University in the early 1920s, Trotter first met Pritchett, who was then an undergraduate. Trotter turned Pritchett's attention northwards to Canadian history and to the possibility of a career in history. When Trotter took up a post at Queen's University, Pritchett followed a few years later in 1926 and began work on a PhD. Trotter took him under his wing: he acquired funding for him; he arranged part-time teaching contracts; he put him in touch with experts in his field; he gave him teaching and research tips; and, of course, he wrote countless letters of recommendation. When Pritchett graduated in 1931, their relationship did not end, since Trotter continued to play an avuncular role. When Pritchett solicited his counsel, he gladly provided it. When Pritchett needed employment, Trotter always managed to secure him a summer-session course. When James Shotwell was planning the Canadian-American relations series in 1934, Trotter submitted Pritchett's name. And in 1935 Trotter ensured that Pritchett would have a spot on the program of the 1936 annual meeting of the CHA. After securing a Social Science Research Council grant in the spring of 1937, Pritchett sent Trotter one of his many thank-you notes. In this one he added a more personal comment: 'Please do not think me maudlin, when I say I admire you above all my friends. You are so unselfish and so fine. You are my ideal of a gentleman. If at any time I can do anything for you I want you [to] know that I am "at your service."'[58] Trotter responded in kind. 'It has always been a great interest to me to watch your academic progress and a joy to see you stepping on from one goal to another,' he said, 'and I am proud to have been a companion along part of the way.'[59] Trotter's careful nurturing of Pritchett continued into the 1940s. When Pritchett wrote what George Brown considered an ill-considered and misguided review of a book by George Wrong, Brown suggested to Trotter that he might want to have a word with his protégé.[60] Trotter agreed. Pritchett, he said, 'is too good a man to be allowed to weaken his own position by taking on such superior airs about the work of better men.'[61] A few weeks later, over the course of dinner in New York City, where Pritchett was teaching at Queen's College, Trotter disciplined his former student, offering him some 'pretty frank' advice. In the long run, he told Brown, it would not be 'without effect.'[62]

Meanwhile, the emphasis on technique in graduate school found its way into the undergraduate curriculum. In 1922, for example, Mack Eastman noted that UBC had already graduated several students in honours history without having been able to offer an honours seminar in historical method. It is essential, he said, to add a seminar 'that would teach Honour students how to do intensive and accurate work in one or more fields ... [that would] involve a study of Bibliography, Research methods, etc.'[63] It would not be until 1927, however, that 'Historical Method' and 'The Writing of History' were listed as two out of five possibilities for the seminar that year.[64] In 1931 a third-year methods course was made a permanent listing. As D.C. Harvey explained, 'The third year seminar for honours students is an examination of historical standards and methods and training in the technique of historical writing. The fourth year seminar affords practice in applying these methods on some subject in which source material is amply available.'[65] Beginning

in 1931, the Manitoba calendar advised students taking Canadian constitutional history that they would 'be expected to be familiar with the
documentary base of this period,' that is, the original sources.[66] In 1933
the calendar stated that both 'Topics in Canadian History' and 'The
French Revolution' would also serve 'as an introduction to methods of
research.'[67] In his annual report, Noel Fieldhouse explained: 'The
Department believes that only by the use of some such method
(whereby the student is given some training in using reliable sources
of information for himself, in weighing contradictory evidence and
opinions, and in discriminating between relevant and irrelevant material) can the teaching of History have any educative value.'[68] In the mid-
1930s Queen's University listed a reading course in 'History and Historiography,' which included readings in nineteenth-century historiography, historical methods, and sources.[69]

Even if a particular department did not offer a course in historical
methods, the method of history was nevertheless stressed. In his 1895
inaugural lecture George Wrong encouraged the use of primary documents in the teaching of history.[70] According to the calendar, if students
in the honours course of modern history hoped 'to secure first class
honours,' their major essay 'must be based on the study of original
materials.'[71] Underhill thought this stipulation insufficient. When at the
University of Saskatchewan, he too had stressed the use of primary documents. 'In my own classes the Documents are made the basis of all the
work,' he told the president. 'In any University history class nowadays
stress is always put on the reading of original documents just as Science
class stresses laboratory work.'[72] In his critique of the Toronto curriculum, Underhill charged that secondary books were used from beginning to end, that 'there was only occasional use of original materials,
and knowledge was acquired throughout in predigested doses. "A polite
veneer of ideas" was the inevitable result.'[73] By 1938 it was stated in the
calendar that, in the fourth year, history would be studied 'in part from
the original sources' and that, in addition to understanding 'the forces
which lie behind the world today,' students would have 'some knowledge of the materials on which historical study is based.'[74] J.M.S. Careless remembered Chester Martin from the late 1930s as 'a deeply
imbued scholar' who could get his seminar students very excited by
what could be done 'with the raw materials of history,' the primary
documents.[75]

Other departments emphasized the use of primary documents as
well. McGill's honours courses were taught as seminars wherein students

were expected 'to submit a really substantial piece of work based wholly on original material.' While E.R. Adair conceded that this 'may not always be profound historical research,' he quickly added that 'it introduces the students to the technique and the trials of the historical writer by giving them a chance to use their critical and literary capacity in performing, though on a minor scale, the same sort of labor as that with which [the historian] is faced.'[76] The University of Alberta's Morden Long began teaching a Canadian history seminar in 1932: according to the calendar, it was to be 'a course based on original sources.'[77] Chester New told the McMaster chancellor that, beginning in 1938, he intended 'to do something in historical method and criticism in a very informal way' for those students intending to go on to graduate school.[78] Although he never got the chance to introduce his plans to Mount Allison's history curriculum in the early 1940s, George Stanley likewise stressed training in the use of primary documents. He wanted to establish a fellowship that would allow a senior undergraduate to do some original research at the Public Archives of Nova Scotia or the New Brunswick Museum 'in the history of the seaboard provinces.' 'I think you will agree with me,' he told John Clarence Webster, 'when I say that the real interest in the study of history comes in handling documents or contemporary source materials ... And that is why I want to encourage suitable students to delve into at least the topsoil of historical research.'[79] Hired at University of New Brunswick in 1938, Alfred Bailey instituted a half-year methodology course: History of Historical Writing, Historical Method and the Philosophy of History.'[80] A few years later, in 1941, he offered two half-year courses: 'Historiography' and 'Philosophy of History.' The latter course was dedicated entirely to Arnold Toynbee's *Study of History*. According to Bailey, his course on Toynbee was the first such course in the world.[81] In 1945 Bailey combined the two half-year courses into a single full-year course, 'Philosophy of History,' and expanded the reading list to include Vico, Hegel, Comte, and Spengler as well as Toynbee, but not Marx.

Graduate programs at Toronto, McGill, and Queen's, the Summer School for Historical Research, and undergraduate instruction in historical methodology and historiography indicate a heightened self-consciousness among historians, a sense that their discipline was unique, that it had its own rules and methodologies, and that it was neither political science nor English literature. It was also in the interwar years that two other important institutions emerged, the *Canadian Historical Review* and the Canadian Historical Association.

III

When he returned from the war, W.S. Wallace 'proposed to Professor Wrong the transformation of the *Review of Historical Publications* into a quarterly. 'My reasons for this were twofold: in the first place the number of publications relating to Canada had increased to such an extent that it was difficult to review them adequately in an annual volume; and in the second place I was convinced that the time had come when students of Canadian history would be glad to have a vehicle for the publication of their researches.'[82] With financial support from the University, the *Canadian Historical Review* (*CHR*) first appeared in March 1920. The editors stated in the inaugural issue that twenty-five years earlier historical research in Canada had been in its 'infancy.' Since then research had become more 'vigorous.' There was 'now a large body of historical students, not only in Canada, but also in England and in the United States, engaged in sifting the vast masses of new material relating to Canadian history which recent years have brought to light.' Yet 'there is almost no medium in Canada through which the occasional work of these historical students may be given to the public.' To this end, the *CHR* would serve 'as a medium for the publication of original articles on Canadian history and allied subjects, of important documents and of correspondence relating to questions of interest to students of Canadian history.'[83]

In terms of the disciplinization of history, the *CHR* performed an incalculable function. By its very appearance it confirmed the existence of a body of knowledge and ensured its autonomy. As a national journal published out of the country's leading university, it conferred authority and prestige on its contributors. Recall Arthur Lower's observation that his early article in the *CHR* boosted his 'professional reputation.' Within the historical profession, the *Review* shrank distances and eased isolation. A historian at Dalhousie could read the work of a historian at UBC and discuss it with a colleague at Toronto. In this sense it not only communicated scholarly information, it acted as a medium through which historians communicated with each other.[84] Reading it allowed historians to imagine themselves connected to other historians in a great project – the writing of their country's history. As Lower remarked, the *CHR* provided 'a focus for Canadian historical studies and Canadian historians, giving them a sense of unity and an *esprit de corps* long before other disciplines.'[85]

Like the *Canadian Historical Review*, the Canadian Historical Association (CHA) performed an integrative function.[86] Its forerunner, the Historic Landmarks Association (HLA), had exhausted its purpose. From its creation in 1907 the HLA had gathered information about Canadian landmarks and provided an arena for men and women to share their interest in Canada's built and natural heritage. The creation of the Historic Sites and Monuments Board and the Quebec Historic Monuments Commission, however, rendered the activities of the HLA suddenly redundant. When Lawrence Burpee assumed the presidency of the HLA in 1920, he intended to transform the association. Its mandate, he said, ought to be broadened, its constitution amended, and its name changed. Taking his cue from the American Historical Association, Burpee envisioned a national historical association for students of all history.[87] In 1922 he presented the Historic Landmarks Association with a draft constitution for a new association to be called the Canadian Historical Association. Its purpose would be 'to encourage research and public interest in history; to promote the preservation of historic sites and buildings, documents, relics and other significant heirlooms of the past; [and] to publish historical studies and documents as circumstances may permit.'[88] Whereas the HLA had focused its efforts solely on landmarks, the CHA would focus on research and dissemination in addition to preservation. After the HLA provisionally adopted the new constitution, W.D. Lighthall moved that Burpee be elected president of the Canadian Historical Association.[89]

A career civil servant, Burpee did not have advanced training in history, nor did he teach in a university. Born in Halifax in 1873, he joined the federal civil service in 1890; he worked as private secretary to several cabinet ministers; he served as the head librarian of the Ottawa Public Library from 1905 to 1911; and from 1912 he was the Canadian secretary of the International Joint Commission. Not surprisingly, Burpee did not see the CHA as a narrow professional association. Its membership was open to anyone interested in history; the first executive and council included a mix of academics, archivists, and non-academics;[90] and its first standing committee was charged with landmark preservation. Furthermore, Burpee envisioned the CHA as in part a patriotic association. As he explained in his first presidential address, 'Not the least important object of the Association would be to associate itself with other patriotic agencies in bringing into more perfect harmony the two great races that constitute the Canadian people.'[91]

At least one professional historian confessed his incredulity. Writing to his wife in July 1923, A.L. Burt lamented the absence of an association for serious scholars doing serious research: 'There are a number of local societies organized for local antiquarian research, but nothing can be hoped for from them.' The newly created CHA, he believed, promised little more: 'It will never be a real Canadian Historical Association, for it has been started on the wrong lines and the best students of Canadian history are not taking it seriously. Indeed, it threatens to prevent the formation of a real Canadian Historical Association, which would be a clearing house for ideas on the study of Canadian history.'[92] Burt's initial, instinctive response to the CHA is understandable. Burpee was not a professional historian; he foresaw the CHA's fulfilling a patriotic role; and the first executive and council included men like Lighthall. In some ways, the new Canadian Historical Association looked not unlike the old Historic Landmarks Association.

But looks can be deceiving. Burpee may not have been a professional historian – he did not do history for a living – but he was an important figure in history's professionalization. That professionalization came from outside the university as well as from within. In 1908 Burpee published an article outlining a modern approach to history. It was no longer possible, he said, 'for the historian to build his structure with secondary material.' Instead, 'he must build his work upon the sure foundation of original sources; and he must leave his foundation exposed so that all who go by may test the character of his material and the faithful use he made of it.' To this end, he called for greater cooperation from individuals, societies, colleges, and institutions in the preservation of manuscript material.[93] When Lighthall nominated him for the presidency, he had published three books and a handful of articles.[94] As president, Burpee deliberately broadened the objectives of the CHA to include research. Each year the CHA sent a delegate to the annual meeting of the American Historical Association. In 1922 Arthur Doughty represented the CHA at the International Congress on the History of America in Rio de Janeiro. In 1923 Burpee reported that the CHA had been represented at the Congress of Historical Sciences in Brussels; five years later, the CHA joined the International Committee of Historical Sciences.[95] In 1925 the CHA negotiated a subscription to the *Canadian Historical Review* and the *Bulletin des recherches historiques* for its members,[96] and it was also in 1925 that the CHA voted to make the president an annual appointment. However, the 'burden of organization' would belong largely to the newly created chairman of the Management Committee, in this case, Burpee.[97] In 1926 the council was expanded from six to nine members in an effort to guarantee better regional representation. Moreover, the make-up of the council changed in the 1920s: Seven out of nine were either academics or archivists in 1926, including Duncan McArthur from Queen's University, Chester Martin from the University of Manitoba, Frank Underhill from the University of Saskatchewan, and Leon Harvey from the University of New Brunswick. Also included was A.L. Burt.

Chester Martin once remarked that it was largely through Burpee's 'persistent efforts' that the CHA was founded at all. It was also through his persistent efforts throughout the 1920s and into the early 1930s that the CHA survived. There was nothing inevitable about the CHA. It was not predestined to be, nor was its survival guaranteed. And Burpee knew it. In a 1923 letter to Lighthall, he emphasized the importance of an interesting program and a good turnout to the upcoming annual meeting: 'Our future success may depend to quite a large extent on the success or otherwise of our meeting this year.'[98] A year later, Burpee visited every province except Prince Edward Island in order 'to discover ways and means of increasing the usefulness of the Association, as well as to build up its membership.'[99] As observed in the *CHR* in 1927, it was a daunting task to maintain a professional association in a country with so few people 'who have a professional interest in history.'[100] Yet through his tireless commitment, Burpee ensured the initial survival of the CHA, first as president to 1925 and then as chairman of the Management Committee to 1934.

Although by the mid-1920s more academics than non-academics sat on council, non-academics continued to serve in the role of president into the early 1930s. In 1929 the Honourable Rodolphe Lemieux was appointed president; he was succeeded by the Right Honourable Robert Borden, who was in turn succeeded by Judge Frederic Howay in 1931 and by Dr John Clarence Webster in 1932. Appointing a French-Canadian cabinet minister and speaker of the House of Commons, a former prime minister, a British Columbia judge, and a New Brunswick medical doctor helped to establish a national profile for the CHA. Moreover, such appointments enhanced the legitimacy and status of a young and not yet established association. It was a means to an end, to increase the CHA's 'credibility in the eyes of the public.'[101]

Take Sir Robert Borden, for example. Prime minister of Canada from 1911 to 1920, Borden enjoyed a reputation as Canada's 'senior statesman' following his retirement from politics. A self-titled 'man of affairs,' he busied himself with business and academic interests until his death in 1937. In 1921 he delivered the Marfleet Foundation Lectures at the

University of Toronto, and in 1927 he gave the Rhodes Memorial Lectures at Oxford. Having 'earned something of a reputation as a scholar,' he was elected a fellow of the Royal Society of Canada in 1928. Borden also assumed the leadership of voluntary associations; for example, he was the first president of the League of Nations Society, and he served as chairman of the Canadian Institute of International Affairs. Borden disliked administrative duties, however, and he 'advised the organizers of the CIIA not to look to him, as chairman, for active promotion of the group.'[102] Likewise, when asked in 1932 to sit on the general committee for the Carnegie Endowment's Canadian-American relations series, Borden agreed, on the condition that his duties be kept to an absolute minimum. No documents pertaining to the Canadian Historical Association appear in his personal papers; administrative tasks fell to Lawrence Burpee. In his diary entry following the first day of the 1931 annual meeting Borden referred to the CHA as the Canadian Historical Society, and his presidential address on patronage and the civil service was, by his own admission, not an academic presentation but 'rather a summary enlivened by anecdotes.'[103] However, Borden was useful to the CHA as a prominent Canadian whose name on CHA stationary conferred authority and legitimacy.

In addition to his status as speaker of the House of Commons, Rodolphe Lemieux brought something else to the CHA in his capacity as president: he was French Canadian. 'To further in every possible way the development of the most friendly relations between the two great races' had been one of Burpee's initial objectives. 'The most effective way of breaking down the walls of prejudice and misunderstanding that still to some extent divide us,' he explained in 1926, 'is to bring members of the two races into intimate relationship, working together toward a common object, as we are doing in the Canadian Historical Association.'[104] Burpee's was, no doubt, an honest effort, but he deluded himself. Certainly his version of the CHA's openness to French Canada was very different from that of Aegidius Fauteux, a prominent Quebec historian and librarian at the Bibliothèque Saint-Sulpice.

In a wide-ranging 1927 letter to Gustave Lanctôt, then French secretary, Fauteux addressed the relationship between the CHA and French-Canadian historians. He observed that in all probability the association would not want Lionel Groulx's participation. Groulx may have been Quebec's leading historian, but his challenge to the widely held assumption that the British presence in French-Canadian history had been beneficial and his musings about an autonomous French-Canadian state were beyond the pale to English-Canadian historians. Fauteux proceeded to give Lanctôt the names of four other French Canadians who might be more acceptable to the CHA, including Groulx's intellectual opposite Thomas Chapais, who emphasized the benefits of British constitutional principles and who admired the spirit of French-English cooperation in Canadian history. Then, sympathizing with Lanctôt, he acknowledged 'la difficulté que tu éprouves à maintenir le principe du bilinguisme dans l'Association Historique.' According to Fauteux, 'il y a trop d'incompatibilité entre les deux races pour qu'elles s'associent avec un peu de suite sur n'importe quel terrain, celui de l'histoire y compris. Cela se modifiera peut-être, mais Dieu sait quand.' Indeed, one need only recall the distasteful experience of the only French-speaking participant at the 1923 annual meeting: 'Il n'y a que quelques instants, je me suis laissé conter comment le seul canadien-français qui était au programme avait été traité lors de la première réunion annuelle de l'Association. Deux ou trois canadiens-anglais venaient de lire à haute voix leurs travaux, lorsqu'il se leva à son tour, mais il avait à peine ouvert la bouche qu'un membre de langue anglaise proposa brusquement que le travail en français fût considéré lu.' It was this experience and others like it, Fauteux concluded, that explained why French Canadians 'ne soient pas chauds pour aller pérorer au milieu de gens qui ne les comprennent pas ni ne les apprécient.'[105]

Despite Burpee's best intentions, it was clear that the Canadian Historical Association was really the English-Canadian Historical Association. Yes, beginning in 1926, there were two secretaries on the executive, one English and the other French; yes, council always included at least one French-Canadian member; yes, there were five French-speaking presidents between 1922 and 1950; and yes, the *Annual Report* always contained at least one and sometimes two articles in French. But like its predecessor, the Historic Landmarks Association, the CHA conducted all of its business in English. The minutes do not contain a single word of French. It would not be until 1962 that the minutes record in French the report of the French-language secretary. Despite the participation of French Canadians at the annual meeting, the program itself was printed almost entirely in English. 'As to bilingualism,' Queen's University's Reginald Trotter explained in 1935, 'I greatly prefer the form such as was used at McGill last year where the title page was set in both languages but the rest of the programme set in English except for the title of the French papers. I suppose we can continue this practice as a matter of course.'[106] Actually, to refer to the participation of French Canadians at the annual meeting in itself is misleading. The program always included a French Canadian, but it was the same three or four people that appeared year after year. For example, before 1950 Gustave Lanctôt presented eleven papers; Francis-Joseph Audet, five; and Arthur Maheux, three. So thoroughly English speaking was the CHA that Audet intended to deliver his 1935 presidential address in English but publish it in French; a minor accident, however, prevented him from attending. Maheux both presented and published his 1949 presidential address in English, with only a concluding nod to his 'French-speaking audience.'[107] Finally, those French Canadians who regularly participated in the CHA were not representative of intellectual life in French Canada; they belonged to 'le petit group outaouais' of *bonne-ententistes* already active in the Royal Society of Canada.[108]

Meanwhile, the annual meeting of the Canadian Historical Association became more recognizable as an annual professional meeting over the course of the 1920s and 1930s. As early as 1924 a gentleman who had been a member of the Historic Landmarks Association warned the Canadian Historical Association that the annual meeting must not become an occasion 'to hear a few eminent historians displaying their learning.'[109] But that is precisely what happened. Although as many non-academics as academics attended the annual meeting in the 1920s, the presenters were professors, archivists, and librarians after 1925. It was Frank Underhill who first suggested that the association turn its annual meeting into something more scholarly and, at the same time, something more social. He wanted to see the CHA emulate the success of the AHA. As he explained in a 1926 letter to the brilliant Toronto classicist and then English secretary, Charles Cochrane, the CHA ought to invite a series of papers organized around a single theme. As well, it ought to provide more opportunity for its members to socialize, although 'judging from this year's experience I don't know that meeting one another would be a particularly thrilling event.'[110] Cochrane agreed. To this end, he invited specific historians to give papers on some aspect of Confederation to mark the Diamond Jubilee of Confederation at the same time as he organized a dinner at Hart House. Underhill accepted Cochrane's invitation to present a paper; he would later describe it as his 'first professional historical paper.'[111] Although Innis complained that the presentations had been average in quality ('some of the papers very good and others beating old straw'), he nevertheless enjoyed the Friday night banquet ('excellent from the standpoint of food').[112] Following the 1928 annual meeting in Winnipeg, an excited George Brown from the University of Toronto penned a quick note to his colleague D.C. Harvey at the University of Manitoba: 'I feel that the Association is really beginning to find itself.'[113]

The annual meeting became an event, something not to be missed, something that historians looked forward to. Before the 1929 meeting, Frank Underhill asked Western's Fred Landon if any of the 'London people' would be attending. Toronto, he said, would be sending at least four or five.[114] The annual meeting provided a forum for historians to present their work, receive feedback, and exchange information; and, equally important, it provided historians with an opportunity to meet their colleagues in a social setting.[115] Professional associations do not exist solely to promote and protect their members' interests. They also exist to allow like-minded people to meet on a regular basis 'for the sole pleasure of mixing with their fellows and no longer feeling lost in the midst of adversaries, as well as for the pleasure of communing together, that is, in short, of being able to lead their lives with the same moral aim.'[116] In his memoirs, Arthur Lower commented on the importance of the CHA annual meeting and the summers spent at the Public Archives in Ottawa: 'one felt genuinely a member of a band that had no local moorings (except Ottawa) and was as broad as the Dominion. It was this sense of wider brotherhood that shored me up during many a dark day in Winnipeg.'[117]

Lower might have added that one of the things that kept this 'wider brotherhood' together was gossip. In her 1985 presidential address, Susan Mann spoke to the question of gossip and its importance to building and maintaining communities in general and the history community in particular: 'What historians gathered at the CHA actually do is GOSSIP. Who's doing what? How is he doing it? Is it appropriate historical behaviour?'[118] Because it contains – either explicitly or implicitly – group norms and values, gossip functions as a form of social control.[119] A.L. Burt's 'post-1918 generation' formed a community and, like all communities, its members liked to gossip; in turn, that gossip reinforced the community.

Harold Innis loved nothing more than 'an hour's gossipy conversation.' 'His study became a kind of clearing-house for the academic gossip of a large part of the English-speaking world,' Donald Creighton writes. 'He had a great fund of stories, for men told their best anecdotes in his presence, and his own humour was rich, and generous, yet delightfully astringent.'[120] Michael Bliss fondly recalls lunch with C.P.

Stacey as 'a treasured time of historical gossip.'[121] Here was the senior
Stacey admitting the junior Bliss into the 'brotherhood.' Of course,
most of these stories and anecdotes have been lost, but the personal correspondence of English Canada's historians contains numerous references to other historians. That is, they contain gossip. For the most part,
the gossip was innocent and involved keeping up to date with others'
comings and goings. Charles Cochrane informed Frank Underhill that
D.C. Harvey had received a temporary appointment at McGill and that
A.L. Burt had been hired by the University of Alberta: 'He has already
departed to carry the gospel of the aesthetic to the Plains.'[122] 'McArthur
tells me that you are migrating again to Ottawa this year,' Manitoba's
Chester Martin told Saskatchewan's A.S. Morton.[123] When Innis heard
that Burt was unhappy at the University of Minnesota and that he might
return to Alberta, he told Arthur Lower.[124] Columbia's Bartlet Brebner
told C.P. Stacey that his name had been frequently mentioned at the
annual meeting; everyone, he said, was delighted to hear of his appointment as an army historian.[125] When it proved impossible for George
Glazebrook to meet Donald Creighton in Washington over the Christmas holidays – at this point Creighton was on a Guggenheim fellowship
in the United States – he began his letter, 'Alas! Our gossip must be
postponed.' Nevertheless, he continued, the Modern History Club had
hosted a splendid Christmas party: 'They did rags on the staff, all good
fun; & four of the staff sang (sic!) equally topically. Richard Saunders
appeared as Santa Claus – a great sight.'[126] Gossip was not always professional; it could also be personal. On hearing from a Toronto historian
that Brebner's wedding plans had been cancelled, Burt promptly told
his wife: 'Glazebrook, my informant, explained it by saying that she is a
Southern girl and like all other Southern girls is very unreliable.'[127] As
word circulated about Innis's deteriorating health in 1950, Fred Landon
wrote to Frank Underhill: 'I heard that Innis was ill. Is this correct? I
wish that you would give me some particulars.'[128]

To be sure, gossip could be more pointed. Duncan McArthur
delighted A.L. Burt with a 'scandalous tale' about W.P.M. Kennedy, the
Toronto constitutional historian. Fearing a negative review of his book,
Kennedy selected his friend Chester Martin to review it in the *CHR*. But
Martin, with assistance from Adam Shortt, wrote a critical review. The
managing editor of the *Review*, W.S. Wallace, showed the manuscript to
Kennedy: 'Kennedy went through it with Wallace, saying every now and
then "Now Wallace, you can't let that go in, for I know Martin is wrong
there, and to let it pass, would hurt his reputation."' When all was said

and done, the book review was 'a salad of Shortt, Martin, Kennedy and Wallace.'[129] Another example of critical gossip comes from the correspondence between Innis and Lower. According to Innis, George Brown had been offered the position of archivist at the newly created Public Archives of Nova Scotia; however, he feared that Brown would use the offer as a bargaining chip with the University of Toronto.[130] When Brown did precisely that, a cynical Innis commented, 'Rather disgusting business but there it is.'[131] Finally, as Arthur Doughty neared his retirement, rumours about his successor circulated. Burt wanted the position. So, too, did D.C Harvey. When Burt received, in his words, 'a disturbing note' to the effect that the prime minister was set to appoint W.S. Wallace, he wrote to A.S. Morton, who shared Burt's concern. Unfortunately, he said, Wallace had 'good political pull,' and his strong publication record might 'lead those who do not know how little he has paid attention to archival research to rate him higher than is just.'[132] In these three examples, the gossip carried an implicit message: do not manipulate the review process; do not bargain one employer against another; and archival research ought to be the mark of a historian's reputation.

Knowing how damaging gossip could be, Arthur Lower attempted to track down the source of 'some old story floating about' in connection with his employment at the Public Archives in the 1920s. Apparently, R.O. MacFarlane at Manitoba had told Noel Fieldhouse, also at Manitoba, that Lower had withheld documents from Adam Shortt when he was in his employ and then used them in a volume of primary documents he edited with Innis. To make matters even worse, gossip had it that Lower then proceeded to review Shortt's volume and criticized it for not containing the documents that he himself had withheld. An obviously upset Lower wrote to MacFarlane asking him to explain himself: 'I cannot afford to have such things circulating.'[133] MacFarlane responded that Lower was right to 'nail down' this story at once; however, he also said that he knew nothing about it.[134] Lower let the matter drop with MacFarlane – Fieldhouse, he said, 'must have got things twisted up in some way'[135] – but he pursued it with others, including Innis and W.A. Mackintosh. Innis told him, 'you can't do anything with pure maliciousness.'[136] Besides, 'the whole thing is too preposterous for words.'[137] Mackintosh advised him to ignore it; the Public Archives was a 'hive of gossip.'[138] In the end, Lower never discovered the guilty party. That he went to such length, however, indicates the importance Lower placed on his professional reputation. At one point Lower conceded that he had probably been wrong to pay attention to the rumours, 'But unless one does, I suppose they can go on festering for a long time.'[139]

When the editors of the *Canadian Historical Review* invited selected readers to comment on past and future editorial policy, two respondents wanted the *CHR* to include more information about historians. Ronald Longley at Acadia requested 'more regular news' about 'the activities of the Canadian historical fraternity.' As he explained, 'I am interested in the activities of my colleagues, promotions, appointments, etc.'[140] UBC's Fred Soward agreed. The *CHR* should add more details about fellow historians, 'their promotions, transfers, etc.'[141] Sherwood Fox, Fred Landon, J.J. Talman, and M.A. Garland from Western were even more direct. From time to time, the *CHR* contained obituaries, they observed, but it would be nice to get 'more information on the personal activities of individuals while they are alive.' In other words, the *Review* 'might loosen up a little and admit that students of history are human beings.'[142] To know who was promoted, who won a prestigious fellowship, and who received an administrative appointment was to be in the know. To be in the know was to feel a sense of membership, a sense of belonging, in the profession.

IV

By the early 1930s the CHA had established itself as the leading historical association in the country, and, when necessary, it would defend its status as the 'National Body.' From its beginnings, the association enjoyed a special relationship with the Public Archives, a relationship that enhanced the CHA's status and authority.[143] This relationship was formalized in 1934 when the Archives made a room available to the CHA free of charge, which the CHA intended to use as a library and board room.[144] In 1935 Norman Fee, an archivist at the Public Archives and English secretary and treasurer of the CHA, learned that the Catholic Historical Association wanted a similar relationship with the Public Archives. To Fee this constituted an encroachment of CHA territory, and he quickly wrote to Reginald Trotter: 'There is also, as you can easily see, a very concerted move by certain interests to link up the Catholic Historical with the Archives. I dare not write more on this point. We must guard against anything that will leave the way open to even a questioning of the right of the Canadian Historical to recognition as the National Body.'[147] In the end, nothing came of the Catholic Historical Association's 'concerted move.' What part – if any – Fee and the CHA played is not known, but as a member of the executive, Fee was set to defend the CHA's self-declared status as the national historical association.

The imperative to defend the CHA, in this case its autonomy, found expression in late 1939 when the Royal Society of Canada (RSC) approached the Canadian Historical Association and the Canadian Political Science Association (CPSA) with a proposal to create a new section that would take in the two associations. According to Columbia's Bartlet Brebner, the suggestion 'provoked a positive explosion.' Council considered the question, but 'the general thesis was that it was no fault of the CHA that the RSC had become moribund and that there seemed no good reason for two vigorous associations to risk their health in going to its rescue.'[146] Thoroughly suspicious of the RSC's motives, the CHA nevertheless agreed to strike an ad hoc committee. However, council also stressed 'that the high standing which the Association occupies in the field of history should be safe-guarded.'[147] Donald Creighton and Reginald Trotter met with representatives from the RSC and CPSA on 25 November 1939. They listened politely, but at the same time, they made it absolutely clear 'that the members of the Association would be ... unwilling to enter into cooperation on any basis that would destroy the autonomy of the CHA or even bind it to any set relationship between its own sessions and the sessions of the RSC.' They agreed that cooperation between the CHA and the RSC had potential benefits. The problem, therefore, was 'to preserve the independence of the professional associations but to do it in a spirit of readiness to cooperate so far as cooperation may have positive values.'[148] In their formal report to council, Creighton and Trotter recommended that no further action be taken in this matter. To subordinate the CHA in any shape, way, or form to the RSC would be wrong-headed.[149]

If defending the CHA's territory and its autonomy was a professional imperative, so, too, was the need to expand the CHA's role. This need, in turn, can be seen in the CHA's desire to promote history in the schools. Interest on the part of historians in what was happening in the schools dates back to the nineteenth century. In 1898 George Wrong delivered a report to the American Historical Association (AHA) on the state of history in Canada's secondary schools. He painted a bleak picture. Teacher training, he said, was wholly inadequate; the curriculum was 'defective'; not enough class time was devoted to instruction in history; and the textbooks were 'inferior in quality.'[150] Wrong's 1898 complaint became a professional lament.[151] According to the Montreal *Gazette*, Queen's historian J.L. Morison 'could not find words strong enough to apply to the current textbooks which he referred to as one of the chief products of the devil.' Morison went on to say that history 'was singularly and almost universally badly taught,' and that 'the students who came to him were absolutely hindered by what they had learned.'[152] In 1921 Wrong reiterated his disregard for the teaching of history in the schools when he complained about the 'abysmal' ignorance of history on the part of incoming students. 'The very name of History repels students coming to the University and this is due to bad work in the schools.'[153] Discussing the question of history in the schools at the 1923 annual meeting of the CHA, McMaster's Chester New urged the association to take a proactive interest: it was 'the experience of probably every teacher of history in Canadian universities that fully seventy-five percent of every freshman class [has] acquired a profound distaste for history in general and a special hatred for Canadian history in particular.' Manitoba's Chester Martin concurred: 'Enthusiasm for the study of history as it exists in the universities is lacking in the lower schools.'[154] A year later, Duncan McArthur commented on the dreadful condition of Canadian history in the public schools. Its defects, according to McArthur, included an overemphasis on constitutional history, a tendency to stress memorization, poor school libraries, and a lack of practical, sound teaching guides. The country, he said, was cheating itself: 'The security of our Canadian democracy is entirely dependent upon an educated and a correct public opinion, which in turn can be obtained only through a knowledge of our nation's history.'[155] Not one to mince his words, Frank Underhill commented on the utter ignorance of first-year students: 'On our first-year university history examination recently ... we put on the question, "What is responsible government, and when was it achieved?" We were surprised to find that not one in ten had the foggiest idea of what responsible government is: it was rather a startling commentary on the manner in which Canadian history is taught in our high schools.'[156] Arthur Lower complained that few Canadians actually read history. And who could blame them? 'The main association Canadians themselves have had with their own history has consisted in the terrifically boring stuff shoved at them in their school days.'[157]

It was in this context that historians attempted to assist teachers in the teaching of history. Not every attempt, however, fully materialized. In 1923, for example, the CHA passed a resolution instructing the executive to investigate the publication of a historical atlas to be used in Canadian schools and to cooperate with the Public Archives' scheme to develop a series of lectures and lantern slides to be used by high school history teachers. Over the next few years the initiative to create a series of outline lectures died a quiet death. Only three were ever completed. Everyone was 'overburdened with other duties,' Burpee explained in 1926.[158] Meanwhile, the CHA could not hope to undertake the publication of an atlas; it simply lacked the resources. On his own initiative, however, Burpee managed to complete an atlas in 1927.[159] In 1930 UBC's W.N. Sage urged the CHA to follow the AHA's lead on the question of teaching history in the schools, and he called for closer cooperation 'between university professors and teachers in normal, high, and elementary schools.' In 1937 historians again considered the question of the CHA's relationship to history in the schools: George Glazebrook wanted the CHA to do more to assist teachers; E.R. Adair recommended that teachers be invited to attend the annual meeting; George Brown agreed with both, but noted that the meeting program was hardly attractive to teachers. The CHA, Brown said, should look into preparing material that might actually be useful to teachers,[160] and as editor of the *Canadian Historical Review*, he followed up on his own suggestion a few months later when he instituted a new section entitled 'Book Notes.' Specifically designed for high-school teachers, 'Book Notes' aimed 'to keep teachers in touch with recent books in the field of historical scholarship, which are not too detailed or highly specialized to be of value to them.'[161] In 1939 council instructed Fred Landon to seek the London school board's permission to invite teachers to the 1940 annual meeting 'without loss of time or salary.'[162] In 1943 all members of council were asked to approach their local schools in an effort to bring the association to the attention of teachers. Three years later council once again considered 'the suggestion that efforts be made to create an interest in the CHA among teachers throughout Canada, and that efforts be made by individual members of council in different provinces to get in touch with the inspectors' and teachers' organizations who might assist in bringing this about.'[163] In 1951 council entertained the idea of putting together a 'representative group of high school teachers' in an effort to determine how the CHA might be made more useful to them.[164]

If council never assembled a group of high-school teachers, it did launch the Historical Booklet series. At the 1951 annual meeting, E.R. Adair proposed that the CHA look into the English Historical Society's pamphlet series on historical revisions. Each pamphlet in this series was written by a historian but aimed at high-school teachers. When he became president in 1952 C.P. Stacey agreed to follow up Adair's suggestion and, after consulting various council members, decided that the association ought to pursue something very similar, something that would be of use to teachers, of interest to general readers, and perhaps contribute to building up the association's membership. Everyone agreed that the first booklet in the series had to be written by a 'big name' and that Donald Creighton was that name; he had just published the first volume of his two-volume biography of Sir John A. Macdonald, and his stock was high. But Creighton declined. Deep into work on the second volume, he did not have the time. Stacey raised the idea of inviting Adair to write on the fall of New France. Council baulked. Adair was too iconoclastic, especially on the topic of French Canada. Stacey then approached George Stanley, inviting him to prepare a booklet on Louis Riel. Stanley agreed. When the Ontario Department of Education learned of the topic, however, it cancelled its advance order of 1,000 copies. 'They are afraid of [Riel's] controversial aspects,' Stacey explained.[165] 'Riel is regarded as likely to stir up old antagonisms,' Dick Preston added.[166] The task of writing the first booklet and inaugurating the series fell to Stacey. In 1953 the CHA published *The Undefended Border: The Myth and the Reality*; the Ontario Department of Education purchased 1,000 copies, and the Historical Booklet series was born. Although Ontario declined to purchase any subsequent booklets, the series survived, and, after some sixty booklets, it marches on.

Professional historians promoted the better teaching of history in the schools because they believed it to be self-evidently important. No one would argue, then or now, that history should be poorly taught in the schools. Historians, however, were not altruistic: they had a professional and pecuniary self-interest in the teaching of history in the schools. To quote Burton Bledstein, 'The culture of professionalism tended to cultivate an atmosphere of constant crisis – emergency – in which practitioners both created work for themselves and reinforced their authority by intimidating clients.'[167] In pointing out the terrible state of history in Canadian schools, professional historians placed themselves in a position to offer a solution: better textbooks written by professional historians.

To this end, historians wrote several school textbooks from the turn of the twentieth century on.[168] George Wrong published five texts, which, in turn, had several printings: *The British Nation* (1904);[169] *An English History, adapted for use in Canadian Elementary Schools* (1905); *Ontario High School History of England* (1911); *Ontario Public School History of England* (1921); *Ontario Public School History of Canada* (1921). With

Chester Martin and W.N. Sage, Wrong published *The Story of Canada* (1929). Duncan McArthur wrote a *History of Canada for High Schools* (1927). A.L. Burt wrote three textbooks: *High School Civics* (1928); *The Romance of the Prairie Provinces* (1930); and *The Romance of Canada* (1937). Chester New co-authored two high-school textbooks: *Ancient and Medieval History* with Charles Phillips (1941) and *Modern History* with Reginald Trotter (1946); and Arthur Dorland wrote *Our Canada* (1949). In 1942 George Brown authored the widely used textbook, *Building the Canadian Nation;* by 1971 some 600,000 copies had been sold to schools across Canada.[170] By 1961 Brown had written three additional textbooks: *The Story of Canada* (1949); *Canada in North America to 1800* (1960); and *Canada in North America, 1800–1901* (1961). With J.M.S. Careless, Gerald Craig, and Eldon Ray, Brown published three texts in 1953 alone: *Canada and the Americas*; *Canada and the World*; and *Canada and the Commonwealth*. Arthur Lower also wrote a book for the high-school market. Based on the success of *Colony to Nation*, publisher Longmans, Green asked him to write a textbook. With J.W. Chafe, a Winnipeg teacher, Lower published *Canada – a Nation and How It Came to Be* in 1948. According to his memoirs, it was still in use in 1967.[171]

Cracking the textbook market could prove lucrative. A.L. Burt boasted to his father that his first royalty cheque from *The Romance of Canada* would be a little over $1,000.[172] To someone who earned less than $5,000 per year, $1,000 was nothing to sneeze at. The best evidence of royalty payments can be found in the papers of W.S. Wallace. The Varsity librarian and history professor had four textbooks in use in Canadian schools: *A New History of Great Britain and Canada* (1925); *A First Book of Canadian History* (1928); *A History of the Canadian People* (1930); and *A Reader in Canadian Civics* (1935). Although the records are incomplete, they nonetheless reveal a healthy income from royalties. Published by Macmillan in 1928 and used in Ontario's schools to 1949, *A First Book of Canadian History* sold roughly 520,000 copies.[173] Receiving 3 cents per book, Wallace earned approximately $15,600 in royalties from this book alone; in a ten-year period between 1925 and 1935 he received a yearly average of $2,400 in royalties from Macmillan.[174] Again, for someone who earned $5,000 per year, an additional $2,400 was a sizeable sum. Professionalization, according to Magali Sarfatti Larson, is 'an attempt to translate one order of scarce resources – special knowledge and skills – into another – social and economic rewards.'[175] In this case it was a matter of professional historians translating their special knowledge of history into royalty payments.

In the aftermath of the Great War a new cohort of historians emerged, defined themselves as researchers, initiated graduate programs, attempted to instil in their undergraduates an appreciation for sources and their use, created a national journal, and founded a professional association. In short, history professionalized. It was something one could do for a living. But it was not a job. Quoting Arthur Lower, history was not about putting in so many days 'just sawing so much wood [and] meeting the nine-to-five routine.' It was now a vocation: 'In a university a man can, and should, throw himself into his work, marry himself to it, feel a sense of vocation.'[176] However, the professionalization of history was neither an inevitable nor a benign process. It encompassed the deliberate – and, as Lower unwittingly indicated, gendered – attempt to mark and police the boundaries between who could and who could not be a historian.

CHAPTER 4

'Mr. Newman, manifestly, is not a historian': the amateurization of history

'Mr. Newman, manifestly, is not a historian.' Thus begins W.J. Eccles's review of Peter Newman's *Company of Adventurers*, published in 1985. He proceeds to dismiss the book for its misrepresentation of the fur trade and the author for his fondness for titillating, salacious details about sexual relations between European men and Amerindian women.[1] Eccles is not alone in his criticism. Academics universally panned it: it was a flawed book, they said. Non-academics, however, universally praised it: it was a great book, 'a significant contribution to our history,' according to the *Globe and Mail*'s William French.[2] In her analysis of the controversy, Jennifer Brown refers to history's two solitudes: in one solitude are academic historians, in the other are popular historians. Brown laments the existence of the two solitudes and urges that the 'chasm be bridged.' As a historian of the fur trade, Brown does criticize the book. But she criticizes it as bad history, not as popular history. For example, she raises the issue of sexual stereotypes of Native women, specifically Newman's handling of the phrase 'bits of brown,' Hudson's Bay Company Governor George Simpson's pejorative reference to them.[3] In his response to Brown's article, an unrepentant Peter Newman asserts that she does, in fact, criticize his book as popular history. It is, he says, a familiar tactic: 'Canadian academic historians have been deriding popular historian Pierre Berton for years, and when June Callwood wrote a superbly readable popular history of Canada a few years ago, they savaged her.' History was big enough for everyone, and the time had come for historians 'to stop pretending their craft is a lofty calling that can be protected from curious outsiders.' As a parting – and surely a gratuitous – shot, Newman concludes that if there is a moral to this exchange it is that 'Canadian history should be made up of bits of Newman as well as bits of Brown.'[4]

The academic response to Newman and Newman's response to academics can be seen as part of a larger pattern that first emerged in the pages of George Wrong's *Review of Historical Publications Relating to Canada*. Newman may have written a flawed book, and, if he did, Brown and Eccles were right to call him on it, but the existence of two solitudes was a product of history's professionalization as both a positive and a negative process of self-definition. Historians defined themselves in terms of what they were – university-trained, university-based experts in history – and in terms of what they were not – history buffs puttering away at their pet projects in their spare time. Useful to an understanding of this process is Thomas Gieryn's conception of boundary-work. Referring to the history of science, Gieryn argues that any effort to identify, categorize, and organize the differences between science and non-science is bound to fail because the differences between science and non-science are not absolute but rather ideological. 'Boundary-work,' he writes, 'describes an ideological style found in scientists' attempts to create a public image for science by contrasting it favourably to non-scientific intellectual or technical activities.'[5]

Engaged in boundary-work of their own, English-Canadian historians made a distinction between what they did as historians and what amateur historians did as historians. By favourably contrasting their work to the work of amateur historians, professional historians raised their status and authority.[6] Or, as one amateur historian said in 1938, 'historians who have shed their amateur status and joined the closed ranks of the professional historians are apt to look down upon the efforts of those who have not got their equipment or their scientific knowledge.'[7] This does not mean that professional historians discouraged amateurs from writing history; nor does it mean that they refused to consult their work. Far from it, in point of fact. Professional historians believed that amateur and local historians had an important role to play in the gathering of facts, the preservation of documents, and the promotion of history in general. But it does mean that the existence of two solitudes, one professional and the other amateur, was deliberate. The professionalization of history was also its amateurization.[8]

I

When George Wrong received his appointment at the University of Toronto, a friend offered his congratulations. However, he also asked: What exactly is it that a historian does?[9] In other words, how can one make a living as a historian? History, as this man understood it, was a pastime, a leisure activity, something someone did in their retirement. For Wrong, history was a career and he was a professional historian, and in his 1895 inaugural address he drew a boundary between the trained and the untrained student of history. Any 'untrained reader can enjoy his Macaulay or his Froude, lounging on a sofa, or toasting his knees before the fire.' As a result, 'men who have not given an hour's serious study to historical questions will assume the tone of experts and critics with a lightheartedness that is amazing.' Although Wrong did not want to discourage the public from reading history, neither did he want to encourage the belief that anyone could write history. The meaning of the past, he said, was 'only to be grasped when the insight and discrimination of a trained student are brought to the task.'[10] McGill's Charles Colby agreed when he said: 'No, history is not the easy subject which many, with insufficient knowledge, deem it to be. No branch of the curriculum requires more sympathy, more imagination, more tact.'[11] According to Colby, history was not something that simply anyone could do; it required training; it required sympathy and imagination. Adam Shortt went further when he compared what he did to what a medical doctor did. Expert advice, he warned, 'must be introduced as through the surgeon's injecting needle, into the proper tissues of the body politic.' After all, 'The wrong serum administered by enthusiastic but misguided amateurs may have disastrous effects.'[12]

The University of British Columbia's Mack Eastman understood the effect of enthusiastic but misguided amateurs. When the province removed W.L. Grant's *A History of Canada* from the list of approved textbooks in January 1920 in response to charges from British Columbia Orangemen that it was anti-British, anti-Protestant, pro-French Canadian, and pro-Catholic, he was livid. In a letter to Grant, Eastman condemned the book's detractors: 'I believe that the general public, as well as the teaching profession, is friendly to your book. Only the wild Orangemen, the Fenian Raid Veterans and some other antiques who will soon die off, refuse to disarm.'[13] Although Eastman, together with his UBC colleague, W.N. Sage, publicly and privately protested the decision, the book was never again approved for use in British Columbia schools.[14] Two years after the banning of Grant's book, Eastman delivered an address to a teachers' convention in Vancouver. Although he did not refer directly to the Grant incident, it was no doubt on his mind when he argued that it was the professional historian, not the amateur, who was best equipped to offer balance and perspective to school children. As he

explained, 'the perspective of the trained professional will be better than
that of the man about town.' Yet it would seem that since the war, 'every
man is his own historian ... Any old man in the street can will [sic] tell us
more of the "true meaning of history" in ten minutes than you and I
shall ever know in all our lives. History is open season and historians are
fair game all the year round and no license is required ... Today, more
than ever before, amateurs and charlatans rush hourly in where professionals fear to tread.' Eastman hit the proverbial nail on the head: unlike
doctors and lawyers, for example, professional historians could not prevent people from doing history, because 'any old man in the street'
could pronounce 'the true meaning of history.' Continuing his critique,
Eastman added, 'Every monomaniac wants a textbook written or sup-
pressed to appease his own special fetish.' But the professional historian
must not retreat: 'The children's only salvation ... is in the calm and
objective effort of the maturest and most gifted historians to place the
recent past tentatively in its setting. If they fail, all fail.'[15]

Reginald Trotter shared Eastman's concern. In a 1928 talk before the
Saturday Club at Queen's University, he stated that he wanted to dispel
the popular impression of history as 'non-technical,' as something upon
which anybody can 'speak with oracular authority.' That just anybody
could do history was preposterous, Trotter argued. He mocked the man
who would claim 'I know nothing, and care less, about so-called scholarly criticism in historical research or about the art of lively but accurate
historical narrative and exposition, but I know what history I like when I
like it.' In the final analysis, not everyone was 'equally competent to pass
judgment in historical matters.' The writing of history was necessarily
complex. For example, using primary material required 'the most criti-
cally discriminating examination before it can become the basis of reliable history.' Indeed, the historian's material – his sources – were 'not a
whit less vital than are the laboratory apparatus and material to the
investigations of the scientist.' Trotter was careful, however, not to claim
any kind of finality: 'Absolute objectivity in historical narrative, whether
or not it be desirable, is an unrealizable dream.' Nonetheless, the historian was infinitely 'more competent than the inexpert layman to speak
authoritatively' about the past.[16]

Alfred Bailey echoed the remarks of Eastman and Trotter. In a 1937
address to the Saint John Vocational School the young historian drew a
sharp line between what he did and what the amateur did. History, he
argued, must have a practical end. It must help us, in the here and now,
to formulate intelligent public policy. Too often, however, 'the study of

history is regarded as a mere hobby, like collecting stamps'; this was hardly surprising, given that 'the so-called historical work in this country has been dominated by the ideas of the genealogist and the antiquarian.' Antiquarians delighted in obscure, unconnected facts: 'For instance, he may piece together the story of a fire that burned somebody's barn in Oromocto in 1852,' but really, who cares? The historian, meanwhile, would take this same incident, the 1852 burning of a barn in Oromocto, and transform it into usable, practical knowledge. First, he would gather statistics on all such fires in the preceding and succeeding years in an effort to determine their frequency. Linking these statistics to changes in the construction of buildings and in the knowledge of fire prevention, the historian would ask if 'the financial burden sustained by the people of this province through economic loss by fire [was] due to ignorance of the proper construction of buildings and of efficient methods of prevention.' If the answer was yes, then the historian must make policy recommendations about what could be done to prevent the loss of money and property by fire. As Bailey stated, the historian's aim 'should be not merely to supply reading material to titillate the jaded curiosity of an effete leisured class, but to direct his studies of the past towards the solution of our present economic and social problems.' In fact, the historian must 'combine the knowledge of the scientist with the fiery zeal of the missionary, and go out over the province with a new story told in new terms.'[17]

If favourably contrasting their methods and results with the methods and results of amateur historians was one means of establishing their authority, professional historians also pursued another tactic: debunking. In 1920 the *Canadian Historical Review* (*CHR*) conceded that 'Historical Revisions are seldom popular. Few people like to be told that Wolfe did not recite the lines from Gray's *Elegy* as he floated down to the Foulon on the night before the battle of the Plains of Abraham, or that Brock did not say, as he fell at Queenston Heights, "Push on, brave York Volunteers."' Popular or not, revision was absolutely essential: 'if Sir Robert Walpole's reproach "Anything but history, for history must be false," is to be removed, the accepted version of history must be constantly revised, and kept up to date, in the light of recent researches, without regard for cherished preconceptions or for the picturesqueness of the discarded details.'[18] The *CHR* might have added that, in addition to arriving at a more accurate version of history, the debunking of time-honoured heroes helped to distinguish professional historians from their predecessors.

II

Saskatchewan's A.S. Morton argued that the French-Canadian explorer, Pierre Gaultier de La Vérendrye, was not the intrepid explorer depicted in popular accounts. 'We have writers, colourists by nature, who are only satisfied with flaming tints,' Morton began. As such, they painted a heroic picture of 'a man whose soul burned to "blaze" the trail to the Western Sea.' However, material in the Public Archives made 'it possible to put our conventional idea of La Vérendrye to the test, and reach out towards a fresh interpretation of his career.' According to Morton, 'the light of the contemporary sources' revealed, first, a commandant of western posts and, only second, an explorer.[19] In a response to Morton's article, Lawrence Burpee strongly criticized his conclusion: 'It is curious, after a man has assumed a certain hypothesis, how neatly all the available facts can be made to fit into it.'[20] However, the veracity of Morton's interpretation is not the point; rather, it is his rhetorical style. He opened his article by mocking the heroic accounts of La Vérendrye. Against this backdrop, he presented himself as the dispassionate expert; uninterested in hero-worship and unmoved by 'the prevailing adoration of La Vérendrye,'[21] his interpretation, he proclaimed, would rely on the archival record. By his style and the tone of his argument he intended to distinguish himself from those writers 'who are only satisfied with flaming tints' and to establish himself as a professional historian interested only in the truth as found in the contemporary sources.[22]

Also in 1928 W.T. Waugh of McGill published a full–length biography of James Wolfe. Wolfe had been lionized in English-Canadian historical writing in the nineteenth and early twentieth centuries.[23] For David Ross McCord, Wolfe constituted an obsession. In addition to renovating the grounds of the family home, Temple Grove, to resemble the famous Plains, he amassed what he repeatedly claimed to be the world's largest collection of Wolfiana. Among other items in his collection were a lock of Wolfe's hair (for which he paid £40 in a 1914 Sotheby's auction), several letters bearing the general's signature, a silhouette of his mother, and, most important, Wolfe's personal diary dated 18 June to 16 August 1759. At one point, McCord likened his labours, the building of a national museum, to those of Wolfe: 'But one thing is certain – Wolfe had to carry Quebec – and I must carry the museum.'[24]

Whereas McCord's Wolfe was unambiguously heroic, galvanic, and dashing, Waugh's Wolfe was more fully human, a man of strengths, to be sure, but also a man of weaknesses. Moreover, his Wolfe was far from dashing. 'He must have been a very ugly little boy,' Waugh surmised. 'His flaming red hair did not go well with his blue eyes. His nose was tilted heavenward. His chin fell away as the chin of no man of action ought to do. He soon began to grow too fast, and throughout his life he was very thin. His legs were much too long, his movements ungainly. From the earliest years he suffered from a delicate chest and other physical weaknesses.' As a young officer in the British army Wolfe proved himself thoroughly average. He could be 'pompous and sententious' and, to the end, 'unpleasantly censorious and over free with advice.'[25] Yet he was ruthless in battle. Although McCord conveniently ignored this fact,[26] Waugh did not. Wolfe, he argued, 'would punish breaches of discipline without mercy, he would record with satisfaction a great slaughter of the enemy, he would advise the massacre of a Highland clan, he would burn villages, he would destroy the nets and boats of poor fishermen: he would, in a word, do anything that the laws of war permitted.' Waugh credited Wolfe with skill as a military tactician, but he also drew attention to his tactical shortcomings. For example, he blamed Wolfe for the British defeat at Montmorency, the first major confrontation between the French and the British in the summer of 1759: 'The whole undertaking, in short, was ill-conceived and ill-prepared.'[27] In the final weeks leading up to the Plains of Abraham, a bedridden Wolfe suffered from tuberculosis of the kidneys and depression at the failure of the campaign to date. Still, Wolfe somehow managed to overcome his poor physical and mental state to lead his army to ultimate victory. In other words, as a man and as a soldier Wolfe had vices and virtues. In his review, an effusive George Wrong declared *James Wolfe: Man and Soldier* a fine example of new biography: 'This is biography as now, in reaction against the picture of the inspired hero, we like to have it; and Professor Waugh has done it skillfully.' The end result, according to Wrong, was a more complete, more balanced picture of the famous general.[28]

E.R. Adair surpassed Waugh in his 1936 presidential address to the Canadian Historical Association. The controversial and outspoken Adair took great pleasure in thoroughly knocking the great James Wolfe from his pedestal. As George Brown once said of Adair, 'He is simply one of those people who like to stir things up.'[29] Adair believed that it was incumbent on the historian to test legends 'by the acid of facts.' When Wolfe is subjected to the known facts, Adair argued, he is little more than an incompetent fool. According to the McGill historian, Wolfe had few friends, he was physically unattractive, and he fared poorly with members of the opposite sex; he was ponderous, platitudinous, and obsequious. His ascension through the British army owed more to nepotism and connections than to actual merit and talent. As a strategist, Wolfe proved positively hopeless; his victories owed more to blind luck than well-executed plans. In the final weeks of the campaign against Quebec, he vacillated. Adair even accused Waugh of hero-worship; after all, it was Wolfe's brigadiers, not Wolfe himself, who engineered the ultimately victorious battle on the Plains of Abraham. Adair conceded Wolfe's romantic appeal: 'but when we come down to earth and study what actually happened, we soon discover how different the real story is.'[30]

Two years later, Adair gave a similar address to the Mechanics Institute in Montreal. Wolfe, he declared, 'had no sense of humour ... and was not popular with the ladies, writing of the Scottish girls: "They are cold – to everything but the sound of the bagpipes."' At the end of the day, Wolfe's victory over Montcalm was as much an accident as anything else.[31] Many years after having studied with Adair, a McGill student could still recount her reaction to Adair's version of James Wolfe. Barbara Whitely remembered her 'shock' at hearing Wolfe referred to as an 'inept bungler.' 'What's more, Professor Adair continued by explaining testily that Wolfe did *not* recite Gray's "Elegy" as they rowed to shore from the English ships.'[32]

Adair's thorough debunking of Wolfe was not his first attempt at deflating myth: a few years earlier he had subjected the much-loved hero of New France, Adam Dollard, to the test of contemporary evidence. Nineteenth-century and early-twentieth-century Quebec historiography had transformed Dollard and his sixteen brethren into the saviours of New France. Aware of an imminent Iroquois attack against the fledgling colony, these young men decided to strike first. Joined by forty-four Hurons and Algonquins, Dollard met the advancing Iroquois war party at Long Sault. After an eight-day battle Dollard and his compatriots succumbed, but in their self-sacrifice, they saved the colony and its Roman Catholic faith. At all of these stories Adair scoffed. Dollard, he argued, never intended to sacrifice himself. His goal was decidedly less noble: to ambush Iroquois hunters; to steal a shipment of furs; and to redeem his damaged reputation in France. That he and his comrades happened to engage an advance party of 300 Iroquois was purely accidental. Moreover, there is nothing to suggest that this larger group of Iroquois intended to attack either Montreal or Quebec. Dollard's folly may have undermined the security of the colony because, as Adair noted, the Iroquois stepped up their attacks against New France in the following year: 'As a saviour of his country, Adam Dollard, Sieur des Ormeaux, must be relegated to the museum of historical myths.'[33]

Adair's account infuriated Quebec historians. Lionel Groulx responded. So, too, did Gustave Lanctôt. In a six-page letter to George Brown, editor of the *CHR*, Aegidius Fauteux stated that Adair's 'vigorous attack' against the 'revered' Dollard was unnecessary. 'There is only one explanation [for] his bizarre coup d'éclat,' he argued: 'I easily gather from other instances that he disdainfully pities our manner of writing history and feels bound to accomplish a necessary reform ... As he himself contends, he is a realistic historian fighting against the old fashioned romantic school.'[34] Fauteux was right: in dismantling the Dollard legend, Adair positioned himself as a 'realistic historian' vis-à-vis the myth makers, the romantics, and the amateurs.[35]

Also in 1932 Toronto's W.S. Wallace published a short, self-consciously iconoclastic booklet entitled *The Story of Laura Secord: A Study in Historical Evidence*. Wallace acknowledged that Laura Secord's intrepid 1813 journey through a hostile forest to warn British troops of an impending American attack possessed 'a romantic quality such as endears it even to the hard heart of the professional historian.' Be that as it may, it was the historian's task to weigh the evidence: 'Fortunately, there has survived an unusual wealth of contemporaneous documentary evidence with regard to the Battle of Beaver Dam.' Wallace highlighted the discrepancies between the 'facts' in Secord's testimony and the facts found in the documents. He concluded that Secord's version of events, told some years later, did not coincide with the account found in the contemporary evidence. As Wallace reminded his readers, the 'human memory is a notoriously treacherous and fallacious medium for the transmission of historical truth.' Wallace also implied that Secord's motives were suspect, and that her story was told with an eye to securing financial security, first in the lease of a ferry at Queenston and later in the form of a government pension. Wallace ultimately concluded that 'Mrs. Secord's narrative fails therefore by all the tests we have applied to it.' That this woman saved the country was 'too absurd for further discussion.'[36]

As the subtitle of his booklet indicates, Wallace also intended the story of Laura Secord to present a lesson in the use of evidence. Cecilia Morgan argues that Wallace wanted to distinguish himself – the professional historian, who understood what constituted evidence and who knew how to handle it – from the amateur historian, who dabbled with 'ephemeral, insubstantial, and unverifiable reminiscences,' precisely the kind of reminiscence that underpinned (or, as Wallace believed, under-mined) the Secord legend.[37] Furthermore, that Wallace was a man and Secord and her promoters were women is not insignificant. As seen in chapter 2, when the *Review of Historical Publications Relating to Canada* criticized the Women's Canadian Historical Societies of Toronto and Ottawa, it criticized them as amateur societies and as women's societies. The male voice was the voice of authority. The female voice lacked authority. Summoning the masculine ideal of man as objective by rein-forcing the feminine ideal of woman as subjective, Wallace, in *The Story of Laura Secord*, sought to distinguish what the professional historian did from what the amateur historian did and, in the process, reinforced the authority of professional historians.[38]

Wallace's booklet set off a tempest in a teapot, as Secord's many defenders rushed to her defence. Summarizing the debate and siding with the author, Hector Charlesworth, the editor of *Saturday Night*, explained, 'Prof. Wallace is one of your modern scientific historians who rely on contemporary documents; whereas the story of Laura Sec-ord was introduced into Canadian history at a time when romance was considered more important than mere records.'[39] Wallace may have been 'one of your modern scientific historians,' and he may have believed in 'the hard heart of the professional historian,' but he was prepared to walk away from the truth as he understood it in order to preserve his lucrative relationship with the Ontario Department of Education. Knowing that his version of Laura Secord's walk would arouse controversy and not wanting to bite the hand that fed him – at this point he had two books authorized for use in Ontario's schools – Wallace cautiously sent a manuscript copy to G.F. Rogers, chief director of Ontario's Department of Education: 'I thought it would be well for me to let you see it, in order that you might advise me whether the Department had any objection to my printing it?'[40] Presumably Rogers had no objections.

Eastman, Trotter, and Bailey; Morton, Waugh, Adair, and Wallace: each in his own way engaged in boundary-work. In denigrating the work of amateurs they raised the status of their own work. The professional-ization of history thus demanded the simultaneous amateurization of history. Amateur historians were a necessary Other. As a strategy of pro-fessionalization, using as a foil the newly created amateur historian was a means to an end: the establishment of authority.[41] Amateurization, how-ever, did not mean contempt for, or ignorance of, local history; in point of fact, at the same time as professional historians attempted to distinguish themselves from amateur historians, they also acknowledged their utility.[42]

III

In a 1932 article entitled 'The Importance of Local History in the Writing of General History,' D.C. Harvey placed local (i.e., amateur) and general (i.e., professional) historians in a pyramid.[43] At the base of the pyramid were the innumerable local historians; at the apex were the far-fewer-in-number general historians. Moreover, 'many local historians must have lived and died before one general historian could undertake to write an adequate general history.' The chief function, therefore, 'of the local historian is to provide the general historian with verified and verifiable facts about their smaller fields and with the most discerning interpretation of these facts as they can offer.' Harvey therefore called for a very clear division of labour, or 'differentiation in function.' 'The local historian must give detailed accurate knowledge. The general historian must select common or differentiating movements, must place them in perspective, and treat them in due proportion to their national importance.' What might this division of labour look like in practice? At the base of the pyramid we would find the many local historians at work on the history of their family or on biographical sketches of original settlers: 'They may tell of the first saw-mill, the first residence. the first town-meeting, the first town officers, the first fire-brigade, the first epidemic, the first church and school, and the first branch road connecting them with the outside world.' Moving up the pyramid, we would find the county historian and then the provincial historian: 'When all these local historians have done their work and the solid base of the pyramid has been built up to the centre, our general historians must be called upon to act.' To the general historian fell the enormous task of synthesis, emphasis, proportion, and perspective. Still, the local historian was enormously important. Knowing that he had a vital role to play, he 'should walk with a firm step, conscious that his part is one of fundamental importance.' His energy must be properly directed, however, if 'the general historian is ever to go beyond the vaguest generalizations.' At the same time as Harvey acknowledged the importance of amateur historians, he deliberately constructed a hierarchical division of labour (professional historians constituted the apex of the pyramid, amateur historians the base) and a hierarchical relationship (professionals must 'properly direct' the work of amateurs).[44]

Western's J.J. Talman would have agreed with Harvey's argument. In an unpublished address entitled 'History Must Be More Than an Adornment,' Talman stressed the importance of local history to the writing of a national history that would serve as a 'dynamic force' in the nation: 'All history, no matter how local, is part of the national record.' In any community, therefore, 'the coming of the first settler, the building of his shanty and later his log house, the erection of the gristmill and sawmill, the building of the first tavern and later a school and churches, the changing of blazed trails to corduroy, plank and gravel roads, the printing of the first newspaper, the coming of the electric telegraph and railways [and] the developing industries' all spoke directly to the national experience. Talman acknowledged that a much work was being done in the field of local history across the country: 'Much of it is of value while much may be of little purpose.' Whatever the case, 'more could be done than is being done.' The trick was to teach those interested persons that 'local history is something more than family trees and antiquarianism.' Professional historians should come to the 'aid and comfort' of amateur historians. Through adult education, community programs and extension work, university history faculties ought to take the initiative and guide 'the amateur along paths of scholarship.' 'No matter how the guidance and aid may come, local history should not be left to wander.'[45]

The desire to acknowledge the significance of local history, to encourage its development, and yet at the same time to preserve the authority of professional history found its clearest expression at the 1952 annual meeting of the Canadian Historical Association. In the fall of 1951 rumours circulated among some members of the CHA that local history associations and societies were planning to federate in order to create a national society. For obvious reasons, the CHA became very nervous: such a group would represent a direct challenge to its status as the national history association. C.P. Stacey, at this point vice-president, explained that the CHA must do something, anything, in order 'to head off the possibility of the malcontents setting up some new organization.'[46] To the president, Jean Bruchési, he predicted a grim future – 'the formation of a new society would be almost fatal to the CHA.' The association must take a proactive stance. Stacey reported that Richard Preston of the Program Committee had agreed to include a session on local history; from this initiative might come some concrete suggestions 'for more effective liaison between [the] CHA and the local societies.' There was no guarantee, of course, but it 'might serve to prevent a serious secession from the Association.'[47] Over the next few months Stacey recruited five panelists: Hilda Neatby, Jim Conacher, Richard Preston, Lewis Thomas, and Honorius Provost.

In their respective addresses, each speaker stressed the importance of local history. Neatby was very honest: for 'intellectual and cultural' reasons, as well as 'practical and sordid' reasons, the CHA must take more interest in local history. Not only did local history refine their understanding of national history, but increased membership and thus improved finances 'should accrue to the national association from active local and regional societies.' Neatby conceded that local history could mean bad history: it tended towards 'the trivial, the picturesque, and the pseudo-dramatic' at the same time as it led to 'endless and aimless counting and listing.' But local history did not have to mean bad history: 'local and regional groups could receive valuable help and support from a national association with a constant concern for scholarly standards.'[48] Representing the *CHR*, Jim Conacher stated that English Canada's leading historical journal already supported local history through its published bibliographies and 'Notes and Comments' section.[49] As editor of the CHA's *Annual Report*, Richard Preston stated that it 'would be most unprofessional if historians' did not study their own history when discussing 'a practical question like the interest of their own national association in local history.' He argued that the CHA had always expressed an interest in local history; because of drift, rotation of officers, and the autonomy of the Programme Committee, however, the association did not necessarily follow up its own initiatives. Valuing a place for local history at the annual meeting, he called for more cooperation between the CHA's Local History Committee and the Programme Committee.[50] Lewis Thomas of the Saskatchewan Archives placed an enormous value on local history ('What, except for biography, brings us closer to human beings as they really are than local history?'), but he also wanted to see the CHA challenge local groups to improve their work. In this way, local historians would see themselves as belonging to 'a larger fellowship of scholarship.'[51]

Linda Ambrose argues that Hilda Neatby harboured a 'disdain' for local history, while Lewis Thomas was much more sympathetic. 'Professional historians,' she concludes, 'were never unanimous in their ideas about the amateurs.'[52] However, both Neatby and Thomas appreciated the many 'important contributions'[53] of local history and both wanted to improve its quality. In point of fact, professional historians displayed a degree of unanimity vis-à-vis local historians. As C.P. Stacey observed, it was 'obviously the sense of the meeting that the CHA should take an interest in and be responsible for the coordination of the activities of local societies.'[54] Established in 1950, the Local History Section of the CHA resumed with new vigour its mandate to promote greater interest in, and improve the standards of, local history. Among other things, the section recommended that the CHA give certificates of merit for outstanding contributions in the field of local history. Although it took eight years, the CHA conferred its first awards in 1960.[55]

If professional historians needed amateur historians as an Other, they also needed them for their assistance in the preservation of source material, for their membership dues in the CHA, and for their efforts at increasing interest in history generally. However, historians repeatedly asserted a hierarchical relationship, while the CHA protected its status as the national historical association. Arthur Lower spoke for his profession when he wrote: 'It is perhaps inevitable that a historical association in Canada should gather round it a number of people who are not professional historians,' he explained to a colleague. 'That would be all to the good if these persons were people interested in public affairs and in history as a genuine force in the nation's growth. They are, however, frequently one or other species of the abundant genus of cranks. Probably they are our cross and we must bear with them, simply preventing them from becoming dominant.'[56]

But drawing and policing the professional/amateur boundary was not the profession's only boundary-work. One way of viewing the historical profession is as a club with a restrictive membership policy, that is anxious to enhance and defend its members' status and determined to protect its members' access to the academic labour market. Given English Canada's history of anti-Semitism, it is not surprising to learn that Jewish graduate students and historians endured discrimination. Based on the counsel of Sir Joseph Flavelle, University of Toronto president, Sir Robert Falconer, did not hire a Polish Jew for fear that he would not sufficiently understand British institutions. But Lewis Namier had the last laugh, since he went on to become Sir Lewis Namier, one of England's greatest historians.[57] In a letter of recommendation for a student, Frank Underhill wrote: 'he is a Jew with a good deal of the Jew's persecution complex, and this makes him unduly aggressive and sarcastic in discussion and writing.'[58] A few months later he described the same student as 'a Jew with the slightly aggressive attitude which marks some Jews.'[59] The principal of McGill stated that, all things considered, the selection committee would prefer a gentile to a Jew for the Kingsford Chair in History.[60] In private, Donald Creighton liked to gossip about 'Jews, kikes and the sons of Abraham.'[61] Harold Innis did not want to hire any Jews because it would only encourage more Jews to enter the social sciences.[62] Arthur Lower confided to a colleague that, 'privately,' he could 'admit that French Canadians seem a good deal more my own people than do Japs or Jews (at least many Jews).'[63] Noel Fieldhouse took too sympathetic a view of European fascism in the late 1930s, according to Ernest Sirluck, and he 'spoke ambiguously about Jews, whose treatment in various parts of Europe was being increasingly reported in the press.'[64] Although the historian-turned-headmaster W.L. Grant attempted to secure a position for Lionel Gelber in the federal civil service, and although he expressed his distaste for anti-Semitism, he nonetheless relied on the anti-Semitic notion of the good Jew. As Grant explained, Gelber 'is the only Jew I have ever known without the least touch of Jewish complex. Physically he is tall and good looking and not aggressively Jewish, though a certain curve in his nose betrays him.'[65] Underhill also relied on the good-Jew argument. He wanted to hire Gelber because it was wrong that a department as large as Toronto's did not have a Jew on board; and, after all, at least Gelber was a Jew that they knew.[66]

As distasteful as the profession's anti-Semitism was, there were not many Jewish students seeking graduate degrees in history, nor were there many Jewish historians seeking positions at English-Canadian universities. There were, however, many women in those situations. Precisely because women were more numerous – as undergraduates, graduate students, and scholars seeking employment – historians were compelled to define and defend themselves as men in ways that they never had to define and defend themselves as WASPS. After all, 'it is a sociological truism that nothing contributes more to the status of a vocation than the extent to which it is seen as a male calling.'[67]

CHAPTER 5

The importance of being sexist: the masculinization of history

When George Wrong said that 'the chief charm and strength of woman is in her being unlike man'[1] he both understood it as a self-evident statement of fact and intended it as a compliment. 'Nature,' he believed, 'dictates in every society that the work of man and woman shall be different.'[2] The representation of woman as the negative of man and the commitment to natural but separate spheres weakened women's claims to historical knowledge and worked against women seeking a career in history. Boundary-work was very much a gendered process as male historians, eager to enhance and defend their status, authority, and privileged access to the academic labour market, excluded women. If the professionalization of history included its amateurization, it also included its masculinization.[3]

In her book, *What Can She Know? Feminist Theory and the Construction of Knowledge,* Lorraine Code maintains that mainstream Anglo-American epistemology 'works from engrained assumptions about *who* can be a knower.'[4] These assumptions are deeply gendered. Far from being transcendent, Anglo-American epistemology relies on a series of binary oppositions: reason/emotion, objective/subjective, and knowledge/experience. In turn, these oppositions are hierarchical and gendered: reason, objectivity, and knowledge are superior and masculine, while emotion, subjectivity, and experience are inferior and feminine. According to Code, the representation of woman as the negative of man dates to the Ancients. For example, with reference to the human soul, Aristotle noted that 'the slave has no deliberative faculty at all; the woman has, but it is without authority and the child has, but it is immature.' This representation of woman 'as a creature whose deliberative faculty – her capacity to think, judge, and know – is *without authority*' has endured in its persistent variations.[5] What can she know? The rhetorical question implies its own answer. Emotional, subjective, and experiential, her voice lacks authority.

In this chapter I will explore the intersection between the professionalization of history in English Canada and gendered assumptions about who can and who cannot not be a knower.[6] Although it contributes to the literature on women in higher education,[7] and to the growing interest in the history of women in history,[8] it most directly complements Alison Prentice's pioneering essay, 'Laying Siege to the History Professoriate.' Prentice studied women as undergraduates, graduate students, and faculty members at six English-Canadian universities prior to 1950.[9] To some extent, what follows covers similar terrain. The experiences of women studying and teaching history are documented, and the sexism – the observable discrimination based on sex – they endured is revealed. However, it starts from the premise that sexism was not simply 'the way they did things back then.' Again, it is Prentice who points in the right direction. In a suggestive remark early in her essay, she notes that as 'historians competed for place as experts and creators of knowledge,' neither the first generation of professional historians nor their mid-century successors could imagine 'women participating in the new professionalism.' 'As some departments grew and specialized, their leaders appeared to worry that too much female involvement might undermine the professional status that academic historians sought for themselves and their more serious students during this period.'[10] Prentice is right. Women could not and cannot be 'accommodated into a cultural ideal [in this case, science and knowledge] which has defined itself in opposition to the feminine.'[11] If women could not be easily accommodated, they were also actively excluded. To professionalize the study of history along rational, objective, and scientific lines, the presence of women had to be minimized.

Sexism not only protected the status of history as a masculine discipline, it also protected the academic labour market for men. Current thinking on sexual harassment is useful to understanding the discrimination women confronted in the historical profession. Sexual harassment is too often understood to mean only unwanted sexual advances by men against women. Vicki Schultz develops a broader conceptualization of sexual harassment, however, when she states that 'the real issue isn't sex, it's sexism on the job. The fact is, most harassment isn't about satisfying sexual desires. It's about protecting work – especially the most favoured lines of work – as preserves of male competence and authority.'[12] Thus reconceptualized, sexual harassment includes: 'characterizing the work as appropriate for men only'; 'withholding the training, information, or opportunity to learn to do the job well'; 'providing sexist evaluations of women's performance or denying them deserved promotions'; and 'isolating women from the social networks that confer a sense of belonging.' 'Harassment,' Schultz concludes, 'serves a gender-guarding, competence-undermining function. By subverting women's capacity to perform favored lines of work, harassment polices the boundaries of the work and protects its idealized masculine image – as well as the identity of those who do it.'[13] Of course, those women studying and seeking a career in history would not have described the discrimination they confronted as sexual harassment. But as defined by Schultz, it remains a useful means of interpreting their historical experience. Furthermore, the sexism Schultz identifies was not incidental to the professionalization of history in English Canada – it was necessary.

I

Women were very much part of the expanding undergraduate enrolment. While it is impossible to determine the precise number of women undergraduates in history at English-Canadian universities, Prentice demonstrates that prior to 1950 women accounted for anywhere from one-third to one-half of the history students at the six institutions she studied.[14] It is similarly difficult to generalize the experiences of women as undergraduates. There is no doubt, however, that women students encountered sexism. That sexism, furthermore, both stemmed from and perpetuated a discursive association of history with masculinity.

For example, when at the University of Saskatchewan Frank Underhill separated men and women students in his tutorials, 'believing that shy females in the group inhibited the men from expressing themselves freely, thus lowering the quality of the tutorial.'[15] As he explained in 1930, 'no university teacher wants to be condemned to teaching women. He knows that that means an old age of pedantry or empty, meaningless aestheticism.'[16] Arthur Lower shared Underhill's reticence. He thought co-education fine for children, perhaps adolescents and graduate students who are adults, but co-education at the undergraduate level only spelled trouble: 'pretty girls [are] always attracting young men, the play goes on every day and all day. The girls, with their unsubduable social instinct, have a genius for turning every occasion into a social occasion and, in small groups where discussion is called for, they nearly all follow the lead of the 'dominant' males, contribute never a point – and write, if not always the best, then invariably the tidiest essays.' To mitigate the effects of the naturally coquettish but also submissive co-ed, Lower 'often informally separated' the women from the men.[17] Yes, he believed separation benefited women as well as men, yet he did not cast blame on any perceived qualities inherent in men for this state of affairs. It was the fault of women, their irrepressible sociability, and their habit, particularly strong in pretty women, of distracting men. How many other professors divided men and women into separate groups is not known.

Meanwhile, women were barred from at least three undergraduate historical societies. Toronto's Historical Club provided the model; founded by George Wrong in 1904, it did not admit women until the 1960s. Membership was limited to about twenty-five third- and fourth-year students from across the humanities. The club held fortnightly meetings (often in the home of a prominent Torontonian, such as Sir Joseph Flavelle, Sir Edmund Walker, and Sir Edmund Osler) and arranged an annual dinner each spring in Hart House (complete with dinner jackets and a guest speaker). There is every reason to believe that the History Department took the club and its members seriously. Two faculty members sat on the executive, and the entire faculty attended the annual dinner. Commenting on the Historical Club's restrictive membership policy in the 1930s, Robert Bothwell observes only that it was 'a very odd development' at a time when more than half the history students were women.[18]

A.L. Burt reproduced Toronto's Historical Club at Alberta in the 1910s. Like Toronto's, Alberta's club was exclusively male, and Burt, like his mentor George Wrong, took it seriously. Writing to his wife from Britain in 1919, Burt enquired about the club and expressed an anxious desire to see it survive his temporary absence due to the war. 'You are a dear old soul to keep up the Historical Club,' he told his wife. 'It is immensely appreciated by the boys.'[19] When he returned from England, Burt began to look for a house 'and the first essential that we laid down was that the house must have a large living room – for the sake of the Club, whose membership was growing.'[20] Like Toronto's, Alberta's Club was not opened to women until the 1960s, when Sylvia Van Kirk became the first woman to join in 1965 and then, in 1968, the first woman to serve as president. As she recalls, there was considerable concern among the members that a woman president would turn the club into a 'hen party.'[21]

McGill, too, had an all-male History Club. Although founded by Charles Colby in 1897, the club experienced something of a rebirth in 1923 – what the yearbook called a 're-organization.' McGill's club also initiated a policy of meeting in the homes of prominent Montreal citizens. In 1925 the members enjoyed a visit from one of England's greatest historians, G.M. Trevelyan. Like their counterparts at Toronto, McGill professors took the club seriously: each year at least one professor, and sometimes two, appeared in the annual photograph and a professor would host one of the meetings. Principal Arthur Currie agreed to be the club's patron, and in 1930 he too invited the members to his home. The club did not open its membership to women until 1956. In an effort to create a similar institution for women, McGill's first and only woman lecturer in history until the 1960s organized the Royal Victoria College Historical Club for women in 1919. In *Old McGill* Vera Brown is described as the 'moving spirit' behind the club.[22] Beginning in 1926, the two clubs met for an annual end-of-the-year meeting. Yet none of the history faculty appeared on the honorary executive, and not until 1942 did anyone from the history staff sit for the RVC Historical Club's annual photograph.

If the all-male Historical Club obviously excluded women at the undergraduate level, it could work against them at the graduate level as well. Writing a letter of recommendation for a male undergraduate seeking a scholarship to pursue graduate studies, Underhill stressed the young man's membership in the department's oldest and most prestigious society: 'I know from my experience of him as president of our Historical Club ... that he has very great social gifts, which are more than just a capacity for being pleasant with people. He has run the Historical Club with greater skill than any of its recent presidents have shown.'[23] Lacking the opportunity to join, women also lacked opportunities to make such an impression.[24] Lower looked back on his membership in Toronto's Historical Club with fondness. He liked the elitism and 'the enjoyable social occasions.' The highlight of his membership was meeting a former American president, William Howard Taft. In a brief, but insightful comment, he noted that the Historical Club, and others like it, 'had a good deal to do with giving an atmosphere of professionalism to the study of history.'[25] Here, young men were trained in the informal rules of academic culture, how to give a learned paper, how to ask good questions, and how to socialize after the proceedings. Burt fondly recalled the Alberta tradition of encouraging every member learn to smoke. Taking his first cigar, one poor lad experienced what probably was a nicotine rush and had to excuse himself. He did not return until refreshment time, his face 'much paler and more serious.' No worse for the wear, he was, in Burt's estimation, henceforth 'a man.'[26]

While in one of the Historical Clubs a young man might be inspired to pursue a career in academia. George Stanley, Morris Zaslow, and Dale Thomson had been members of Alberta's club. The list of historians who had been members of the Varsity Club before 1960 is impressive: W.S. Wallace, G.M. Smith, W.N. Sage, A.L. Burt, Frank Underhill, Fred Soward, David Spring, J.M.S. Careless, Gerald Craig, Paul Cornell, Kenneth McNaught, William Kilbourn, Laurier Lapierre, and Graeme Patterson.[27] Careless explicitly recalled that it was the friendships he formed with the staff that encouraged him to think about a career in history: 'Coming to know the staff pretty well, after all it was a very small department then, and liking them and I think generally admiring them and thinking they had a very good life,' I decided upon graduate school.[28] McNaught clearly understood the club's raison d'être: 'Its purpose was to establish closer, informal relations among professors, "promising" students, and members of the Toronto establishment.'[29] Although he was not a member of the club, it was also through his friendships with the Toronto staff that C.P. Stacey decided to pursue a career in academia. Upon completing his BA, he had decided on two things: 'I wanted an academic career, and one in history. The friendships I had formed among the University of Toronto's teaching staff influenced me in both matters. They were a pleasant society, I thought, the sort I would like to belong to, and while I should never grow rich pursuing such a career, riches was not what I was after.'[30]

These examples – the separation of men and women in tutorials and the all-male historical clubs – should be read as more than examples of sexism. True, exclusion communicated an unmistakably sexist message – young men are more important than young women. But it also communicated another message – only young men are capable of doing history. The exclusion of women at the undergraduate level indicates that a gendered understanding of the discipline as history was being constructed along masculine lines: young men alone embodied the attributes necessary for historical investigation. Recalling his undergraduate years at Toronto in the 1910s, Arthur Lower said that history attracted more men than, say, English, because it was regarded as being of 'masculine fibre.'[31] Early on in their university lives, therefore, some women received the message that they could not be historians, that they did not conform to the ideal type.[32] In other words, there was nothing 'odd' about Toronto's Historical Club, as Robert Bothwell notes. Borrowing Vicki Schultz's language: 'isolating women from the social networks that confer a sense of belonging' protected both the discipline and the profession.

This is not to say that exclusion was practised in every university (women were welcome in the various undergraduate historical clubs and societies at UBC, Saskatchewan, and United College); nor is it to say that women did not go on to graduate school. Indeed, some women did receive encouragement to pursue graduate studies. Of course, it was not easy to win funding. Certainly, the very prestigious Rhodes Scholarship was closed to women, as was the Parkin Travelling Scholarship. Founded in 1924 and named in honour of Sir George Parkin, the latter allowed young Canadian men in any discipline to study in England. When the criteria were being defined, it was W.L. Grant who suggested that it be restricted to 'members of the male sex'; 'my reason is that I think that the recipient should be someone whose aim in life we might hope would resemble that of Sir George himself.' Since women could never resemble Parkin, it did not make sense to fund their studies in England. At least three young men who received the scholarship went on to enjoy a career in history: C.P. Stacey, Gerald Graham, and R.O. MacFarlane.[33] Moreover, women experienced discrimination in open scholarship competitions. In a revealing letter of recommendation, Underhill admitted that while the woman in question had written a superior MA thesis, she did not get a scholarship: 'She was considered very seriously for another scholarship but it was finally given to a man student who, in my opinion, hasn't half the intellectual ability that she has.' As Underhill explained, she is a 'very quiet retiring girl and this rather told against her with some of the staff who hadn't seen much of her.'[34] Yet despite the patent discrimination, women did receive scholarships. Based on the number of awards women won, and the number of scholarships women received, Prentice concludes that women were encouraged to study history and to go on to do graduate work at the master's level in particular. At the next and most important level, however, the 'numbers (and proportions) of women students dropped dramatically.'[35] Prior to 1960 women completed five out of thirteen history PhDs at McGill and six out of forty-one at Toronto.

As at the undergraduate level, it is difficult to generalize about the experiences of women at the graduate level. McGill's E.R. Adair is reputed to have been particularly mean spirited. Writing about his graduate student experience at McGill after the Second World War, W.J.

Eccles remembers that Adair 'could be unfair in his criticism of his students' work, even cruel at times,' and that he aimed his cruelty at women students in particular: 'He seemed to enjoy reducing female students to tears, and they, it seemed to me, took masochistic pleasure from the experience; at least they always came back for more.'[36] How many women Adair's aggressive teaching methods deterred from academia is impossible to determine. Still, women could and did enjoy support at graduate school. Even Adair went to bat for one woman doctoral candidate, Alice Lunn. In support of her 1936–7 application for a Royal Society fellowship, he referred to her as 'One of the best women students I have had at McGill,' stressing her 'Sound judgment and great capacity for work.'[37] In the end, Lunn received the fellowship, which allowed her to conduct research in both Ottawa and Paris.

Two men in particular stand out as supportive of women graduate students. Except for his re-creation of Wrong's all-male History Club at Alberta, A.L. Burt consistently adopted a progressive position on the so-called woman question. While in England during the closing months of the war, he wrote his wife a series of long, detailed letters. Occasionally he would comment on women and their status in society. He once worried that, while the army was not entirely 'lewd,' it nevertheless had a 'coarsening influence' on men in 'their attitude toward women.'[38] On another occasion he said that women should have careers, and that they should not be compelled to abandon them upon marriage. He could even imagine that in some situations it would be better for the woman to be the wage earner and for the man to stay home. In any event, he concluded, a wife 'should be more than a housekeeper, as too often she only is.' Several years later he said that marriage must be an 'equal union' between husband and wife, and that he refused to believe that men are predators and women parasites in a marriage. Given that he viewed marriage as a partnership and that he believed women ought to have careers, it is not surprising that Burt should have encouraged his brilliant women students to continue their studies. Recognizing Aileen Dunham's capacity for graduate work, Burt sent her to Toronto, where she completed her MA in 1920. From Toronto Dunham went to the University of London, where she completed her PhD in 1923. Writing on behalf of Dunham in 1922, Burt stated unequivocally: 'She is by far the most brilliant student that I have ever had and I expect that it will be many years before I encounter her like again.'[40] A classmate of Dunham, Lillian Cobb, similarly went on to an academic career in England with Burt's support.[41] Finally, he supervised Hilda Neatby's PhD thesis at

Minnesota from 1931 to 1934. She even became an honorary member of the Burt family, Burt's children referring to her as 'Aunt Hilda.'

Like Burt, Alfred Bailey of the University of New Brunswick assisted female graduate students. Having secured a 1943 Rockefeller Foundation grant to work on the history of New Brunswick, Bailey used a portion to fund the MA work of three women, including Katherine MacNaughton, a teacher in Campbelton, New Brunswick. Although clearly intelligent, she lacked self-confidence. In a 3 June 1943 letter to Bailey, MacNaughton presented him with the opportunity to rescind his offer. After all, she said, 'My lack of knowledge of New Brunswick history, or indeed of any history, is disgraceful, and the mediocrity of my ability undeniable.'[42] Bailey responded immediately with an encouraging letter: 'I am quite convinced you are the best person for the job.'[43] MacNaughton began her research on the history of education in New Brunswick in the fall of 1943. Although she completed her degree requirements, and although her thesis was published in 1946, her self-doubt remained unabated.[44] Even as her book was delivered to the binder, it was all she could do to steel herself to attend an interview for a Beaverbrook Scholarship for a year's study in London. Exasperated, Bailey responded: 'For goodness sake! ... Such humility humiliates your friends and supporters who have faith in you.'[45] Two years later, MacNaughton summed up her relationship with Bailey: 'Anything I have ever done, you pushed me into it, and the push has always been to my advantage.'[46]

However, even if a woman was encouraged to do graduate work, and even if she did find a supportive adviser, her sex followed her. Recall Adair's recommendation of Alice Lunn: 'One of the best women students I have had at McGill.' In otherwise very strong letters, Underhill referred to one woman as 'best girl student I have had in history for some years'[47] while he referred to another as 'the ablest girl we have had for a long time.'[48] Arthur Lower said of one student, 'she is among the best women students I have had.'[49] Western's Fred Landon once described one of his female MA students as a 'nice kid.'[50] Although his letters of recommendation for female students were always positive,[51] even Bailey on at least one occasion reported: 'if you need a good girl' on staff, then he was 'happy to recommend' his former student. In a separate letter of recommendation for the same woman, he commented on her 'very good appearance.'[52] Even when recommended positively, then, women continued to be identified as women historians.

Sex was an indelible and negative marker of difference that set women apart from their male counterparts. William Aiken, a lecturer in modern history at McMaster University from 1938 to 1940, commented on the differences between 'boys' and 'girls' in a particular history class. The boys, he said, are for the most part 'much better' than the girls. Boys have 'more speculative minds – more imagination,' while 'girls are quick on the facts, but rarely go farther than the facts.'[53] In other words, the female mind was immediate and focused on particulars, while the male mind was transcendent and capable of abstraction. In at least three letters of recommendation Underhill unwittingly revealed his understanding of woman as the opposite of man. Of one woman he wrote, 'she has shown a capacity for grasping political ideas which is not usual in girls.'[54] Of another he wrote, 'she appears to differ from most girls in having a good political mind.'[55] In what Underhill considered high praise indeed, he said of a third woman: 'She has a good clear political mind like a man.'[56] The capacity for political thought, he believed, was masculine. Arthur Lower once wrote of a female graduate student: she 'seems to have rather more than the average feminine difficulty in making up her mind, and she does not seem to know her ultimate aim.'[57] Indecisiveness was feminine, decisiveness masculine.

Again, it would be a mistake to read the above comments as only sexist comments. That these male historians felt compelled to rate women according to a preconceived standard of masculine capabilities and strengths shows a representational system in which women were categorized as 'unlike men,' to borrow George Wrong's phrase. The success or inclusion of women in history was contingent on their ability to conform to the masculinized ideal of the historian. Marked not-male and thus set apart as different, women could not compete at the next level, the labour market.[58]

II

Formal competitions, job advertisements, and hiring committees did not exist in the historical profession before 1960. Rather, the labour market worked informally, by word-of-mouth, reputation, nepotism, networks, and attempts by supervisors to secure positions for their students. This informality worked against women.

Anticipating an appointment, department chairs and sometimes university presidents would send letters to senior colleagues in Britain, the United States, and, because of its graduate school, the University of Toronto. The letters were explicit: we are looking for a new man; can you give us a name or two? 'I am looking for a young man for the position of lecturer in History ... We would like a young man with natural ability and growing power,' wrote J.H. Riddell to the acting head of history at Toronto in 1919.[59] 'Each year for the last five, I have been hoping to get another man,' Burt wrote to Underhill in 1927.[60] Seeking a replacement for Jack Pickersgill, Arthur Lower approached his alma mater in 1937, asking for information 'about young men available at Harvard to teach mainly European history.'[61] He made a similar request of Underhill two years later: 'Have you any bright young men who may be wishing a junior post next fall? ... I must have a man of personality and a reasonable range of knowledge.'[62] Writing to Underhill in December 1939, the president of the University of Saskatchewan stated, 'I want a man who could become a junior professor. ... Have you any names you could bring to my knowledge?'[63] To Reginald Trotter, Thomson explained, 'I should like a younger man who could make the teaching of Canadian History a special contribution to the work of our Department.'[64] Anticipating another appointment in the fall of 1946, Lower again wrote to Underhill: 'I suppose you yourself can find work for almost all your young men, but if there is anyone you think could be spared, I would be glad to have his name.'[65] In the early 1950s Western's J.J. Talman requested a list of potential candidates for a possible opening. Of the nine qualities the candidate should possess, that he be 'a man with an agreeable personality' topped the list.[66] To no one in particular, the acting dean at Waterloo College informed the Toronto History Department in 1953: 'We are looking for a qualified man to give the general under-graduate History courses.'[67] Writing to Sir Lewis Namier, Noel Fieldhouse outlined the ideal candidate: 'What I want is a man who would be at least on the "short list" for a Chair in the United Kingdom and who would, as soon as he had time to settle in here, take over the Chairmanship of the Department.'[68] And on the basis of 'some personal recommendations, including an informal but very satisfactory one from Donald Creighton,' Western's Wallace K. Ferguson offered an appointment to Donald Kerr: 'I am sure that you are the man we want.'[69]

Within this context, how many women were hired? That depends on how one counts. Certainly, departments hired women to fill low-status, temporary positions. McGill's Charles Colby allowed the warden of Royal Victoria College, Hilda Oakeley, to teach Ancient History from 1901 to 1906, when she returned to England. As she recalled in her memoirs, however, 'The path of the women members of the McGill staff was not altogether smooth.' The 'very conservative' dean of arts, Alexander Johnson, was less than enamoured with women teaching at the university: 'He saw every encroachment of the monstrous regiment of women with disfavour.'[70] McGill then listed Oakeley's successor, Ethel Hurlbatt, as a tutor in the History Department between 1907 and 1915. The department also hired graduate student assistants from 1928 to 1930 and from 1933 to 1938 when the calendar stopped listing assistants. Unfortunately, the departmental records are incomplete, but there is evidence to show that the department employed women assistants in the 1940s and 1950s as well. However, for only four years did it employ a woman as a lecturer: Vera Brown from 1916 to 1920. Her time at McGill ended on an unfortunate note. Although she had an MA, in 1920 the Faculty of Arts passed a resolution condemning the Department of History for allowing Brown to lecture to third- and fourth-year honours students. Rumour had it that the BA Advisory Committee was preparing a resolution for the faculty to suspend first-year lectures in history until Brown stopped lecturing. 'But one thing seems clear,' C.E. Fryer explained to Colby, 'we really must have more weight in the department next year – someone in addition to Miss Brown if she remains.'[71] The issue was not her lack of a PhD. At the same time as Colby argued that the department should retain Brown for another year as a courtesy to her while she looked for another appointment, he also recommended the appointment of another McGill alumnus with an MA, T.W.L. MacDermott.[72] MacDermott came to McGill three years later as a lecturer; significantly, his career was singularly unimpressive as a scholar, and in 1935 he left the university altogether to become headmaster of Upper Canada College. Meanwhile, McGill hired Basil Williams in 1920. He, too, had an MA, but he had other attractive qualifications. In a revealing letter, Principal Arthur Currie claimed that he had hired Williams because of his 'scholarly productiveness.' However, he admitted his attraction to Williams's record of military service: his 'general experience as a soldier in the South African War, and as a Major of the Artillery in the late War also appealed to me.'[73] Military service as an informal skill necessarily excluded women. In a 1924 letter to Principal Currie, one woman wrote, 'It does seem as if it should be possible for a Canadian woman with a Ph.D. degree to find work in a Canadian University. I, therefore, hope that it will be possible for you to consider this application favourably.'[74] She was not considered.

The situation at Ontario universities was similar to that at McGill. Queen's regularly employed female assistants from the 1920s through the 1950s. However, only Anna Wright worked as an instructor and then for only three years, from 1943 to 1946. In working as an instructor at a university, Wright surpassed the expectations of Toronto, where she had received her PhD. According to the Department of History, 'Miss Wright's performance in her "fields" last year was the best we have had in recent years. She has a real gift for exposition and ought to have a career before her in secondary education in this province.'[75] The University of Western Ontario employed only two women: Ruth Davis was a reader in 1926–7 and an assistant from 1929 to 1931, and Helen Hughes also worked as an assistant from 1927 to 1929. McMaster hired Gwendolen Carter as a reader in 1932. She had a BA from Toronto and a BA from Oxford and stayed at McMaster for three years. The minutes of the Board of Governors make it clear, however, that her third year would also be her last year: 'Miss Carter has been reappointed Reader in History for next year, with the intimation that, in the judgment of the [Executive Committee of the Board of Governors] it will then be better to secure the services of a man who has completed more post-graduate work.'[76] The necessity of a graduate degree was eminently reasonable; the insistence on securing the services of a man, however, was clearly the product of a sexist and epistemological bias against women historians.

Toronto certainly hired women, but never to a permanent position. From 1914 to 1926 there was always at least one woman listed as an instructor in the calendar: they included Winnifred Harvey, Helen McMurchie, Marjorie Reid, and Margaret Wrong, daughter of George Wrong. However, George Wrong viewed women's employment in general with trepidation: what would befall men as women entered the labour market? 'Now all but extinct is the young lady whose education was 'finished' at eighteen and who then waited at home for her marriage. Many of these now look for jobs exactly as do their brothers, engage in works for social betterment and exercise in politics influence backed up by the vote. Sometimes I wonder a little how, since they hold positions formerly held by men, the man will be able to find employment that will make possible his taking a bride and making a home.'[77] In any event, not until Hilda Neatby's appointment as a special lecturer in 1944 did Toronto employ another woman above the rank of tutor. Throughout the 1940s and 1950s Toronto regularly employed women as readers to assist professors with grading.

In the Maritimes, Dalhousie did not hire women historians, Acadia employed a woman lecturer for two years in the 1920s, and the University of New Brunswick hired Frances Firth as an assistant for three years (1946–9). Mount Allison was an exception in that it employed two women as lecturers throughout the Second World War. Although one of the women, Ella Smith, remained until 1951, it was by default rather than by design, when George Stanley decided not to return to Mount Allison after the war. As a Catholic women's college, Mount Saint Vincent was staffed chiefly by members of the Sisters of Charity. Although a 1951 fire destroyed all university records, it is clear from surviving calendars that from 1938 through to her retirement in 1965, Sister Francis d'Assisi taught history in addition to performing administrative duties, first as dean and later as president. Sister Francis d'Assisi earned her doctorate from Fordham University, but her career was primarily as an administrator. Indeed, she was the driving force behind the Mount's survival as a women's college.[78] Moreover, Elizabeth Smyth argues that women religious 'represent a unique subset' of women historians in English Canada.[79] Although some were serious, even accomplished, historians, women religious were not part of the historical profession that was unfolding in the first half of the twentieth century.

Only at western Canadian universities were women hired to full-time positions; the numbers, however, are hardly staggering. At the University of Manitoba, Dr Ursilla Macdonnel lectured in the Department of History from 1922 to 1931 at the same time as she also served as the dean of women. When Chester Martin replaced George Wrong at Toronto in 1928, Macdonnel was appointed acting head until H.N. Fieldhouse's appointment in 1930. Alberta had only one woman on staff; after completing the course work for her doctorate at Chicago, Jean Murray worked as an instructor for two years from 1928 to 1930 at Alberta before heading east to Saskatchewan. Indeed, Saskatchewan listed Isabel Jones (1918–21), Elsinore MacPherson (1922–3), Hilda Neatby (1928–31), and Jean Murray (1931–5) as instructors. The University of Saskatchewan also gave permanent appointments to women. For Neatby and Murray the breakthrough came in 1936 and 1937, respectively, when they made assistant professor, Neatby at Regina College and Murray at Saskatoon. In the 1930s UBC had women assistants: Gwen Musgrave in 1930–31; Margaret Ross in 1931–2; Margaret Ormsby in 1935–6 and 1936–7; and, finally, Patricia Johnson in 1937–8. Another woman, Sylvia Thrupp, was an instructor for several years, from 1935 to 1944; eventually, her career took her to the United States. Meanwhile, Margaret Ormsby returned to British Columbia as a lecturer in 1943. Like Saskatchewan, UBC also gave a full-time appointment to a woman when Ormsby was appointed assistant professor in 1946.

The Canadian Federation of University Women understood the

closed door that confronted women academics. Writing to Reginald Trotter, Dixie Pelleut noted, 'The Committee [on Academic Appointments] feels that it is rather disappointing to offer scholarships to encourage women to go on to graduate work, if there is to be little opportunity to give the recipient a chance to pursue her profession when she is adequately qualified.'[80]

Because women could not expect open and fair competition in the Canadian academic labour market, it was in their best interests to leave the country altogether for doctoral studies. That was the advice George Wrong gave to a young woman in 1925. If you did well at Radcliffe, he advised, 'they would back you for an appointment.'[81] A few years later, Hilda Neatby received the same counsel. Although she very much wanted to do her doctorate at Toronto with Underhill, she resigned herself to the reality of the academic labour market in Canada and anticipated a career in the United States, where it was important to have an American degree. 'It has recently been pointed out to me,' Neatby informed Underhill, 'that it might be wiser for me to apply for a fellowship in an American university as my having studied in the United States would make it easier to secure a position there if I wished to do so later on.' While there is no record of Underhill's response, it is clear from Neatby's next letter that he advised her to pursue doctoral studies in the United States. 'It is a great disappointment in every way ... to give up the idea of coming to Toronto. I feel, however, that if a Toronto student has not a good chance of a position in the United States it would be better to try for an American university as in Saskatchewan at least, even the better high school positions seem to be more or less closed to women. All the same, although common sense makes me follow your advice, I can't help hoping that some chance may yet take me to Toronto.'[82] Neatby went to Minnesota. On at least two occasions, once in 1933 and again in 1934, she told her sister that she had little hope of securing an academic appointment in Canada because of her sex.[83] The assumption that women should set their sights on the American academic labour market seems to have been common, at least in the 1920s and 1930s. After completing her doctorate at London, Aileen Dunham secured a position at Ohio's College of Wooster in 1924. Here she taught history for over forty years.[84] In an unsigned and undated letter, McGill's Department of History attempted to secure a teaching position in one of America's women's colleges for one of its female graduates who had returned to Canada with a higher degree. Effusive with praise, copies of the letter were sent to Bryn Mawr, Wellesley,

Mount Holyoke, Smith, Vassar, and Barnard. None was sent to any Canadian universities.[85]

The answer to the original question – how many women were hired – is three: Jean Murray, Hilda Neatby, and Margaret Ormsby. According to Prentice, Saskatchewan's and UBC's focus on regional history may have been a factor in their decisions to hire women at a time when permanent academic appointments for women were few and far between: 'History department heads like Walter Sage [of UBC] and Arthur Morton [of Saskatchewan] may have been able to perceive women as potential fellow workers in a way that their counterparts in central and eastern Canada could not, perhaps in large part because of their interest in promoting local and regional history.' As she quickly points out, however, 'this was by no means the whole story.'[86] After all, departments that taught regional history did not necessarily hire women. There were no women at Dalhousie, for example. Prentice credits D.C. Harvey, a member of the graduate program in history at Dalhousie, with a certain progressiveness on the question of female historians. Certainly, Harvey promoted the history of British Columbia when at UBC from 1928 to 1931 and the history of Nova Scotia when at the Public Archives of Nova Scotia and Dalhousie from 1931 onward. But when it came time to select a protegé who would eventually succeed him at the Public Archives of Nova Scotia, he made it clear that he wanted a man, despite the presence of two very capable women on his staff, both of whom he had supervised as MA students.[87] Furthermore, there were no permanent appointments for women at the University of New Brunswick, despite Alfred Bailey's interest in regional history in the 1940s and 1950s. Although the Second World War interrupted George Stanley's plans for a regional history program at Mount Allison University, he considered his two female wartime replacements as strictly temporary appointments. He did not think he could work with his wartime replacement. As he explained to a friend, 'I doubt very much whether Miss [Ella] Smith and I would get along together in the same department. Nor have I a great deal of respect for her qualities as a University Lecturer.'[88] Moreover, as Chad Reimer suggests, Sylvia Thrupp's experience at UBC was exploitative. For nine years, from 1935 to 1944, Sage hired Thrupp on year-to-year contracts. Intimidated by her intelligence and thus reluctant to have her in the department on a permanent basis, Sage also knew that Thrupp had no choice but to accept one-year contracts because she needed to be in Vancouver to care for her ailing father.[89]

Still, Saskatchewan was an exception to the otherwise very strict rule that women not be given permanent appointments. Why? Because there were unique circumstances at Saskatchewan that did not exist elsewhere: Jean Murray was the daughter of the president. Although not incompetent, she was not brilliant either. She did not excel at Toronto, and, given who her father was, she actually received more attention.[90] Likewise, she was reputed to have had some difficulty in completing her dissertation at Chicago.[91] She never produced a monograph. Nevertheless, she was employed as an instructor at Saskatchewan in the winter of 1926 and between 1931 and 1935; she was hired as an assistant professor in 1937. How much influence her father brought to bear is impossible to determine, but since his daughters did not marry, he must have worried about their financial welfare. Indeed, we do know that he paid from his own pocket her instructor's salary in 1932.[92] Moreover, Murray, A.S. Morton, and their respective wives were good friends; perhaps Morton felt a loyalty to the Murray family and agreed to Jean's appointment. Kate Nicoll, Hilda Neatby's sister, always believed that Murray and Morton had been 'keeping the place warm' for Jean.[93] Given the closed doors women confronted at universities across the country, it would seem that having a university president for a father undoubtedly helped.

As for Hilda Neatby, she was uniquely brilliant. In his 1923–4 annual report Morton noted that 'Miss Neatby was so far ahead of the others I took her by herself once a week.'[94] A.L. Burt thought Neatby to be one of the two best students he had ever encountered.[95] Even Frank Underhill, who disliked teaching women and believed that Saskatchewan's Historical Association was poorly served by its open membership, conceded that Neatby was brilliant: 'On the whole she was the best student that I had while in the West.'[96] Indeed, they remained lifelong friends. After teaching in the department on a part-time basis from 1927 to 1931 she decided to pursue doctoral studies. In 1934 Neatby received a teaching position at Regina College, and in 1936 she was appointed assistant professor. In 1944 she went to Toronto as a special lecturer in history, but her appointment was never considered permanent. The simple fact is that Toronto refused to give a permanent position to a woman, even one of Neatby's obvious calibre. The departmental minutes for 16 September 1944 reveal Toronto's blindness: despite Neatby's presence on campus, the department looked past her in its discussion on 'the problem of future staff appointments.' The names of four men (all of whom had done at least one degree at Toronto) were bandied about in relation to a junior, but permanent, position; one member of the department even suggested that 'letters of inquiry be sent to several English and American universities with regard to young men who might be available in future for limited temporary appointments.'[97] Neatby's future did not include Toronto.

When a position opened at Saskatoon in 1946, Neatby expressed a desire to return to her alma mater. Charles Lightbody, who had been an undergraduate at the same time as Neatby and who was at this point working as a lecturer in the department, also sought the appointment. According to James S. Thomson, the president, George Simpson, who had replaced A.S. Morton as chair in 1940, wanted to hire Lightbody: 'Simpson still wants Lightbody – to avoid excessive femininity on his staff – Burt of Minnesota thinks Lightbody would be a mistake, Frank Underhill thinks the appointment would be all right.'[98] But in the end, Neatby got the appointment. Lightbody lacked her publication record. Besides, he was by all accounts a strange and at times difficult bird: an odd combination of brilliant and petulant, he embodied the absent-minded professor, the eccentric egghead.[99] Neatby herself once referred to him as a 'freak.'[100] As a result, argues Michael Hayden, 'the university invited [Neatby] only because it could find no other suitable candidate.'[101]

Clearly, Jean Murray, Hilda Neatby, and Margaret Ormsby were exceptional. Also, they never married. Careers and marriage and children were mutually exclusive to women: a career or a family, but not both. That was the rule. As Dalhousie historian George Wilson explained in 1953, 'Having a baby ends a woman's appointment. She can't have her cake and eat it too.'[102] The constraints this placed on women historians, constraints that men did not experience, cannot be overstated. The understanding of what a historian should be was based on the male experience. By definition, pregnancy and motherhood cast women outside what it meant to be a historian. Although not a historian, Irene Spry was a graduate student and lecturer in Toronto's Department of Political Economy in the 1930s. There she worked closely with Harold Innis, encountering his deep, almost monastic devotion to the scholar's vocation. It was Innis who arranged her participation in the Canadian-American relations series funded by the Carnegie Endowment for International Peace. In 1938, however, Spry's career arrived at the crossroads: one path led to a life of scholarship, the other to marriage and family. As Spry recalled, 'I let Innis down. He was training me to carry on the work that he thought should be done by social scientists. And instead I went out, got married and had children and did war work; I never produced the book I was supposed to write about the energy sources in Canada. And I perfectly understand why Innis wrote me off; he had every right to do so.'[103] They never spoke again. Neither Innis nor Spry understood that the ideal social scientist was gendered masculine; male social scientists simply never found themselves having to decide between a career and a family. Although he had four children, Innis was freed from the sphere of necessity in a way that Spry could never be. Recounting the circumstances of Innis's expedition to the Mackenzie River basin – 'the last great surviving region of the fur trade' – Donald Creighton wrote: '[Innis's] first son, Donald, was born in April, 1924. And nearly a month later, when the examination papers were finished and he was finally free, he left for Winnipeg.'[104] To be a new parent and to be free was not a contradiction for men in the way that it was for women. Innis supported Spry's graduate work, but he did not want to hire women in the same way as he did not want to hire Jews: it would only encourage more women to enrol as students, 'and there were already too many in the social sciences.'[105]

The presence of so few women in history departments hurt at least one woman seeking a career in history. Obviously bright – she graduated from Varsity in 1950 with a gold medal and first-class honours – Bridget Moran was accepted into the graduate program. Having served in the armed forces, she was entitled to financial support from Veterans Affairs to pursue her education. However, 'the poltroons in Ottawa' refused to support Moran's graduate work in history because, as they argued, there were no female historians in Canada. To them it would be money wasted. Why not teaching or nursing, they asked? Determined to be a historian, Moran forged ahead, but without financial support, she found that graduate school proved impossible: 'Two months into my second year as a graduate history student, I had had enough. I gave the whole thing up.'[106]

III

To say that the labour market to 1960 was informal and male reveals only part of the story. The gendered epistemology underlying the discipline of history and the desire 'to claim [historical] work as masculine turf,'[107] as Vicki Schultz writes, necessitated that male historians, seeking to protect the boundaries of their discipline and their profession, work against women's inclusion in the profession.

The exclusion of women could be a matter of policy. Looking for an appointment for his daughter, George Wrong wrote to the principal of McGill in 1915. He was summarily informed that no 'additional appointment will be made in the way of a woman teacher.'[108] Wrong could not have been surprised. His own department had the same policy. Although Marjorie Reid had lectured at Toronto for several years, in 1925 she came to the unhappy realization that she would have to look elsewhere for advancement. In a long letter to Frank Underhill, then at Saskatchewan, Reid acknowledged the impossibility of ever getting a full-time job at Toronto: 'I have been re-appointed Lecturer at Toronto for 1924–25, but my appointment here has never been considered permanent, and I think that it is high time I began to work up in a new place.' When she heard of Underhill's move to the Department of Political Science, she thought there might be a vacancy in the Department of History. In a magnanimous gesture, however, she expressed her reluctance to encroach on another woman's territory: 'To be quite frank, I am very reluctant to become a rival of Miss McFarlane or Miss Murray for any position that might be open to a woman. I do not know whether they are looking forward to University work, but I think they are able and well trained for it, and they might find it difficult, because they are women, to make a beginning elsewhere.'[109] Underhill promptly responded that, no, there would not be an opening at Saskatchewan. Reid was absolutely right about her status at Toronto: not only did Toronto not consider her appointment permanent, it refused to give permanent appointments to women. Writing to the University of Wisconsin on behalf of Marjorie Reid in 1925, W.P.M. Kennedy wrote: 'As she is one of my old pupils who has had a distinguished course, I am only anxious that she be given a fair chance to develop her academic ability as a teacher.'[110] However, Kennedy's definition of 'fair chance' did not include Toronto. As he had explained in an earlier letter, 'our policy is not (whether rightly or wrongly does not matter) to give higher appointments to women.'[111] Reid left Toronto in 1926 and never again taught at an English-Canadian university. While Kennedy's remarks were uniquely explicit, the policy was not. Only because it was possible not to accept women could Burt write the following to Reginald Trotter: 'If you are willing to accept a woman into your department, you would find Miss Hilda Neatby, now teaching in Regina College, far superior to either of these men.'[112]

The exclusion of women persisted well into the 1950s and, for that matter, well into the 1960s.[113] The example of Margaret Banks illustrates this policy. On completing her MA with Underhill in 1950, Banks decided to pursue a doctorate under his supervision. While Underhill was encouraging, he did caution her: it was unlikely that, as a woman, she would get an academic appointment.[114] What he did not tell her was that he, as her supervisor, would make it impossible. Looking to make a junior appointment for September 1952, UNB's W.S. MacNutt asked Underhill in early January for a list of suitable candidates.[115] Meanwhile, Banks also had learned of UNB's opening and approached Underhill for a letter of recommendation. In her diary, Banks recorded the following: 'January 22 – Saw Professor Underhill at Baldwin House in the morning. He had already heard about the vacancy at UNB and had told several people who might apply. [Because he did not tell me] I expect my chances of getting the job aren't very good. However, he would write about me.'[116] Banks's instincts were accurate. A week later, Underhill responded to MacNutt's letter with a list of six names, five men and one woman. On balance, he thought Lovell Clark would be the best bet; he is a 'most promising man.' Then, almost as an afterthought, Underhill mentioned his 'girl' graduate student: 'We have a girl, Miss Margaret Banks, who has done most of her work under me in Canadian and British History. She came to us from Bishop's. She is a very good student, but very mousy and quiet; and I doubt whether she would serve your purposes as well as one of the men, though I expect she'll do the best Ph.D. thesis of the lot.'[117] On the one hand, Underhill recognized the superiority of Banks's intellect and acknowledged her competence as a historian. On the other hand, the masculinity of the historical discipline was so deeply ingrained in Underhill that he could not envision Banks as a member of the profession, and to protect the profession from women, Underhill recommended inferior men. Banks did not get the job. Lovell Clark did. In an interview, Banks confessed her initial shock at Clark's appointment: 'I was very surprised when Lovell Clark got the job at UNB. Of course, I congratulated him when he told me. That was how I found out I did not get the job. But it surprised me. He had failed his orals! I passed mine but he failed and had to redo them.'[118]

Between 1952 and 1961 Banks launched an annual search for a university appointment. Applying to every English-speaking college and university in Canada and to several colleges and universities in the United States, her search amounted to an annual ritual of rejection. Obviously unaware of Underhill's damning letter, Banks enquired about possible vacancies at UNB in 1953 and 1954.[119] Twice Bailey responded politely: thank you, but no thank you.[120] In the winter of 1954, however, he had been looking to line someone up to replace MacNutt should he decide to take a year's leave of absence. Although aware of Banks, Alfred Bailey did not consider her. Moreover, Donald Creighton did not recommend her in his response to Bailey's initial general enquiry to Toronto.[121] That Creighton did not recommend a woman is not surprising. He once told Banks that women could not teach in a university because, owing to the high pitch of the female voice, they could not be heard in a large lecture hall. In any event, despite the importance of a PhD and the fact that Banks had earned the degree, Bailey considered two men, neither of whom had completed their doctorates. In the spring of 1954, however, Queen's considered her for the McLaughlin Lectureship, a one-year appointment in British history. At first the interview was to take place in Kingston, but she received a telegram asking her to meet with Arthur Lower, who was in Toronto and staying at the King Edward Hotel. In the lobby of the King Eddie, Lower proceeded to ask a series of unacademic questions, in Banks's words, his 'great blue eyes piercing into me.' One query in particular stood out: 'Have you any other girlfriends who have gone into academia?' The subtext of the question is forever lost; it is clear, however, that women and academia were incongruous to Lower. According to Banks, Lower could not understand why she would want to leave her job at the Ontario Archives to teach at a university. Upset by the meeting, Banks left the hotel and walked a full two blocks before realizing that she was walking in the wrong direction.[122]

On 19 January 1955, her frustration mounting, Banks wrote a pointed letter to Sidney Smith, president of the University of Toronto. Smith had been quoted in the *Globe and Mail* about an approaching crisis in university staffing: because the university could not offer competitive salaries, he warned, there would be too few professors to meet the expected increase in enrolment: 'We must attract and train men and women now to be ready for that crisis when it arrives, or else we will fail in our duty to the nation's youth.'[123] Banks could not help but wonder if Smith appreciated the real problem. Based on her experience, she believed that the difficulty was not low salaries; it was lack of academic positions. Banks felt that women had to contend with the added reality of sex discrimination: 'You say that the university must attract and train men and women now to be ready for the crisis when it arrives. This will constitute a marked change in policy, especially with regard to women. If men have been discouraged in the past, it is doubly true of women, who are told quite openly that most universities, if given the choice between employing a man and a woman, will appoint the man, even when his qualifications are the lower of the two.'[124]

In the fall of 1959 Banks travelled across western Canada in order to visit each history department. At the University of Saskatchewan she had lunch with Hilda Neatby. Neatby was pleasant but not hopeful. As de facto chair of the Saskatchewan History Department in the winter of 1958, she had conceded that she could not hope to hire a particular female candidate because she was not only of the wrong field but of the wrong sex as well.[125] As chair throughout the 1960s, a decade when there were more openings than scholars, Neatby hired only one woman to a permanent position. It was as if she had forgotten her own frustration at the hands of discrimination. In a 1961 letter she sketched her thoughts on the question of hiring women, in particular women who might have children. She clearly pathologizes pregnancy, likening it to pneumonia at one point and a physical disability at another.

> It seems to me that a department head or dean has a perfect right to 'discriminate' against a woman who might have a baby in March, as he could 'discriminate' against a man likely to develop pneumonia in January. I cannot see any unfair discrimination in taking into consideration all factors relating to the efficiency of the individual. Other things being equal, it is surely fair to choose the person not liable to physical disability for whatever cause. In fact, choosing between two young men of apparently equal qualifications, it would be natural to give some consideration to health.

Although she quickly added that she personally did not subscribe to such a view and would 'accept the babies as they come,' she also said that, at the same time, she would 'defend the administrator who hesitated to take this risk.'[126] Such an ambivalent answer to the question of women, pregnancy, and academia might explain her track record on female appointments.

In December 1960 Banks launched her final search for an appointment in history. In a letter to the principal of Bishop's University, her alma mater, she explained that for many years she had been seeking a university appointment. Echoing the frustration of Marjorie Reid's 1925 letter to Underhill, Banks explained: 'Before admitting defeat and proceeding to train for other work I am making a final attempt to secure an appointment for the fall of 1961.'[127] There was nothing at Bishop's. A few months later, in February 1961, Banks accepted the position of law librarian at the University of Western Ontario, where she remained for the next twenty-eight years.

The example of Margaret Banks is unique only insofar as it is well documented. Placed in the context of history's professionalization in English Canada to 1960, it corresponds to an observable, demonstrable pattern of discrimination in the labour market. Whereas women could be, and were, historians when history was understood as an avocation, they confronted a much different reality when history was understood as a vocation. The example of Banks also corroborates the argument that there was a deeper, gendered epistemology underlying the discipline. This epistemology emerged first in the pages of George Wrong's *Review of Historical Publications Relating to Canada*, and it continued over the course of the first six decades of the twentieth century as women studied history at the undergraduate and graduate levels and as they pursued academic careers. True, the barriers women confronted were not impermeable, since many did study history and a handful even managed to build successful careers, but 'Where the position of women is clearly subordinate, a few exceptional achievers do not threaten the system and their achievement gains salience over their womanhood.'[128]

To say that sexism indicates an unenlightened generation or that it was 'just the way they did things back then' is unsatisfying. It fails to account for the very real disciplinary and professional boundaries historians erected and policed. History's professionalizing drive made claims to reason, objectivity, and knowledge. Gendered masculine, these attributes made sense only in opposition to their 'feminine' inferiors: emotion, subjectivity, and experience. In minimizing the presence of the feminine in the discipline of history and in minimizing the presence of women in the profession of history, the profession was not incidentally sexist. It was necessarily sexist.

In the final analysis, boundary-work constituted an important strategy in the professionalization of history. Related to boundary-work, but distinct in its own right, was the imperative to protect scholarly independence.

CHAPTER 6

Protecting scholarly independence: a professional imperative

Frank Underhill had been a thorn in Varsity's side since his arrival in 1927. Throughout the 1930s he was regularly called into the president's office to explain himself. Each time he escaped dismissal. But with the spectre of war in Europe on the immediate horizon, the anti-imperialist Underhill became an easy target. In April 1939, for example, leading members of the Ontario legislature launched a vicious attack against Underhill for remarks he had made some four years earlier. Premier Mitch Hepburn announced his personal disappointment 'that the University Board of Governors has not up to now disciplined Underhill in a manner befitting the crime he has committed. It smacks of rank sedition.'[1] McGill's E.R. Adair also found himself in hot water when he described British Prime Minister Neville Chamberlain as 'stupid' in a November 1939 talk to the Montreal Rotary Club. His remarks ignited a debate on academic freedom and freedom of speech in wartime, but his job was never in jeopardy. His life, however, was menaced when the principal's office received a cryptic death threat: 'This is a call to tell you [that] you had better put a guard on Adair at once. And I ask you to make a record of this call.'[2] Meanwhile, back in Toronto, President Henry Cody threatened Underhill with dismissal. As Underhill recalled, Cody was 'terribly worked up when I saw him first and abused me as a trouble-maker who was costing the University untold sums of money.'[3] In the end, however, Underhill was saved by the intervention of his colleagues, in particular Samuel Beatty, the dean of arts, Malcolm Wallace, principal of University College, Chester Martin, Head of the History Department and Harold Innis, who collectively promised Cody 'a hard time' if Underhill were dismissed.[4] Innis, in particular, stood as 'the chief tower of strength on my side,' observed Underhill.[5]

Underhill's reprieve proved a short one. In August 1940 he delivered an address at the Couchiching Conference – the annual meeting of the Canadian Institute of Economics and Politics on the shores of Lake Couchiching – which landed him in the hottest water of his career. Canada, Underhill noted, must reconfigure its defence policy in the light of the war: 'We in Canada are now committed to two loyalties, the old one to the British connection involving our backing up of Britain, and the new one to North America involving common action with the States ... And so we can no longer put all our eggs in the British basket.' Anodyne in any other context, Underhill's remarks were acidic in the context of war. The *Toronto Telegram* accused him of treason.[6] Again, pressure mounted against Cody to rid the university of its perpetually unpatriotic professor once and for all. Underhill, too, felt the heat: 'Altogether the whole thing has been as nasty as possible. People call up on the phone to denounce me, and yesterday a car load of young fellows (students presumably) passed me on St. George St. and, recognizing me, one of them shouted "Down with Underhill!"'[7] Yet the beleaguered Underhill was not without friends. When a special committee of the board of governors asked Underhill to resign on 2 January 1941, his fellow academics rallied to his defence and urged him to stand firm. Six days later Underhill submitted his response: he would not resign.[8] Facing an adamant faculty, the president and the board of governors backed down, and Underhill – although shaken – was again saved.[9]

The Underhill affair constituted a question of academic freedom and scholarly independence. To defend him as his colleagues did was a professional imperative.[10] As Donald Creighton told him, 'your dismissal will be a black reflection upon the state of Canadian universities in general and, indeed, upon the whole intellectual life of the country.'[11] To protect universities and intellectual life, it was necessary to protect Underhill. Professions – by definition – seek freedom from 'lay evaluation and control.'[12] The Underhill affair, however, was only the most striking example of that imperative. The defence of scholarly independence was an ongoing process. One way to study this process is to examine the relationship between historians and money.

I

Historical research requires money. In the 1890s poor William Kingsford nearly bankrupted himself in the writing and subsequent publication of his ten-volume history of Canada. Having mortgaged his house and furniture, 'he was saved from ruin, and the project completed, only by the intervention of such friends as Sandford Fleming.'[13] Things were not much better for English-Canadian historians in the pre-Canada Council era, since research dollars were few and far between.[14] It was no accident that the 1905 organizing meeting of the Champlain Society took place 'in the [Toronto] board room of the Canadian Bank of Commerce.'[15] With the assistance of the bank president, Sir Edmund Walker, George Wrong and Charles Colby raised the necessary money through individual subscriptions. In 1924 Wrong floated the idea of expanding the mandate of the Champlain Society to include publication subsidies for academic monographs. As he explained to John Clarence Webster, if the Champlain Society could convince 'a few rich men' to create a fund of $50–100,000, the interest generated could be used to publish books that, as things stood, were not being published: 'I have already approached one rich man, who is pondering the problem, and I shall hope to do some more work on the scheme later.'[16] In the end, nothing came of Wrong's plan.

For that matter, every attempt to raise money for historical research and publication proved fruitless. In 1920 W.S. Wallace expressed his (ultimately unfulfilled) hope that the Public Archives would create a research fund for university teaching staffs.[17] Out of his desire to see a 'revolution' in historical research, A.L. Burt suggested that professional historians undertake to convince 'a group of moneyed men' to put up 'the necessary money to support a serious organization to conduct research in Canadian history.'[18] Similarly, in 1929 Arthur Lower told his colleagues that they could do worse than asking Canada's wealthy citizens to support the publication of academic research: 'There is plenty of money in Canada if it can only be got at,' he said. 'Historians might pursue less worthy objects than devising means of getting at it.'[19] In 1930 Chester Martin lobbied the National Research Council to include history within its mandate. Playing the nationalist card, he explained that the centre of historical research on Canada might well shift to the United States, where the availability of 'unlimited wealth' would allow both large and small universities to create graduate programs in Canadian history. Already, 'Many universities and libraries in the United States are accumulating some of the most valuable "Canadiana" on the continent.' Martin recommended that the National Research Council provide travel and living allowances for work at the Public Archives: 'This is a national problem and it ought to be dealt with on a national scale.'[20] His effort failed.

Historians, therefore, survived on what little they could scrape together from their universities and their own pocketbooks. Commenting on his early career, Donald Creighton remarked that he had undertaken a 1928 research trip to Paris on his 'own meagre savings.' There he lived in 'abject poverty,' surviving on *les sandwiches au jambon*.[21] With their money running out and their health weakened by an inadequate diet, he and his wife returned home – in steerage: 'I desperately wanted to write something, but I knew I had to give up European history. So I decided to find a Canadian subject. It was a poor second. I had a real sense of deprivation.'[22]

It was in this context that Canadian historians sought to tap America's 'unlimited wealth.' Beginning in the late 1920s, for research and publication grants historians turned to the Carnegie Endowment for International Peace and the Rockefeller Foundation. Since the creation of the Endonment in 1911 the Carnegie Corporation had provided over $7 million to Canadian universities, colleges, libraries, museums, and art galleries.[23] Similarly, since its creation in 1913 the Rockefeller Foundation had provided nearly $14 million to similar institutions and projects.[24]

In his seminal book on the history and function of intellectuals, Lewis Coser argues that foundations function as the gatekeepers of ideas: 'With the power of the purse, they are in positions to foster certain ideas or lines of inquiry while neglecting or de-emphasizing others.'[25] As an analogy, the foundation as gatekeeper is helpful, because it reminds us that foundations retained real power, that they were not what they projected themselves to be: disinterested patrons of research. Donald Fisher argues that as the only game in town, American foundations in the 1930s were able to set the objective of the game: 'to prevent the collapse of liberal democratic capitalism.'[26] However, the foundation-as-gatekeeper analogy is unhelpful, because it implies that foundations retained complete control, when, in fact, scholars exercised and defended their autonomy.

Studying the Canadian context, Jeffrey Brison argues that the story of American philanthropy and Canadian arts and letters is not a straightforward story of American domination. If it is not the crude story of cultural imperialism, however, cultural imperialism is a recurring theme in the story, since 'foundations selected Canadians who shared their visions, agendas, and ideologies.' Brison acknowledges the agency exhibited by Canadian artists and scholars in their dealings with American foundations, but he concludes that it would be too easy to say that

they took the money and ran. The reality 'was that there was no fundamental contradiction between the nationalist agendas pursued by the
Canadian cultural elite and the foundations' pursuit of the scientific
management of culture.' In the end, 'potentially oppositional models'
to liberal capitalism 'were marginalized.'[27]

At least in the case of university historians, however, the foundations
did not have much choice in their selection. Not only was it a small community, to an individual its members believed in the objective of the
game: to prevent the collapse of liberal capitalism. Stanley Ryerson, a
communist, was an exception, but he was a only marginal figure in the
English-Canadian historical profession, independent of American philanthropy. In the early 1930s he abandoned an academic career because,
as he told his parents, 'University work & political work are mutually
exclusive.'[28] As for Frank Underhill, he was a democratic socialist, not a
communist, and was not anathema to American foundations. He was an
early participant in the Carnegie Endowment's Canadian-American relations series – although he never completed his manuscript on Canadian
political leaders and the United States from 1850 to 1890 – and in 1942
he received a Guggenheim Fellowship, which took him to Manhattan for
the academic year. In other words, there were no oppositional models to
be funded, let alone marginalized. To quote Theodore Hamerow on the
relationship between philanthropy and American historians, 'all of the
tendencies in history which philanthropy encouraged originated within
the discipline itself.'[29]

It is against this backdrop that we examine two different case studies:
the Social Science Research Council's Frontiers of Settlement Series
and the Carnegie Endowment's Canadian-American relations series.
What unfolds is a pattern of gate-keeping and gate-opening between
American foundations and English-Canadian historians. The foundations had their own agendas, but historians had theirs as well and – with
three minor exceptions – they successfully protected their independence.

II

Conceived in the mid-1920s and published in the 1930s, the Frontiers of
Settlement Series represented the first collaborative social science
research project in Canada to be funded by American research dollars
and to involve the participation of English-Canadian historians. The
project itself was the brainchild of American social scientists eager to

demonstrate their utility.[30] In 1926 the Social Science Research Council (SSRC) – an American body funded by the Laura Spelman Memorial Fund of the Rockefeller Foundation – constituted an Advisory Committee on Pioneer Belts. Its purpose was to devise a study of pioneer belts, or frontiers of human settlement, from a variety of disciplinary angles – historic, economic, social, and geographic – with an eye to developing a science of settlement.[31] After all, the problem of immigration and frontier communities was not unique to the United States. It was a global problem. Africa, Asia, Australia, South America, and North America all had experienced, and were experiencing still, the problems associated with human settlement in previously unsettled territory. As a 1926 committee memorandum stated, what was needed was 'disinterested advice' from experts to guide public policy.[32]

This was very much Isaiah Bowman's vision. As director of the American Geographical Society and the intellectual force behind the study of pioneer belts, Bowman wanted to bring together researchers from all the social sciences in an organized, coordinated effort to develop a 'science of settlement.' In turn, this body of knowledge would function as 'a guide to *the makers of government policies.*'[33] The SSRC Advisory Committee recommended that western Canada be made the focus of any study. According to Marlene Shore, 'pragmatic' considerations led American social scientists to consider Canada, since understanding its history and its policies would cast new light on the American experience. In addition, Canada had become something of a 'back door' for immigrants seeking entry into the United States while Americans from the western and southwestern parts of the United States were migrating to western Canada.[35]

There was another reason why at least one Advisory Committee member wished to focus on Canada. An economic analyst in the Department of Agriculture in Washington, O.E. Baker, argued that in the future America would increasingly depend on Canadian agriculture: 'Canada is almost certain to supply us with a considerable quantity of bread stuffs and dairy products in the near future, not only because of her natural resources and proximity, but also because her land is lower priced and she can produce grain and milk cheaper than we, while our cities our growing in their food requirements and their political influence.' At an Advisory Committee meeting a few weeks later, Baker re-argued his case for a study of western Canada: 'It would be valuable also because the Canadian North West, with its great wheat producing potentialities, is the reservoir upon which before long the people of the United States must depend for their food.' Because some members were uncomfortable with the purely practical considerations that seemed to be determining the decision, the Advisory Committee decided to study Rhodesia as well; here, the investigation would follow 'more theoretical and abstract lines' in an effort to arrive at an understanding of the 'fundamental laws of human behavior.'[35] Because Baker's proposal was so much more developed and the Rhodesia proposal so embryonic, it was the former that received the most attention – and, by extension, the most money. Led by Bowman, the American Geographical Society (AGS) assumed responsibility for the study of pioneer belts in 1928. In addition, in 1929 the SSRC approved a $15,000 grant to the AGS to be followed by a second grant of $30,000.

At around this time, in 1928, the AGS struck the Canadian Pioneer Problems Committee (CPPC). Headed by W.A. Mackintosh, it included two historians, Duncan McArthur at Queen's and Chester Martin at Manitoba and, after 1929, at Toronto. The CPPC was further divided into five disciplinary subcommittees; Martin chaired the history subcommittee. The subcommittees worked closely together, the goal being not simply to avoid overlap and duplication but to bring as many different social-scientific perspectives to bear on the problem of pioneer settlements. It is important to note that the CPPC enjoyed its independence. Although Baker had expressed his desire for the research to be of such a nature as to be useful to American interests, he did not press his wishes on Canadian social scientists. He left the picture altogether when he took a position at Stanford. Shore rightly observed that 'the committee was given full control over the direction of the Canadian study.'[36] Moreover, Canadian social scientists, including historians, welcomed the research dollars and the opportunity to show their usefulness. As stated in a CPPC memorandum: 'This plan again aims to conduct research in a manner that will affect matters of practical policy.'[37] For Chester Martin, Duncan McArthur, A.S. Morton, Arthur Lower, and Harold Innis, the series represented a wonderful opportunity to undertake important research, to publish the results and, ideally, to influence policy decisions.

The Frontiers of Settlement Series, however, highlighted an outstanding problem in Canada: academic publishing.[38] In July 1932 Mackintosh approached Hugh Eayrs, president of Macmillan Canada. Mackintosh acknowledged that it would be highly unlikely that any publisher would assume the cost of publishing the series. If a subsidy could be arranged, however, would Macmillan be interested?[39] Eayrs responded that he was 'keen' on the idea, but he would need a subsidy of $1,000 per volume.[40] In December 1932 the SSRC approved a $9,000 subsidy for the publication of the series. Of this grant, $4,500 would be a direct subsidy to the publisher, while $4,500 would cover 'the cost of editorial work and the preparation of maps.'[41] The subsidy did not prove nearly enough. In 1935, with three volumes published and a fourth at the printer, Eayrs expressed his dissatisfaction with the series: Macmillan was losing money, he said.[42] Mackintosh responded that any further subsidy was out of the question and he pleaded, 'For the sake of both our reputations we cannot allow the work to fall through.'[43] Macmillan agreed to continue the series and, in total, it published eight volumes. Duncan McArthur never completed his manuscript. In 1944 the decision was taken to give up on the dilatory McArthur and not to publish a ninth volume. 'I do not need to tell you that on the whole scheme we have lost money,' a Macmillan executive informed Mackintosh.[44]

As the first large-scale social science project to be funded by American research dollars, the Frontiers of Settlement Series is important for three reasons. One, it demonstrated a pattern that would be repeated in subsequent projects, both large and small. The SSRC had a research agenda when it selected western Canada as its focus of research; in this sense, it functioned as a gatekeeper. However, Canadian academics insisted on, and won, their independence: no one policed their research or their conclusions. Two, the series highlighted the desire of Canadian social scientists to be relevant and useful. They were not drawn into an informal alliance with the state through American philanthropy – they wanted to prove their social utility. For example, in 1928–9 Chester Martin 'had acted as an adviser to the Manitoba Government in its negotiations with the Manitoba Resources Commission.'[45] Not surprisingly, Martin dedicated the final chapter of his book to what he termed 'Federal Policies and Provincial Problems.' Similarly, Arthur Lower identified the early phase of his career by its emphasis on science. As a young historian working on settlement and the forest frontier in eastern Canada, Lower spent, in his words, 'many a month compiling price indexes, tables of imports and exports, and the like.' He wanted to be a scientist; he wanted to be 'useful.'[46] In his contribution to the series, *Settlement and the Forest Frontier in Eastern Canada*, he commented on public policy and urged the authorities to learn from the past and 'keep the settler off the land from which he cannot earn a living.'[47] Even Innis, who viewed with extreme caution the idea of a government/ academic alliance, remarked on the usefulness of the project to Canadian policy formation: 'These volumes constitute a first preliminary in the attack on the difficulties of provincial-federal relations, and their importance is enhanced by the opportune date of the study and their appearance in the years of the depression.'[48] Three, the series underscored the problem of academic publishing in Canada. Without a sizeable subsidy, commercial publishers were reluctant to take on academic projects.

These three themes would resurface in the next – and much larger – project: 'The Relations between Canada and the United States,' which was funded by the Carnegie Endowment for International Peace.

III

Throughout the 1930s and early 1940s the Carnegie Endowment for International Peace (CEIP) organized and funded an enormous research project on the Canadian-American relationship. Under the leadership of James Shotwell, a former Canadian who built his career at Columbia University, the project brought together historians, economists, sociologists, political scientists, and legal scholars from across Canada and the United States. At its peak in the second half of the 1930s, there were sixty-three scholars working on the projected forty-three-volume series. Almost every English-Canadian historian was in some way involved. Between 1936 and 1945 three different publishing houses produced twenty-five volumes, known collectively as 'The Relations between Canada and the United States.' The series included classics such as Donald Creighton's *The Commercial Empire of the St. Lawrence*, Harold Innis's *The Cod Fisheries*, and Arthur Lower's *The North American Assault on the Canadian Forest*. In addition, CEIP sponsored four conferences on Canadian-American relations between 1935 and 1941. Held at St Lawrence University on the American side of the border and at Queen's University on the Canadian side, these conferences were well attended by both Canadian and American academics, journalists, civil servants, and politicians.[49] In total, the project cost $215,000, a staggering sum for social science research in the 1930s.[50]

As is the case with the Frontiers of Settlement Series, it would be naive to assume that American foundations represented disinterested patrons of research. All action is interested. To understand CEIP's interest in the series, it is necessary to understand that of James Shotwell. Although born in Strathroy, Ontario, in 1874, James Shotwell never saw himself as a Canadian. Nor did he see himself as an American. Rather, he felt he was a 'North American.' On the opening page of his autobiography, he metaphorically located western Ontario on a continental map. His hometown, he said, was part of the 'Middle West.' The many interconnections between Canada and the United States figured prominently in his boyhood recollections. Burning Pennsylvania coal, the trains that passed through Strathroy opened doors 'to the far-off world of Toronto or Niagara Falls in the East, or Chicago in the West.' Each summer his family travelled to Sarnia by train and then by boat down the St Clair River to Walpole Island or sometimes to Detroit. Young men from his community, in search of farm land of their own, went to Michigan, the western states, and the Canadian northwest 'in what was the last chapter in the great westward movement for the conquest of the continent.' Later, the young men would go to Detroit and Chicago for the high wages of an industrial economy. Although Shotwell remembered reading 'Shakespeare, Milton and a galaxy of classic English poets,' it was the American magazine *Century* that captured his imagination. In its pages he found himself swept away by Civil War stories. Yet he was not unaware of Canada's separate political existence. When he and his friends refought the Battle of Queenston Heights, no one wanted to be on the American side: 'The school yard was as flat as a table, but one could charge up the woodpile with gallant General Brock.'[51] For Shotwell, there was an essential unity to North America even if there happened to be two political units, Canada and the United States; although he never proposed erasing the political boundaries, he did speak of a 'North American nationality.'[52]

In his final year at the University of Toronto, Shotwell decided to continue his studies. Because there were no graduate history programs in Canada in 1898, he set his sights on American universities. Columbia offered him a scholarship, and there he studied with James Harvey Robinson. History, Robinson believed, should not separate itself from the other social sciences; rather, it ought to embrace other approaches and methods.[53] Robinson's New History was very much related to Progressive History in its championship of progressive reform. He had no patience with the notion of history for its own sake; history should tell us about our world, about who we were, and about who we wanted to be in the future: 'History, the New Historians argued, is not a celebration of past heroes but an instrument for controlling the future.'[54] Robinson's New History left an indelible impression on Shotwell.

Invited to join Columbia's prestigious faculty of History and Political Science in 1904, Shotwell established himself as a highly regarded medievalist and faithful disciple of New History. When the United States entered the First World War, Shotwell took a leave of absence to assist with the war effort. He chaired the National Board for Historical Service, a controversial body dedicated to explaining the historical causes of the war to the American public.[55] A few months later he joined the Inquiry, a panel of experts charged with surveying the legal, economic, political, and historical questions related to future peace negotiations. In 1919 Shotwell and twenty-two other Inquiry members attended the Paris peace talks as an advisory team to President Woodrow Wilson and the American Commission to Negotiate Peace. Although he was a marginal figure in the negotiations, the experience confirmed Shotwell's commitment to the utility of history and of the social sciences. Rational planning by trained experts was essential to progress and peace in international relations. Very much a Progressive, Shotwell's belief in the professional, scientific management of society by experts never waned.[56]

It was after the war that Shotwell's association with the Carnegie Endowment began. In 1919 he assumed the position of general editor of CEIP's *Economic and Social History of the World War.* Five years later, Shotwell was named director of CEIP's Division of Economics and History. From his office he promoted a vision of liberal internationalism and American participation in the League of Nations, the World Court, and the International Labour Organization. He also broadened his contacts with the social science community, and in 1927 he was named the first chairman of the SSRC's Advisory Committee on International Relations. It was in this capacity that he proposed a blueprint for the scientific study of international relations in June 1931.

Entitled 'Scientific Method in Research and Discussion in International Relations: A Proposal for Institutes of International Relations,' Shotwell's blueprint was an unambiguous statement of scientific progressivism. The war and the Depression were irrefutable evidence of the growing interdependence of nations, he began. Nineteenth-century assumptions about nation-states and national economies were profoundly out of touch with twentieth-century realities. The social sciences must step into the breach. The 'supreme task of the social sciences,' he wrote, is to undertake 'creative thinking and constructive planning' in order to secure the 'intelligent consideration' of human problems. The field of international relations offered enormous possibilities; after all, the problems of war and peace and depression and unemployment were international problems. To study these problems, he maintained, a new technique was required. Teams of researchers from different countries must be brought together in some kind of federal arrangement, and they must be allowed to study international problems from a variety of angles. Only on the basis of careful, deliberate research could intelligent, scientific planning proceed. The social scientist – dispassionate, objective, and factual – must answer the call of duty and provide the state with expert knowledge and disinterested advice.[57]

Shotwell saw in the Canadian-American relationship an opportunity for the sort of coordinated research he envisioned. In the aftermath of the Great War, Canada's principal trading partner had become the United States. Canada enjoyed a period of prosperity and expansion in important sectors such as pulp and paper, base metals, hydroelectricity, and automobile manufacturing. Of course, the 1920s closed with the stock market crash of 1929 and the 1930s opened with a global depression. Canadian-American relations worsened. In an attempt to protect American industry and agriculture from foreign competition, a protectionist Congress passed the Smoot-Hawley Tariff in 1930, the highest tariff in American history. In response, Mackenzie King raised Canadian tariffs; shortly thereafter, the government of R.B. Bennett raised tariffs even further while it sought to reinvigorate trade with Great Britain and the other dominions. Although it took two years, an agreement on imperial preferences was reached at the 1932 Imperial Economic Conference in Ottawa. The coalition thus formed appeared to the United States to be a British Empire trading bloc from which it would be shut out. To an ardent free-trader like Shotwell the state of affairs was grave. As he wrote in an April 1932 memorandum, 'I believe that the time has come for a very important shaping up of Canadian-American questions.'[58] A few weeks later, he reiterated his point: 'The underlying relations with Canada are very serious in the future with possible breakdown of the situation.' Rightly or wrongly, he believed Canadians would blame the United States for its 'interference with their economic life.'[59]

By the fall of 1932 Shotwell had prepared a discussion paper in which he outlined the context and his plans. 'From the standpoint of economic interest,' he began, 'the most important of the foreign relations of the United States are those with Canada.' For too long, however, sentimental references to 3,000 miles of undefended frontier had governed relations between the two countries. The time had come for hard-headed analysis. Fortunately, conditions for scientific investigation were very promising, 'with experts on both sides of the line who have identical technical training, and with no barrier of language or diverse customs to confuse the issues or misinterpret the results.' Shotwell insisted that the 'scope of investigation' be very broad, that it 'be planned to cover all phases of Canadian-American relations, because no one subject exists wholly apart from the others.' Tariff policy, capital mobility, transportation and communication networks, the fisheries, population movements, national attitudes, and legal systems: all must be studied in their economic, political, sociological, and historical contexts. He therefore proposed a federal committee structure. A General Advisory Committee made up of eminent Canadian and American citizens would provide long-range vision; it would neither conduct research nor interfere with the results. The actual research would be supervised by a series of international and national committees, that is, a History Committee, an Economics Committee, a Sociology Committee, and so forth. As a provisional budget, Shotwell estimated $185,000, which would be spent over a two-year period of research and a one-year period of publication.[60]

What did Shotwell hope to achieve? Simply, he wanted to better Canadian-American trade relations. Measures, countermeasures, and imperial preferences jeopardized America's economic interests. As he explained at the outset of his 1932 discussion paper, 'From the standpoint of economic interest the most important of foreign relations of the United States are those with Canada. Not only is our trade with Canada larger than with any other single nation, but we have four billion dollars invested in Canadian industries.' Likewise, he justified the study of Canadian-American transportation systems 'in view of our interest in the proposed waterways treaty.'[61] In a letter to Nicholas Murray Butler, president of the Carnegie Endowment, Shotwell reiterated his point: 'We have taken for granted far too much ... the attitude of Canada toward the United States, and the economic and financial considerations that are involved.'[62] When a formal motion was put before the CEIP Executive Committee in May 1933, the question of business and economic interests was emphasized: CEIP had a rare opportunity to fund a research project that could count on the willingness of 'the outstanding leaders of Canadian big business and academic life to cooperate with similar groups in the United States.'[63] In passing the resolution, the Executive Committee provided an initial $25,000 for the project. Shotwell did not have a hidden agenda: rather, he openly wanted to improve economic and business relations between Canada and the United States.

In addition to improving trade relations between Canada and the United States, Shotwell also intended the series to demonstrate how superior the Canadian-American relationship was to other bilateral relationships. As a result, history gradually assumed a greater prominence in the series. At the organizing meeting in the fall of 1933, Shotwell asserted that while the series would respect the different academic disciplines, each volume ought to include the pertinent 'historical background.'[64] A few months later, in a letter to the president of the Carnegie Corporation, Shotwell stated that an agreement had been reached 'on all sides that the underlying synthesis, the scheme around which all of the special studies group themselves, is to be History.'[65] Despite differences between the two countries, theirs was fundamentally a relationship that worked. Here, along the 49th parallel, was what Shotwell once called the 'largest single laboratory for the study of international relations in the world today.'[66] To study the Canadian-American relationship was also to study the sources of peace.

A liberal internationalist, Shotwell intended to 'purchase' a body of knowledge that 'proved' the rightness of liberal internationalism. In this sense, Shotwell was very much a gatekeeper. In Lewis Coser's words, with the power of the Carnegie purse Shotwell hoped to foster a certain line of enquiry and thus neglect or de-emphasize others. At the end of the day, however, the series was very different from the one Shotwell had envisioned. In large part, the explanation lies with Harold Innis.

IV

Shotwell's decision to include Harold Innis in the project was not surprising. Innis's books on the Canadian Pacific Railway and the fur trade had established his reputation as a brilliant and original thinker. As Canada's leading social scientist, Innis knew everyone and everyone knew Innis. He therefore offered Shotwell both intellectual authority and entry into the Canadian social scientific community. As early as March 1931 Shotwell had conferred with Innis about his possible participation in a proposed study of 'American interests in Canada.' Although Innis expressed an interest, he also added that he could not commit to anything for at least a year.[67] In the following spring Shotwell invited him to New York City to attend an important meeting with the Social Science Research Council to discuss the proposal for a study of Canadian-American relations. Innis attended, although he did not feel he added anything of value to the discussion.[68] He went to a second and similar meeting a few months later in July 1932. It was after this meeting that he spelled out the conditions for his participation.

Innis was adamant on two points. First, he did not intend to surrender the autonomy of Canadian scholarship. It was not for sale. Except for Shotwell as the series general editor, he would not tolerate any American interference in Canadian projects. As he explained, 'So important do I regard this principle and with such difficulty has it been conceded in the case of similar projects directed from Great Britain and from the United States [that] I cannot afford, for the sake of my position in the University and in the project, to be charged with conceding a principle which has been gained at considerable costs.'[69] In a draft version of the letter, Innis made specific reference to the principle's having been 'fully conceded in the Pioneer Belt project.'[70] Second, the series must make sense in terms of Canadian research needs. Shotwell responded: 'From my knowledge of Canada I agree with you heartily about the misunderstandings that may arise if our work looks like an investigation of Canadian things by an American corporation of any kind, even a scientific one.'[71] A few months later, he wrote to Innis again: 'I heartily agree with you that research is not a thing to be bought and sold on the money market.'[72]

What were Canada's research needs, according to Innis? Research must focus on the history of the country's key staple industries. The Canadian economy was unique in North America. As he tried to explain to Shotwell, 'I have argued that at considerable length elsewhere ... that the boundary line is not accidental and that the economic background is fundamentally different in the two countries.'[73] A year later, at a New York meeting of the Economics Committee, Shotwell and Innis staked out their positions. Shotwell opened with a comment on what the series was and what it was not: it was for the betterment of Canadian-American relations; it was not 'purely a study in economics.' However, and obviously, studies had to be done. He asked those at the meeting to consider, therefore, which made more sense: studies of comparisons or studies of relations. Innis stressed that both the comparative approach and the relations approach were flawed when it came to understanding the history of the Canadian economy: 'there is an autonomous Canadian economy which must be considered apart from the problems of American or British influences upon [the] Canadian economy.' Later in the meeting Shotwell reiterated his concern that the studies be relevant and practical; 'they must,' he said, 'be focused upon the realities of the present situation.' Innis disagreed. Perhaps in the United States the basic research necessary to policy formulation had been completed; in Canada, however, 'it is still necessary to build up the basic studies' on the key staples.[74]

Upon returning to Toronto, Innis put his thoughts on paper and sent them to Shotwell. The series must make room for specialized monographs on Canadian staples: fish, lumber, minerals, and pulp and paper. The comparative method introduced a 'danger.'[75] The two economies could not be compared until the Canadian economy had been studied. Shotwell showed Innis's letter to J. Bartlet Brebner, another Canadian-born Columbia historian and his principal adviser on the series.[76] Brebner hit the proverbial nail on the head: 'Innis is likely to think in terms of Canadian economic history and temporarily lose sight of our study of relations.'[77] When Innis submitted his proposed outline of studies a few months later, in January 1934, Brebner's concerns were realized: 'This program seems to be designed to produce materials of a research character for chapters in a book on the basic industries of Canada. These chapters might be very useful in an economic history of Canada without reference to its relations to the United States.' Brebner explicitly recommended dropping Donald Creighton's study on commercial organization – what did it have to do with Canadian-American relations?[78] But Innis insisted. As he had reported a few months earlier, Creighton was 'alive' and doing 'excellent work.'[79]

When the economic studies were finally approved in June 1935, Innis had succeeded; through dint of will, he had effectively turned a series on the economic relations of Canada and the United States into a series of monographs in Canadian economic history. The project outline listed ten 'Special Industrial Studies.' For the most part, the studies were organized by staples: lumber, fish, pulp and paper, hydroelectricity, minerals, and agriculture. In addition, there would be Creighton's study of commercial and financial organization before the concentration of capital and two regional economic studies, one on the Maritimes and the other on British Columbia. The latter two projects reflected Innis's interest in marginal economies vulnerable to the economic policies of the centre. The project outline explained the new focus on Canada: 'While it is true that the major objects of investigation in this field are North American in character, it has proved profitable to include some particular examinations of separate elements in the Canadian economy because it is the weaker of the two and has been deeply affected by the economic and political policies of both countries.'[80]

Shotwell did not complain. On one occasion, he himself insisted that the comparative focus be dropped, although for a different reason. Originally, Irene Spry's study of hydroelectricity was to have been a comparative study of its development in Canada and the United States. Spry was a brilliant graduate student and part-time lecturer in Toronto's Department of Political Economy. However, Shotwell grew uneasy. As he explained to Innis, allowing a Canadian to write about American hydroelectricity 'would open us to an attack that would get us into domestic politics here' at a time when 'the power problem is one of the most serious issues' in American politics. 'I don't wish to pussy-foot on any of these questions if they are absolutely within the orbit of Canadian-American relations, but I don't want to rush headlong into this without having some idea where we are coming out.' On the whole, it would be better if Spry concentrated her research on the Canadian side of the line. Actually, Shotwell wanted to drop Spry in order to cut costs,[81] but Innis insisted that Spry be included, and Shotwell agreed.

Shotwell's caution was typical. His repeated pronouncements on the 'scientific objectivity' of the project notwithstanding, he proved more a politician than a social scientist. Unless he was more or less certain of the conclusions, of 'where we are coming out' to repeat his phrase, it was best to avoid the subject altogether. In this case, he subordinated the interests of scholarship to the interests of politics. According to the logic of Shotwell's politics, it was better to keep the research topics safe than it was to ignite controversy. Controversy would only undermine his ultimate goal: to improve economic and business relations between Canada and the United States by highlighting North America's natural and historic affinity.

In addition to securing funding for the historical studies he deemed important to Canadian scholarship, Innis also arranged for the Canadian volumes to be published by a Canadian house. Again, it was a matter of considerable importance to him. In February 1935 the Endowment circulated a memorandum on the status of the project to date. In addition to the usual lists of who was doing what and where they were doing it, the document contained a remark about spelling: 'In order to ensure uniformity in copy for the printers, it has been decided to follow American rather than English usage. The latter has become rare in Canada and Canadians are accustomed to American forms and spelling.'[82] Canadian academics were affronted. George Glazebrook complained to Brebner in a letter: 'Personally I am rather vague about American spelling except that honour is spelt honor, etc. Does this memo mean that Canadian writers have to change their MSS into US style? If so, I shall personally have a good deal to do.'[83] But it was Innis who led the charge. He explained to Shotwell that the series ought to follow both English and American spellings, since 'Considerable controversy' had erupted over this point.[84] Shotwell was genuinely surprised that something so trivial could matter so much. I must confess, he said, that I am 'a little puzzled about your suggestion of following English spelling. Is it really so important?' Besides, there was to be a single publisher for the entire series, 'and we may get into a terrible snarl if we spell half the volumes one way and half the other.'[85] Innis admitted that it was much ado about nothing, or 'nonsense to a very great extent,' but it mattered nonetheless.

Upping the ante, Innis doubted the 'advisability of having all the volumes published in Canada or in the United States and [he thought] it would be safer to divide them between Canadian and American publishers.'[86] There matters stood for a few weeks: Innis wanted a Canadian publisher for the Canadian volumes; Shotwell wanted a single American publisher for the whole series – he wanted a series, not a collection of books that happened to be subsidized by Carnegie money. However, Innis gradually wore Shotwell down. As Brebner explained, 'I think Shotwell is coming around to the idea of publishing some of the volumes in Canada. He has a very low idea, however, of the quality of printing and book-making in Canada, and I wish there were some way of demonstrating that on a project of several volumes with some subsidy, a Canadian publishing company could do a decent piece of work.'[87] Five days later Shotwell gave in; if the Canadian volumes must be published in Canada, then so be it. He even accepted Innis's recommendation of Ryerson Press and its editor, Lorne Pierce. In addition to being a good friend, Pierce had published two of Innis's books as well as his wife's book on Canadian economic history. Meanwhile, Shotwell cautioned Innis that his funds were not limitless and that he would 'drive as hard a bargain' as he could on the question of subsidies.[88] In the ensuing memorandum of agreement between the Endowment and Ryerson Press, it was agreed that the Canadian volumes 'shall conform in spelling and English usage to the Oxford practice,' while the American volumes shall conform 'to the University of Chicago hand-book.'[89]

The association with Lorne Pierce and Ryerson Press turned out to be unfortunate, and Shotwell's low regard for Canadian publishing was realized.[90] Authors and editors alike complained about interminable delays, the quality of the production, and the high price Pierce set for each volume. Arthur Lower's volume, in particular, caused headaches for its author, its publisher, and its sponsor. In October 1937 a frustrated Lower complained in rather harsh terms to Pierce about the quality of a particular map: 'Apart from the omissions, a long list of which I enclose, it is amateurish in execution with its great sprawling lettering.'[91] Shotwell, too, was frustrated with Ryerson Press and in November 1937 he sent an editor to Toronto to assist Pierce and Innis with the editing of manuscripts and the correction of proofs.[92] It bought Ryerson a temporary reprieve.

Meanwhile, there was another problem in the late fall of 1937; again, it related to English versus American style. A full year earlier, Shotwell had asked George Glazebrook to adopt a different style of capitalization in his volume on the history of transportation in Canada; 'the text will seem queer to the American reader,' he explained. Glazebrook complied. Thus, the great lakes became the Great Lakes. A year later, Shotwell made a request for further changes. This time an indignant Glazebrook resisted. When Innis was informed, he drew the line: In Canada, he told Shotwell, we dislike excessive capitalization. Canadian authors, therefore, ought to be allowed to follow the style of the *Canadian Historical Review*; 'we should not be compelled to adopt any American style.'

> I do not need to remind you again that we are fighting continually against the danger of being labeled pro-Americans and we cannot afford to have authors disgruntled with an actual grievance against us because of a trivial matter of type. These are danger spots which are very real to us and may seem trivial to you. My advice would be emphatically to the effect that the Glazebrook volume should go on as it has been begun, and it would help much, if you can see your way clear, to write a letter to Glazebrook explaining the difficulties.[93]

In the interests of maintaining the peace, Shotwell conceded the point to Innis. However, he also made it clear to Glazebrook that his 'desire for capitals was not an invasion of Canadian sovereignty.' In Shotwell's opinion, the use of capitals was more British than American. Nevertheless, Glazebrook could follow any style he desired as long as it was uniform.[94]

Of course, solving the problem of capital letters did not solve the problem of Ryerson Press. In March 1938 Innis sent a confidential letter to Shotwell. Alluding to 'problems' with Ryerson, he admitted that it would be best to switch publishers entirely. The remaining Canadian volumes should be published by the University of Toronto Press (UTP).[95] Shotwell responded that he would have Norman Donaldson of Yale University Press (YUP), the publisher of the American volumes in the series, write a 'stiff' letter to Pierce, especially focusing on the high price he was charging.[96] Innis was not satisfied: 'We have made more than our contribution to Ryerson Press.' Besides, 'Such a move would strengthen enormously the position of the University of Toronto Press .... From the standpoint of intellectual development I can think of few more important steps than the building up of the University of Toronto Press as a national press for University work.'[97] A year later, a weary Shotwell decided that the 'infinite trouble' with Ryerson Press must end.[98] Donaldson gave Pierce six months' notice that YUP and CEIP would be terminating their contract with Ryerson.[99] Of course, Pierce protested.[100] When a compromise was struck to the effect that YUP would edit all of the remaining manuscripts and Ryerson would print the Canadian volumes, it was Innis who was furious. True, he had wanted to remove Ryerson Press from the editorial process for some time,[101] but he did not want to concede that process to Yale. 'We cannot afford to give the general impression that we have become a branch office of American concerns,' he told Brebner. 'I don't need to tell you this but we are in a sensitive mood and always ready to raise the cry of American domination. I think a solution could be reached by which the U of T Press did the editing and the Ryerson Press the printing and distributing.'[102] A few days later, in early October, Shotwell gave in to Innis's demand that UTP become the editor.[103] Innis was pleased: 'I would like to look at this development as an opportunity of building effective editorial work in Canada.'[104] UTP thus edited the final four volumes printed in Canada.[105]

Innis's insistence on a Canadian publisher and a Canadian editor was part of his larger concern about biases in the social sciences. In a 1935 article he had identified a series of biases that exerted 'persistent corroding effects' on the position of the social scientist. For example, a 'danger to social science has arisen from foundations to subsidize research, because of the statement of objectives and of the extent of the subsidies.' In addition, poorly paid social scientists were 'attracted to the prospects of remuneration from foundations with standards of research adaptable to the achievement of an objective.' Although he did not mention any names, there is no doubt which foundation Innis had in mind in the spring of 1935: the Carnegie Endowment. Aware of the potential bias in foundation grants, Innis made every effort, in his words, to tear off its 'mask' and to 'correct' it.[106]

Against this backdrop, his early statements on the independence of Canadian scholarship, his insistence on historical studies in Canadian economic history, his determination to have a Canadian house publish the Canadian volumes, and his passionate defence of the right to keep editorial responsibilities in Canada may well add up to what Sandra Campbell calls 'a gritty pragmatic nationalism.'[107] But they also point to an ongoing struggle in the professionalization of history in English Canada: to both gain and retain control over the work environment and the labour process. Innis wanted to secure the right of historians to govern historical work. Considered in this light, his early statements about the independence of Canadian scholarship were actually statements about the independence of scholarship; his insistence on historical studies in Canadian economic history constituted a declaration of the right of scholars to set their own research agendas; his determination to have a Canadian publisher edit and publish the Canadian volumes was part of a long-term goal to develop the institutions necessary to autonomous scholarly activity. In short, his desire to spell 'honour' with a 'u' and his wish to limit the number of capital letters were expressions of his fierce commitment to do things his way, to control the production of scholarship. Campbell's scrappy nationalist was also a self-conscious professional who jealously protected and enlarged the independence necessary to intellectual life.[108]

Yet there is an obvious irony. In working against the bias of foundations to define 'the statement of objectives,' Innis himself became a bias. He set the research agenda (studies in Canadian economic history), he selected the individual topics (commercial organization, lumber, and hydroelectricity), and he selected the researchers (Creighton, Lower, and Spry). In addition, Innis secured the publishing contract for his friend, and he later secured a contract for his university's press. Despite his intellectual disdain for careerism, for 'leaders,' 'strong men,' and 'the frictions which accompany them,'[109] Innis used the Carnegie Endowment to become a powerful man and to build an academic empire. Because of his intimate contact with Shotwell, he was able to direct the flow of a large share of the money.[110]

However, there were limits to the Innis empire. Although he was the key Canadian player in the series, there were other Canadian historians directly involved.

V

In its optimistic beginnings the series included projected volumes from W.N. Sage, Judge Frederic Howay, and Arthur Lower in the west and

D.C. Harvey in the east; en route, there would be volumes from Fred Landon, Reginald Trotter, Duncan McArthur, Gustave Lanctôt, George Brown, Frank Underhill, George Glazebrook, Chester Martin, and Donald Creighton. C.P. Stacey at Princeton, A.L. Burt at Minnesota, and the always wandering Menzies Whitelaw had been drafted as well.[111] Like Innis, they attached their own agendas to their involvement.

At first, Arthur Lower hesitated. The project, he explained to Innis, 'would be by no means a labour of love for me'; it would take him away from his current interests, and 'I think [Shotwell's] terms would have to be decently attractive if I were to undertake it.'[112] But when the poorly paid United College historian heard the terms, he was delighted; as he had confessed earlier, he was 'quite unashamedly willing to write for money.'[113] Indeed, the honorarium of $500 equalled about two months' income. Although he did not write for the money per se, Donald Creighton could not believe his good fortune when he received an advance of $200 on his honorarium, because it made possible an extended research trip to Ottawa.[114] A young C.P. Stacey certainly needed the honorarium, but he also liked the opportunity the series presented. It would mean getting a book in print, which was important: 'It's a fine scheme from my point of view, but don't let's start cheering until it's a certainty,' he told his mother.[115] When applying for a job, Stacey was careful to note his association with the Endowment and the series.[116] Reginald Trotter, who was a member of the Historical Committee overseeing the Canadian history volumes in the series, used his clout to advance the career of his star graduate student, John Pritchett. Pritchett had completed his doctorate with Trotter in 1931 and was precariously employed by the cash-starved University of North Dakota. Knowing that a book would help Pritchett's cause in a tight labour market, Trotter secured his participation, despite his junior status.[117]

For the most part, Canadian historians wrote the books they wanted to write. Conceived before the series itself, Creighton's research project focused on commercial organization in the St Lawrence valley in the first half of the nineteenth century. Although Creighton agreed to add more 'biographical and explanatory material' in order to make the book more accessible to American readers, and although he 'expanded passages dealing with the United States,' he was not prepared to alter its focus. 'But, as you say,' he told Shotwell, 'the book has its focus in Canada rather than in North America as a whole; and to make it otherwise would, I am afraid, have involved writing another book.'[118] Although Shotwell occasionally expressed concern over the Canadian focus of the series,[119] he was genuinely ecstatic about *The Commercial Empire of the St. Lawrence*; he called it 'high literature'[120] and 'a splendid contribution.'[121] Like Creighton, Fred Landon wrote the book he wanted to write on western Ontario. Brebner was troubled when he received the manuscript: 'The great problem is, of course, that Mr. Landon naturally wants to write a social history of western Ontario and, therefore, brings in other than American influences.'[122] The manuscript went forward nonetheless and became *Western Ontario and the American Frontier.* Calling it 'an exceptionally fine contribution to Canadian history,' Shotwell tried to get it reprinted (albeit unsuccessfully) in 1944.[123] As for Pritchett's volume, it was, in effect, a reworked and expanded version of his doctoral thesis on the Red River settlement. He even commented on its Canadian focus: 'The reason why the part played by the Americans is given such comparatively little space is a simple one: Americans played little part in the story.'[124]

In only three instances – all minor – did Shotwell exert his editorial prerogatives. When he received Lower's manuscript, for example, he commented on its remoteness from contemporary issues and concerns. He therefore explained to Lower that Innis's introduction must make the connection: 'I have been very anxious that [Innis] should cover the history right up to the day before yesterday, as it were. The interest in Canadian-American commercial relations is one of the most valid reasons for undertaking this volume in the first place. So we must meet that obligation as fully as possible.'[125] Lower was unapologetic: 'I am afraid however that my text will not impress the public as emphasizing the present state of the trade. As a matter of fact my interest has been almost purely historical, not current.'[126] To Innis, Shotwell repeated his point about the purpose of the project: 'One criticism which is sure to be made of our whole enterprise is that it gives a lot of information about the nineteenth century and not enough about the drift and current of affairs today.'[127] Through Innis's introduction and an added chapter and appendix by Lower, *The North American Assault on the Canadian Forest* brought the story up to the reciprocity agreement of 1935.

In the Sage-Howay manuscript on British Columbia and the United States, Shotwell exerted a heavier and much needed editorial hand. From the beginning this particular volume had caused Shotwell grief. Judge Frederic Howay was not an academic, but he was the leading authority on the history of British Columbia and a past president of the Canadian Historical Association. As such, it was the Canadian historians themselves who insisted that the judge be associated with the B.C.

volume.[128] As Chester Martin explained, 'Howay is indispensable and Sage must contrive somehow to work with him.'[129] Between the two west coast historians, it was agreed that Howay would write those chapters dealing with the period up to British Columbia's entry into Confederation, and that Sage would write those chapters dealing with the period following Confederation. The partnership was anything but fruitful. Howay thought little of Sage as a historian[130] and, indeed, Sage proved dilatory.

When the Howay-Sage manuscript was finally submitted in 1940, it was a mess of unclear meanings and errors in syntax and spelling. At this point, Shotwell secured the UBC economist H.F. Angus as an editor and co-author. Although Shotwell promised Howay that he would never 'doctor' history 'in the interests of any political tenet' – not even for 'one so valid as that of good relations between Canada and the United States' – he authorized Angus to clean up the manuscript.[131] Harsh and to the point, Angus concluded that Howay and Sage 'did not cooperate in the least and they have produced a series of disjointed papers. 'Even within the papers the arrangement of material is unsystematic. No general themes are developed. There is no introduction and no conclusion. There is some overlapping and some unaccountable omissions, e.g. lumber and fisheries. The uncorrected slips of typing and even of spelling are numerous.'[132]

But there was a more troubling matter. Judge Howay had written his chapters in what Shotwell referred to as a strong 'nationalist tone.'[133] Although Shotwell did not refer to any specific expressions of nationalism, Brebner was explicit: 'There is no adequate account of the Alaska Boundary Award. Howay includes it in his last chapter, but briefly and in a way which Canadian and American scholars would certainly deplore. He pretty well confines himself to Canadian indignation over Roosevelt's methods.' Moreover, Brebner explained, Howay was 'obsessed' with British Columbia's apparent preference for 'law and order and general decency north and south of the international boundary.' It was 'overdone.' 'It is as if he were presenting a long legal brief for the Hudson's Bay Company and British institutions generally.'[134] Indeed, the judge liked to compare the Americans with the British to the detriment of the Americans.[135] It was Angus who 'modified'[136] the tone of Howay's chapters through the occasional and judicious addition of a 'cheery continentalism.'[137] In a memorandum for Shotwell, Brebner reported: 'Angus has been very successful in cutting out Howay's homilies on the virtues of the British and the vices of the Americans, and in interjecting sections of comment which give proper setting and interpretation to the early expressions of rivalry. The handling of San Juan and Alaska boundaries is no longer invidious.'[138]

In addition to his editorial changes to the Lower and the Howay-Sage-Angus volumes, Shotwell cancelled one volume in the interests of Canadian-American amity. C.P. Stacey had been invited to participate in the series through a volume on Canadian-American military history. The purpose was, in Stacey's words, to present 'a completely realistic examination of the historical process which has produced the present demilitarized boundary between Canada and the United States.'[139] Through this semi-popular book, he would survey the Canadian-American military relationship from its colonial beginnings to the present. It was Shotwell who wanted the study brought to the 1930s and to include a discussion of the 'Japanese menace.'[140] Stacey consented. He found the going slower than he had anticipated, however, and in 1939 he informed Shotwell that it was unlikely that his manuscript would be ready in the near future: 'We would be lucky to publish the book in 1940, even if Hitler doesn't upset the applecart, as seems so likely.'[141] Of course, Hitler did upset the applecart, and in 1940 Stacey joined the Canadian army as a military historian.[142] Before doing so he submitted a manuscript to Shotwell that covered the story of Canadian-American military relations to 1871. As he had said all along, to bring the story to the present would create an excessively long book. Although Shotwell the editor liked the manuscript, Shotwell the politician decided against publication. As Brebner explained, Shotwell decided to set the manuscript aside until after the war: 'I do not think that I am breaking any confidence when I say that one serious consideration in this decision is [Stacey's] feeling that it would probably be undesirable to publish a study which concludes with the last really bad period of Canadian-American relations at a time when those relations are unprecedentedly close and trusting.'[143] When the war ended and Stacey made enquiries as to the status of his book, he was summarily informed that the project had exhausted its funds and that he could pick up his manuscript in New York at his convenience.[144] It was never published.[145]

Shortly after he decided not to publish Stacey's manuscript, Shotwell found himself having to defend the series. When the United States entered the war, after Japan attacked Pearl Harbor, the CEIP board of trustees appointed a special subcommittee to review the Endowment's programs. In its report the subcommittee questioned the relevance of the Canadian-American relations series to the promotion of international peace. In particular, it singled out Lower's volume, *The North*

American Assault on the Canadian Forest.[146] An indignant Shotwell responded. The series, he argued, had done much to clear away 'age-old prejudices that have kept opinions bitter north of the line.' Moreover, Arthur Lower 'was one of the strongest nationalists in the northwest and, as a result of his contact and study of the situation as a whole, he has become a leader in Canadian-American rapprochement.'[147] From Shotwell's perspective, it was money well spent. Had Lower read these remarks, he would have dismissed them as so much nonsense. After all, he was never anti-American and his participation in the series did not transform him. To the end of his career, he reamained a strong nationalist. The subcommittee's assessment of the series was closer to the truth: *The North American Assault on the Canadian Forest* fell outside the Endowment's mandate to 'hasten the abolition of international war.'

Forcing Shotwell to make compromises and concessions, Canadian historians took the money and ran. Sometimes the simplest explanation is the best explanation. Had the subcommittee been aware of the extent to which Canadian scholars manipulated the series to their own ends, its comments might have been even stronger.

If the war provided an opportunity for the Carnegie Endowment to review its programs, it also presented an opportunity for English-Canadian historians to look at themselves with a critical eye. Perhaps, they wondered, their task was not only to be immediately useful and practical; perhaps their task also included a consideration and defence of western civilization's values and a consideration and definition of what it meant to be a Canadian.

CHAPTER 7

'History cannot be too much professionalized': professionalization reconsidered

The situation in Europe was bleak when historians gathered at the University of Western Ontario in May 1940 for the annual meeting of the Canadian Historical Association. Denmark, Norway, Holland, Belgium, and France had fallen to Hitler's advancing army, and Great Britain appeared to be next in line. 'The news of the war these days is alarming,' Fred Landon confided in his diary. 'The 10 pm broadcast reported the Germans moving along the coast opposite England. This was a rainy day all through.'[1] On the surface, the profession continued with business as usual throughout the war. Agreeing with a 22 May 1940 editorial in the *Winnipeg Free Press* urging academics to 'carry on,'[2] the *Canadian Historical Review* reported that Canadian historians were 'fully conscious' of their responsibilities to a country at war. Scholarly work and intellectual debate must not be suspended.[3] The CHA organized a lobbying effort designed to raise awareness about the need for 'governments, historical societies, libraries, newspapers [and] business leaders' to preserve 'records not only of the war effort but of the effect of the war on every aspect of Canadian life.'[4] Future historians, according to the CHA, would depend on these records when it came time to write the history of this most momentous struggle. As the war progressed and political leaders called on Canadians to make voluntary sacrifices, historians decided not to cancel the annual meeting of the CHA. It was more important for intellectuals to gather and to share their work; scholarly life must not be allowed to decay.[5] Individual historians, therefore, carried on with their research; departments continued their active programs of undergraduate and graduate instruction; and the Universities of Saskatchewan and New Brunswick undertook Rockefeller-funded initiatives in regional history. In many ways, it was business as usual, but the commitment to 'carry on' belied a more fundamental change – precipitated by the war – taking place within the historical profession.[6]

During the 1940s and early 1950s historians were taking stock of a professionalization project that began in the late nineteenth century. Of course, there was much to which they could point with satisfaction: history was a well-established undergraduate program at every university; Toronto, McGill, and Queen's boasted graduate programs; the *Canadian Historical Review* was a respected academic journal; the Canadian Historical Association was vibrant and fully committed to the protection and promotion of history and historians; when the University of Toronto threatened Frank Underhill with dismissal, his colleagues successfully rallied to his defence; and, in addition to several individual monographs, historians participated in two multi–volume series, the Frontiers of Settlement and the Canadian-American relations series. There were outstanding issues, to be sure: professors' salaries were meagre at best;[7] pensions were inadequate;[8] and academic freedom, despite Underhill's survival, was not guaranteed.[9] On balance, however, history had been established as both a discipline and a profession.

Yet historians began to question what they had wrought. What is history? they asked themselves. What is the role of the historian? Had history become too privatized? The answers to these questions varied. For example, Arthur Lower turned his attention to writing a classic survey of Canadian history, *Colony to Nation*; Harold Innis pondered the meaning of time and space and the rise and fall of civilizations; Hilda Neatby worried about the destructive effects of extreme rationalism; and Donald Creighton turned to biography as a way of re-inserting the individual into history. Examined collectively, the answers were variations on the same theme: history needed to recover its association with moral judgment and historians needed to connect with a broader audience, to provide a vision, or what Edgar McInnis called a myth. History, Creighton believed, was not only technique, it was a civilizing mission; it was a humanity, and 'the real function of the humanities is the production of civilized men and trained and cultivated minds.'[10]

The 1940s and early 1950s can be best characterized as a transition period, as an older generation of historians began to reconsider the historical project while a younger generation had yet to come into its own.

I

Bartlet Brebner opened his 1940 presidential address to the Canadian Historical Association on a solemn note: 'Since November, the course of world affairs has been like the angry, urgent accumulation of towering storm clouds which is so familiar a feature of our Canadian summers. Tonight we are in the midst of an awe inspiring storm which can only be described as a general crisis in world affairs.' The historian, he said, could not but ask himself what he could 'bring to bear on a present which seems unprecedented.' Answering his own question, Brebner opined, 'The historian can bring history to bear, a history which is not mere antiquarianism, but the living stuff, the marrow of a nation and its peoples.' Historians must not give into inflated rhetoric. Jingoism and emotional appeals were best left to the politicians and the generals. Nonetheless, the historian must make every effort 'to present the successes and failures in the story which he records, so that the living may know and profit by what their predecessors have been able to do, and unable to do, with their land and its peoples.' To this end, historians ought to consider what it meant to be a Canadian. They ought to define 'Canadianism' in order that Canadians would be able to confront the future united in a guiding knowledge of itself. Canadianism 'is no mean instrument' with which to face a difficult and uncertain future: 'for it is made up of over three centuries of successful struggle with a recalcitrant environment, of over a century's original and successful political adaptation and inventiveness, and of a kind of conservatism which history has shown can be converted by adversity into stubborn, indomitable will.'[11]

Brebner struck a resonant chord. After the First World War, historians had transformed history into a discipline, into something useful and practical. In the 1940s, however, historians grew less satisfied with history as technique, through which they prided themselves on research, presentation, footnotes, and bibliographies. It was lifeless and uninspiring. It spoke to experts. It did not speak to Canadians.

As early as 1936 Arthur Lower began to doubt what he did as a historian. To a colleague he wrote that Canadian history would 'always remain a dull and unattractive subject ... as long as it continues to be a mere discipline in method.' If it was to 'live,' it must be made more 'imaginative.'[12] Lower's misgivings about the historical project only increased. 'One wonders these days whether the research worker is not just fiddling while Rome is burning,' he told James Shotwell in 1938. 'It is very hard for me to keep in the remote regions of the academic [sic].' After all, what 'we are doing just now [the Canadian-American relations series] may have no meaning within a few years. It seems to me that we are actually witnessing the second world war: it is going on bloodlessly at present but it is being fought none the less.' The fate of western civilization, he continued, might well hang in the balance: 'Few people seem to see that a revolution is proceeding under our eyes, a revolution perhaps as significant as the fall of Rome itself.'[13] As events unfolded in Europe and Canada found itself drawn into a second European war, Lower continued to agonize. Too old to join up, he felt impotent. As he recalled in his memoirs, 'We older men had to play the parts usually reserved to the women – to stay at home and worry.' In May 1940 he confided to a friend his fears for the future. Humanity, he said, seemed determined to destroy itself: 'One sometimes believes that would be small loss. Just clever enough to commit suicide, we are, just clever apes.'[14]

Yet Lower did not give into despair. Instead, he began to rethink the role of the historian. In the summer of 1940 he organized an informal but urgent conference on the teaching of history and the other social sciences. Held at Frank Underhill's Muskoka cottage in August 1940 and attended by George Brown, Gerry Riddell, Alex Brady, D.C. Masters, Underhill, and, of course, Lower, the agenda included a discussion of 'The Nature of the New World [and] the Social Scientist's Place in It.'[15] No one took minutes, but George Brown invited Lower to write an article on this very topic for the *Canadian Historical Review*. 'The subject is very timely,' he told him.[16]

In his March 1941 article entitled 'The Social Scientists in the Post-War World,' Lower opened with a eulogy to the post-1918 world. Marked by 'indecision, apathy, irresponsibility ... economic cataclysms and political earthquakes,' these two decades of 'malaise' had ended. The new social, political, and economic order would be – indeed, must be – rooted in greater state control. Although he had no absolute objections to this likely future, Lower did implore his colleagues to do more than merely describe and record. The economic historian, he wrote, in a thinly veiled reference to himself, was 'like the man who cuts the grass or cleans the windows: he performs meritorious but somewhat external services, and he certainly does not get into the life of the family ... one economic historian, at any rate, is about ready to stop cleaning windows.' The social scientist, he concluded, 'must be more than a mere scientist,' 'a mere dissector of society.' He must cease pretending that he was somehow removed and detached from his community. In other words, 'The social scientist will have something to do with creating and affecting society as well as describing it.' One of the primary tasks confronting the social scientist, he said, was to articulate what he called the 'enduring values that western civilization has created.'[17]

At the May 1941 CHA annual meeting, historians met in a special session to discuss Lower's article. There was a general consensus that

Lower had sounded the right note. Frank Underhill observed: 'The social scientist had discovered that the community had values, now under attack, and that he must go out and take his part in their defence.' George Brown thought that, as historians, 'we have dealt with the more specialized aspects of a subject, and have not dealt with the more fundamental assumptions of the society in which we live.' Historians, he said, had ignored altogether the place of religious values. Harold Innis, who disagreed with the idea of the social scientist as planner, argued that the scholar's function was not to provide answers but to undertake 'fundamental research ... in some problem of far-reaching importance.' 'When anyone appears who claims that he has found an answer, he should be regarded with great suspicion.' Reginald Trotter said that as a student he was taught that the historian must refrain from taking sides, but 'this was a kind of negativism, a retreat from the obligation of drawing a conclusion.' Summarizing the discussion, Lower noted that, as they spoke, 'Power is passing into the hands of those who are strong enough to wield it, and we must ask ourselves the question whether or not, in this process, there is any chance of preserving the values of our civilization.'[18]

In a second article, published in 1942, Lower continued this line of argument. 'In Canada,' he began, 'the Philistine is always just around the corner.' Everyone demanded utility. In wartime, that demand became deafening: '"After all," [the Philistine] would say, "you can't make guns out of history."' True enough, Lower responded rhetorically, but that was not the job of history or any other social science. When a civilization hung in the balance it needed liberal education more than ever: 'Yet surely never was there a time when the people were more in need of the guidance which can come from those whose knowledge enable them in some measure to see the experience of humanity as a whole, whose special business it is to have that vision without which the people perish.' Cast from its moorings and set adrift, Canada could not hope to govern itself, Lower argued, 'unless we can provide our own version of western civilization, our own national culture.' Of course, the fault lay not just with the Philistines among them: 'Perhaps the failure is that of the scholar.' He wrote important books and he attended learned meetings. But he did not reach a broad audience: his 'fellow countrymen ... go their way, serenely unaware of the books he writes and the point of view he entertains.'[19] For Arthur Lower, the attempt to provide Canada with its 'own version of western civilization,' to provide Canadians with something more than clean windows and a trim lawn, was a new synthesis of Canadian history – *Colony to Nation*, written in the early 1940s and published in 1946.

By his own admission, Lower wrote *Colony to Nation* in an attempt to inspire Canadians, to move them, to actively assist them in the search for a Canadian narrative that would bind them together. Many years later, in a interview with Ramsay Cook, Lower responded unequivocally when asked if he had written *Colony to Nation* 'with a wish that Canadians would read it, understand their history better, and consequently become more self-conscious, more nationalist.' 'Of course I did,' he replied.[20] Lower was well aware of the French-English divide, or what he called the primary antithesis of Canadian history. English Canadians, he said, were 'more numerous, but as a group, and with many honorable exceptions, they have not been magnanimous.' French Canadians were 'Parochial, oversensitive, and self-centred ... [and] so conscious of their rights within Canada that they have had no adequate sense of their duties towards Canada.' Faced with this antithesis, Lower sought to transcend it altogether. He looked not at Canadians, but at Canada, at the land itself: 'If the Canadian people are to find their soul, they must seek for it, not in the English language or the French, but in the little ports of the Atlantic provinces, in the flaming autumn maples of the St. Lawrence valley, in the portages and lakes of the Canadian Shield, in the sunsets of the relentless cold of the prairies, in the foothill, mountain and sea of the west, and in the unconquerable vastness of the north. From the land, Canada must come the soul of Canada.'[21] Lower's notion of a Canadian soul was, at the same time, a religious conviction. If from the land – from the little ports of the Atlantic provinces and the relentless cold of the prairies – came the soul of Canada, then that soul was a Christian one. 'We have fought two wars, not on majority votes,' he said, 'but in defence of our conviction that man is an individual, with a unique value, that he must not be deprived of his natural dignity as man or of his fundamental human rights: we have fought for the Christian conception of man, with which the English-speaking peoples have closely bound up the concept of freedom and the traditional guarantees they have worked out to safeguard it.' By 'the Christian conception of man' Lower meant that all men 'are equally the children of God.' Here were Canada's values; here was its myth. Lower had set out, in his words, to reveal to Canadians 'that self-knowledge so necessary if they are to take their rightful place in the world, and still more, if they are to be a happy people, at peace with themselves.' This was also the task of the statesman, the novelist, and the poet, but 'on no one is the duty of revealing to the people reasons for the faith that is in them more directly laid than on the historian, for by its history a people lives.'[22]

Colony to Nation represents the fruition of Lower's larger intellectual project. As he had written some twenty years earlier, 'We must ... have a national soul, as have all great nations, a rallying point, a common something of which every citizen unconsciously feels himself a part, which typifies him and marks him out for other people, we must have this soul or disappear.'[23] However, he could not have written a book like *Colony to Nation* in the interwar years. The profession demanded *Select Documents in Canadian Economic History, Settlement and the Forest and Mining Frontier,* and *The North American Assault on the Canadian Forest.* It demanded that he follow the path of the 'scientist,' that he spend 'many a month compiling price indexes, tables of imports and exports, and the like.' His early work was, in his words, 'the extreme of aridity.' His volume in the Canadian-American relations series was 'objective, statistical [and] based mostly on original material,' and it was useful, 'in the sense that snow shovels or cars are useful.'[24]

Ten years after the publication of *Colony to Nation* Lower warned that history without myth 'is dead.' Scientific history, he argued, 'is removed too far from its roots, made too rarefied and those who write it discover themselves left without readers. I doubt if the "scientific" historian can have much of a run: few men can live in the full glare of intellectualism. Man will have his myths. Let us hope they do him less harm than certain by-products of the pure intellect which, whether from the study of the eroding critic or the laboratory of the scientist, seem to have as his effect or end, his destruction.'[25] He was not alone.

II

While Lower busied himself with the writing of *Colony to Nation,* other historians also commented on the state of the discipline. One was Noel Fieldhouse from the University of Manitoba. When Frank Underhill invited Fieldhouse to give a paper at the 1942 annual meeting of Canadian Historical Association, he told him that he wanted a general paper, one that would serve as a springboard to discussion: 'Most historical papers, being collections of detailed facts, don't serve this purpose, and I should like to get something on the ideas by which men live.'[26] Fieldhouse quickly agreed. As he explained to Underhill, he wanted to begin 'from a query as to why we study history.'[29]

Over the course of the next few months Fieldhouse wrote, then circulated among CHA members, an essay entitled 'The Failure of Historians.' That failure, he believed, was the failure 'to contribute to the discussion of current international affairs.' He did not mean, however, that historians should plead this or that case; nor did he think that historians should seek to solve international problems. Indeed, he rejected the proposition that 'we should use history as a source from which to draw practical lessons which will enable us to construct a science of politics.' In other words, 'history for history's sake is a perfectly tenable position.' Studying history for its own sake produced, he believed, a recognition of difference, a tolerance of that difference, and a deep sense of continuity. This, he said, was why we study history. To do otherwise was to continue in their failure to contribute to the discussion of international differences.[28] Chester New agreed with the main point of the paper – 'that we, whose training enjoins tolerance, allows us to perceive differences, and creates a sense of tolerance, have used these qualities less than we should' – but he went even further. The historian, he said, 'must take sides, condemning what he [thinks] worthy of condemnation and approving what he [finds] worthy of approval.' Richard Saunders echoed his colleagues. Scientific history was impossible, he said; everyone had 'convictions.' Therefore, 'we should find some ideals in history that we prefer to others and [we should] express these preferences.' George Brown believed that the historian must retain his willingness to judge. For example, the development of the parliamentary system in the English-speaking world was a matter of 'great importance,' and he refused to 'surrender his right' to say as much.[29]

Continuing its practice of hearing an introspective paper on some matter of general importance to the profession, the CHA invited Reginald Trotter to discuss the teaching of history in the contemporary world at its 1943 annual meeting. The fact that this session had been arranged at all, he began, was 'indication enough that we who profess history are aware that we need to re-examine our relation to society.' Historians' work was self-evidently important to them but not to 'the mind of the general public.' Moreover, despite the remarkable advances made in the study of history throughout the interwar decades, Canada now found itself in a second world war. Trotter did not want to suggest that historians could have prevented war; however, he wondered aloud if in some way they had failed society by not providing 'a prompter view and a clearer view of the issues that were at stake in the growing world crisis. Have we – again I mean those of us who have got our living out of society by professing history in one way or another – have we been worth our salt? Perhaps we have been innocuous, but I fear that at times we may also have been inept ... Is it possible that sometimes we have been little more than misers in antiquarianism, interested in our own preserve and valuing it in proportion as it could be kept exclusive?'[30] These were tough questions, and the answers were even tougher.

The historical profession prized facts, footnotes, and bibliographies, Trotter proclaimed. It was the *apparatus criticus* that the profession valued, not the ability to make judgments. As a result, historians had 'abstained from raising fundamental questions as to the values at issue.' In their refusal to make judgments, historians had refused to see their 'professional calling as involving any larger responsibility than a recording clerkship.' The emergence of graduate programs and the insistence on technique only exacerbated the problem: 'The resulting tendency was for young PhDs to belittle the historian's main task, in his relation to his students and the public, of helping them to a truer understanding of the large and permanent elements and values in civilization.' As a profession, he concluded, they need not be ashamed; after all, they had done good work and produced valuable scholarship. But history risked falling 'into technical pedantry despite the greatness of its opportunity and its responsibility for ensuring due place in our world for the permanent values of civilized life.'[31] In the ensuing discussion W.N. Sage doubted that there was an overemphasis on technique; he did agree, however, that the real trouble with the current generation of historians was that it lacked vision. W.L. Morton pointed to the commonality of the poet and the historian: 'Each is a maker of myths; only the historian has neglected his job of making myths in this decadent, analytical age.' Frank Underhill suggested that Trotter had not stressed enough the question of values. 'What is needed,' he said, 'is a much deeper contact with poets and philosophers.'[32]

It was in this direction that the University of Saskatchewan had been moving since the late 1930s. Appointed president in 1937, James Thomson believed that the times had transformed the student and the university alike. In his first annual report he complained that the 'primary objective' in attending university had become 'getting a job.' 'The disinterested pursuit of learning is a rare appearance even in mature life, and we can hardly look for it in youth.' But was that not the essence and mission of the university? To cultivate 'a certain culture of spirit and character whereby truth becomes an ideal and the source of mankind an ethical principle'? However, the 'temper of the age,' the uncertainty and economic dislocation, made for a preoccupation 'with the present and immediate' rather than an engagement with 'some classical period of settled attainment that has passed securely into the region of permanence that belongs to the past.' Thomson thus called for a 'miniature renaissance' at Saskatchewan, whereby art, dance, and music, along with the study of history and literature, might be pursued 'simply for their own sake.'[33] In his next report, Thomson again stated that 'the domination of study by the narrowly practical and useful has tended to defeat the ends for which a University ought to exist.'[34] In his third report Thomson outlined changes to the curriculum of the College of Arts and Science. In a deliberate attempt to recover the 'cultural ideal' of an educated individual, one broadly steeped in the liberal arts, there would be mandatory courses in English and at least one other language, in one of the pure sciences, and in one of the social sciences, which included history. When for the second time war engulfed Europe, Thomson's vision was brought into sharp focus. He spoke of a 'crisis in civilization' and the need to pursue a course 'informed and inspired by a belief in the noble purpose of existence which ought to be the working faith of the wise and the good.' The modern university could 'conceive of no higher aim than to provide the leaders.'[35]

George Simpson, chair of the Department of History, was a keen participant in the changing College of Arts and Science curriculum detailed by President Thomson. As part of the initiative, the department changed History 2 in 1941: no longer 'Introduction to European Civilization,' it became 'Historic Background to Contemporary Civilization.' The shift in emphasis was subtle but important. Stressing continuity, the new course presented contemporary civilization as heir to enduring values. Simpson was also concerned about the declining enrolments in both the humanities and the social sciences. He accepted that the war effort's demand for scientists and technicians was insatiable, but he refused to accept it on all-or-nothing terms: that the university either concentrated on science and technology or concentrated on nothing. Society must not be allowed to neglect its traditions, its culture, and its history. The university must commit itself to the liberal arts precisely because the world was at war. The need had never been 'more apparent,' he said. 'It must become one of the first tasks of post-war reconstruction to revive [the humanities and social sciences] if the proper balance in university education is to be restored as between technical and scientific training on the one hand and the liberal Arts on the other.'[36] A year later he argued that the 'emphasis on science, and various public plans envisaging large scale social transformations, tend to produce an anti-traditional frame of mind.'[37] Society was losing its traditions; it was losing itself.

In a letter to George Brown and Donald Creighton, Simpson suggested that the *Canadian Historical Review* ought to place more emphasis on philosophy. By necessity, historians must dig up 'vast quantities of historical material,' but they need not operate in a philosophic vacuum: 'Few are naive enough to believe that a definitive philosophy is possible, but the subject itself should be kept alive as necessary for the vitalizing of history. Philosophy, moreover, is the real storm centre of the social sciences.'[38] History must be accompanied by philosophy, a consideration of the good. Although Simpson never offered a sustained answer, he nonetheless asked the question animating his profession: had history as a discipline failed itself and society in its neglect of moral good?

Yes, said George Wilson. In point of fact, the Dalhousie historian had always seen history as philosophy teaching by example: 'Whatever else the study of history may do it ought to make a man a philosopher. The student is forever brought face to face with the most profound questions that can enter the human mind. Why and whither?'[39] He once described himself as 'more of a philosopher than a historian.'[40] History was a humanity, a civilizing, liberalizing, humanizing discipline. It was a consideration of the good. After spending an enjoyable evening with Wilson, Donald Creighton commented, 'he is one of the most sensible liberals I've met, with a really philosophical approach to history.'[41] Never truly a part of the profession in the 1920s and 1930s when it defined itself in terms of scholarly research and writing, Wilson was appointed president of the Canadian Historical Association in 1950. In his presidential address he argued that history was actually poetry. It was art. It was philosophy. It sowed humility. But it was not a science. Sadly, 'A dry, meticulous, accurate, noncommital account of the past has become the ideal of a great many historians who have all too easily tried to ape their scientific brethren in a scientific age.'[42]

Edgar McInnis agreed. In an unpublished, undated address entitled 'The Contribution of the Social Sciences to the Importance of Living,' the University of Toronto historian stated that historical investigation was, in essence, 'a scientific process and calls for the application of scientific methods.' Yet if history 'must make full use of scientific methods in establishing its data and checking its conclusions,' it did not follow that history was a science: 'History is an art, and it is an art that it makes its most vital contribution.' The justification for history would not be found in its utility and its practicality, in its supposed capacity to solve problems. Rather, its justification would be found in its capacity 'to illuminate in the clearest possible way some aspect of essential truth, even though it may be one that appears to be remote from the problems that immediately beset us. If that can be achieved, the question of its practical value can be left to take care of itself.' In this light, history would help to make a new myth. By myth, McInnis meant the 'focal point of reference that expresses the basic qualities and the inherent goals which characterize a given society at a given time.' The historian, moreover, must not retreat from the obligation to make judgments. The average reader, he believed, was not strong enough to draw the correct judgment from so many facts. If the historian retreated, however, the void would be filled by others less qualified and at least potentially more dangerous: 'Perhaps more than any other group, the social scientists have a responsibility for helping us to avoid the maladjustment into which we have fallen or with which we are threatened. Their guidance may not always be welcomed, still less accepted; but unless they are ready and able to offer it, we shall have an even harder time in getting out of our present slough of despond.'[43] In other words, when there is no vision, the people perish.

James Kenney, the historian and archivist, would have agreed with McInnis, but, at the same time, he went even further. In a 1943 paper entitled 'The War and the Historian,' Kenney asked the question so many others were asking: What is the historian to do when the only scholars who are noticed 'are those who obviously, directly, and materially contribute to the fighting power'? Historians could do a great deal, he said. They had a unique and important role to play, because only they could offer a sense of depth and a larger scale of time to a country caught up in the immediacy of the here and now: 'The historian above all should see the life of our poor humanity steadily, see it whole, see it in the perspective of ten thousand years, and see it cleared from the clap-trap, the prejudices, the hysteria, and the panic of the present.' Moreover, and more important, the historian must engage in a self-conscious defence of western civilization against those who would destroy it. At the centre of our civilization, he said, lay Christianity. The country was at war to defend 'the fields of morals and religion as well as those of politics and economics.' It was fighting against 'a fanatical assault on that whole Christian way of life which has constituted, up to now, the progress of the human race.'[44]

When two leading university principals suggested that arts faculties be curtailed for the duration of the war, it appeared as if Kenney's fanatical assault had come from within as much as from without.

III

Because science, engineering, and medicine would contribute to a stronger war effort, the university must direct its energies to the creation of more scientists, more engineers, and more doctors: this argument could be heard over and over again throughout the war. So great was the demand for scientists and technicians and laboratory workers that entire graduating classes in science, 'such as that of McMaster University in 1941, were absorbed by the Wartime Bureau of Technical Personnel for domestic war service in production plants and laboratories.' In this context, the social sciences and the humanities were seen as unnecessary, and therefore expendable, luxuries: 'The trend today is to science, applied science and medicine, and our best students follow that path,' Principal R.C. Wallace of Queen's University said in 1942. 'The humanities are in eclipse in university life.' He had a point: enrolment in the sciences increased throughout the war, while enrolment in the humanities decreased. In the fall of 1942 Wallace, together with Principal Cyril James of McGill, suggested that arts programs be 'severely curtailed' for the duration of the war. Enrolment in the arts might be limited to two years – after that, students would 'be released for full-time military service.'[45] The *Globe and Mail* supported the idea. In an editorial the paper acknowledged the importance of arts faculties but, at the same time, questioned their utility in wartime. There is always a future danger to cutting university programs, the *Globe* argued, but 'it is needless to repeat that there will be no future unless the war is won. And those thousands of young men taking non-essential courses are not making any immediate contribution to the winning of the war.' The day would come when 'The Government at Ottawa, together with the universities, will have to make up their minds about fitting the universities into the total war picture.'[46] Meanwhile, a special meeting of the National Conference of Canadian Universities (NCCU) was planned for early January 1943. Rumours quickly circulated that the NCCU would make a formal recommendation for cuts to the social sciences and the humanities. According to Watson Kirkconnell, a professor of English at McMaster University, 'it was understood by the grapevine that the Prime Minister was ready to implement the scheme immediately thereafter.'[47]

As the rumour mill worked overtime about the possible closure of all arts faculties, historians rallied to defend their interests. Arthur Lower was furious. Such talk only confirmed his suspicion that in Canada 'the Philistine is always just around the corner.' He implored Harold Innis to get involved, to lend his status and authority to the cause. Reginald Trotter was already active in a campaign aimed at the highest level of government to forestall any attack on the social sciences and the humanities. A founder and leading member of the Canadian Social Science Research Council (CSSRC), Trotter was an obvious choice.[48] But Lower did not think him up to the task. Confidentially, he told Innis, Trotter was 'much too deferential to make a good case by himself.' You must get involved, he continued, you must 'strengthen' Trotter's hand. Unless they acted now, unless they went straight to the prime minister, 'the axe will have fallen at least on senior years in Canada, possibly junior years as well.' The stakes were high: 'If we lose, barbarism seems to lie ahead.'[49]

Innis did not need convincing. He, too, was appalled at even the suggestion of cutting back the country's arts faculties. As president of Section II of the Royal Society of Canada, Innis took it upon himself to organize the humanities along the lines of the social sciences. In the fall of 1942 he established an ad hoc committee, with the well-known and well-respected Watson Kirkconnell as chair. For his first task, Kirkconnell circulated a memorandum among his colleagues in November 1942 and elicited overwhelming support: the arts faculties must not be allowed to become a casualty of the war.[50] The humanities, Kirkconnell told Innis, were vital 'in leavening a civilized state and preventing a mechanized "fascist" type of mind.'[51] Innis, of course, could not have agreed more. As a scholar, he was already moving away from economic history towards a broad consideration of civilization and communication. Talk of the curtailment of the country's arts faculties only intensified his commitment to the university as a detached community of intellectuals involved in that process of face-to-face communication necessary to the ongoing search for truth. As he told Kirkconnell, 'It is not easy to find a solution but the attitude is to let this generation go down the drain the way ours went down. Civilization will not stand this process very long.'[52]

Both the social scientists and the humanists, therefore, submitted a strong defence of the country's arts faculties to the prime minister. Comprising a special subcommittee of the CSSRC, Innis and Trotter stated that to dismember or disband arts faculties would be a grave mistake; nothing less than 'the interests of civilization for which we are fighting' were at stake, they concluded.[53] Kirkconnell submitted a memorandum signed by forty-one humanists. 'Everyone,' according to the document, 'recognizes the inevitability, even the necessity, of an increase in natural and applied science in the new world. Yet science brings its own hazards to the human mind, and requires its antidote in social and humane studies.'[54] Mackenzie King did not commit himself one way or the other but he did acknowledge the importance of 'the Liberal tradition of education in the humanities.'[55]

In the end, the country's arts faculties were not curtailed. Ironically, the suggestion even had a positive result. Out of the struggle to defend the arts came the effort to organize for the humanities an equivalent to the CSSRC. In May 1943 Section II of the Royal Society of Canada passed a resolution authorizing Innis, as outgoing president, and R.H. Coats, as incoming president, to appoint a committee 'to consider the desirability of organizing a Humanities Research Council in Canada.'[56] This they duly did, and in December 1943 the Humanities Research Council of Canada was born in the Upper Club Room at Hart House.[57] Innis, of course, was present; as the country's leading scholar, he had played an 'obstetrical' role throughout.[58]

Innis's participation in the campaign to protect Canada's arts faculties confirmed his 'decision to recover the religious foundations of individualism as the bulwark against the new idolatry of the modern state in the social-science disciplines.'[59] According to Michael Gauvreau, Innis's Baptist faith had always been present in his scholarship. However, if in the early phase of his career it lurked in the background, then in the later phase it occupied a more prominent place in the foreground. This transition began in the second half of the 1930s as he grew more and more disillusioned with the present-mindedness of the social sciences. By the 1940s the transition was complete. It was at this point that Innis turned his attention away from economic history and towards the consideration of a question first put to him by James Ten Broeke, his undergraduate philosophy professor at McMaster University: 'Why do we attend to the things to which we attend?'[60] Innis's answer was vague, difficult to discern, enigmatic, and often opaque.[61] However, that he asked the question at all is important for what it reveals about the social sciences in the 1940s and early 1950s in English Canada.

In the last decade of his life, Innis harboured an abiding scepticism of the social science project. In a 1944 convocation address at the University of New Brunswick, Canada's leading academic lamented the current fate of academia. Besieged by political, business, and ecclesiastical interests, the battle-weary university no longer functioned as 'a repository of the highest traditions of western culture.' For Innis, the highest tradition of western culture was not the truth; rather, it was the pursuit of the truth.[62] The pursuit was altogether neglected, however, in the demand for solutions, for finality. In his wooden prose he explained, 'Growth of science meant an interest in laboratories and buildings: also the neglect of the humanities and of an interest in individuals. The social sciences followed science and talked of organization and planning.'[63] It was precisely this predisposition in the social sciences for utility, for 'organization and planning,' that worried Innis. As he explained in a 1947 letter to John Marshall of the Rockefeller Foundation, he was 'disturbed at the trend in the social sciences towards the methodology of the natural sciences and in turn by what appears to be a widening gulf between the social sciences and the humanities.' Standardization and routine in the social sciences 'deadens the sensitivity' to the humanities and led to 'sterility' in both.[64] In an important essay written in 1950, Innis wrestled with these issues. 'Work in the social sciences has become increasingly concerned with topical problems,' he wrote, 'and social science departments become schools of journalism.' There was more. The exaltation of science, he explained, led to the mechanization and specialization of knowledge in both the social sciences and the humanities. In turn, the mechanization and specialization of knowledge marginalized morality. Consideration of the good could not be accommodated. Innis quoted with approval the work of the nineteenth-century Swiss thinker, Henri-Frédéric Amiel, who wrote in 1852, 'It is curious to see scientific teaching used everywhere as a means to stifle all freedoms of investigation in moral questions under the dead weight of facts.' Society needed more investigation into moral questions because, Innis said, 'Without vision the people perish.'[65]

In an attempt to re-privilege values in the social sciences, Innis created what he called the Values Discussion Group. Throughout the winter of 1949 a group of University of Toronto academics – with Innis at the centre – gathered to discuss questions of objectivity, values, and empiricism in the social sciences and the humanities. 'The consensus of the Values Discussion Group,' Michael Gauvreau observes, 'was that the methods of the physical sciences could contribute only to a limited extent to the development of the social sciences.' Yet even if absolute objectivity was impossible, it was still possible to discern 'the underlying moral principles of individual and social behaviour.'[66] As Innis declared, new means of mass communication had 'upset the old [value orders] and leave no means for controlling them.' 'One of the results of this situation is an obsession with the immediate. Our civilization is dominated by this. Nothing lasts. Everything must change. Civilization becomes cut off from a concern with continuity, with the long term approach. Values in this situation take on the same complexion as their surroundings.'[67] From a condition where values 'take on the same complexion as their surroundings,' it was a short step to nuclear annihilation. The atom bomb, Innis believed, 'belonged to the same knowledge network that had nurtured machine industry. Its hallmark was specialization, a thoroughly modern condition that was now in danger of destroying Western scholarship.'[68]

Innis's concern for human values emerged from his larger concern for the sanctity and the dignity of the human individual. Although Donald Creighton wrongly believed that Innis ceased to be a Baptist after the First World War, he nonetheless appreciated the lasting influence of the Baptist faith on Innis's life. Innis, he wrote, 'clung tenaciously to certain convictions and values which have always been characteristic of his sect. He believed in the independence, dignity, and self-sufficiency of the individual.'[69] Monopolies of knowledge, narrow nationalisms, centralized bureaucracies, mass communications, fanatical political movements: in the 1940s the autonomy of the individual seemed in peril. Innis criticized his colleagues in the social sciences who rushed off to Ottawa to develop public policy that served, in his words, only 'to thwart the human spirit and to fasten the chains more tightly.'[70]

Hilda Neatby was sympathetic to Innis's larger argument. In 1944 she expressed her unease with what she called 'the generally mechanistic approach of other social studies – economics, sociology, and psychology.' History ought to move against this trend through a focus on biography, on 'case studies' of individuals. Such detailed studies 'might be a useful corrective to the dangers inherent in the attempt to weigh, measure, and classify human activities in the mass.' It was the individual who mattered, but it was the individual whom historians ignored. A biographical approach to the past, Neatby believed, was not simply about understanding the past; it was about the present. Biography affirmed the dignity and worth of the individual in a world that worshipped collective abstraction in the name of the state or the proletariat. It affirmed freedom over totalitarianism.[71]

Central to Neatby's larger intellectual project was her faith. Her 1953 book, *So Little for the Mind*, was an extended critique of progressive education – anti-intellectual, progressive education aimed at and achieved a uniformly low standard in the name of democratic equalitarianism – but it was also a plea to re-insert Christian values into public education. The education system had failed, she argued, because individual students were unable to choose good and refuse evil.[72] For Neatby, the failure of progressive education marked only the tip of the iceberg: 'western society today is fundamentally dissatisfied, restless and insecure' because it 'has lost, or almost lost the Christian faith.' She suggested not that society abandon the quest for knowledge, but that it renounce 'the false rationalism which implicitly denies the power of faith.' Rational enquiry must take place within an unquestionable recognition of a transcendent good. She called, therefore, for 'a return to the habitual and deliberate contemplation of greatness.'[73] Truth without good and rationalism without contemplation of greatness were dangerous and misguided concepts and would lead inevitably to the collapse of western civilization.

What did all of this mean for the historian and the practice of history? Neatby did not believe that historians should abandon the archives for contemplation unencumbered by primary documents and long hours of research. History, she explained, must remain 'an objective examination of all the available evidence with a view to an imaginative (but *accurate*) reconstruction.'[74] But by objective she meant research tested by empirical evidence; objective did not mean value-free research. After all, historians 'can never achieve the natural detachment of the man who surveys a colony of ants and whose observations on them may be sublimely free from the influences of time and space.'[75] Neatby – and here she was explicit – believed that historians should abandon the fruitless attempt to compartmentalize reason and faith, vowing 'that never the twain shall meet.' Not only was it intellectually impossible, it was undesirable. Christian faith and historical research, she argued, 'must ultimately be completely integrated if they are to be real.' The two must meet and mingle and inform each other. Not compartmentalizing Christianity but taking it into the archives, Neatby maintained, would necessarily allow the historian to uncover the deeper patterns to the human story. Without Christianity the historian would be 'confronted with questions which all his historical method, all his particular science and art are powerless to answer. What are men? Why are they what they are? What destiny really governs their lives?'[76] Taking Christianity into the archives would allow the historian to judge right from wrong, thereby defending Christian values in the present. Neatby's present was the age of anxiety and uncertainty and unease. Science and technology – embodied in the atom bomb – might well destroy humanity. Civilization, if it were to survive, needed to recover its core Christian values, and the historian had a role to play in that process.

Donald Creighton did not wear his faith on his sleeve, but he did share Innis's and Neatby's commitment to the individual. Not coincidentally, it was Innis who encouraged Creighton to consider a biography for his next project.

IV

While Innis was undertaking his work on communications, civilization, and individualism, Creighton was at work on what remains, perhaps, his greatest contribution to Canadian historiography: a biography of Sir John A. Macdonald. He was aided by a Rockefeller grant. During his trip to Ontario in November 1942 the Rockefeller Foundation officer John Marshall met Creighton and was instantly struck by his intelligence and strength: clearly, this was someone worthy of support. Anne Bezanson, another Foundation officer, came away with the same impression. 'There is no question, either in AB's mind or JM's, that [Creighton] is one of the ablest if not the ablest of historians they have encountered in Canada,' Marshall recorded.[77] It then became a matter of deciding how the Foundation could best support him and his work.

Oddly enough, it was Frank Underhill who answered this question, albeit unintentionally. In the 1942–3 academic year Underhill was living in New York City on a Guggenheim Fellowship. Coming on the heels of the concerted attempt by the board of governors and the president of the University to fire him, the fellowship proved a godsend. Arranged by Harold Innis,[78] it allowed Underhill to leave Toronto and lie low for a while. It also allowed him an opportunity to study Canada at a distance. From his Morningside Heights apartment at the corner of West 121st Street and Amsterdam Avenue, he sent a long, ten-page memorandum to John Marshall. Living in New York City had convinced Underhill of two things: first, Canadians mattered very little to the outside world; and second, Canadians themselves were out of touch with the 'centre of things.' As an example, he argued that in the present world crisis, 'when all the inherited values of our civilization are under challenge, no Canadian has said or written anything about the great themes of our day – democracy and liberty – which goes beyond the conventional clichés of newspaper editorials or politicians' speeches. Once again we are reading what Englishmen and Americans have to say on the subjects, the fundamental issues of our generation.' He therefore wanted to find a way to 'fertilize Canadian intellectual life ... My main thesis is that Canadian universities in the field of the humanities and social sciences might have their life quickened and made more fruitful by closer relations with their American fellows ... Something might be done to bring Canadian universities into the fuller current of intellectual life of this continent.'[79] Underhill had sounded the right note, and Marshall promptly invited him to lunch. In the meantime, an excited Marshall altered a funding proposal he had already initiated. He now wanted to include senior Canadian scholars in his plan to free a select group of historians and literature professors from their teaching and administrative obligations so that they might concentrate on the study of human values in history and literature. In an internal memorandum Marshall called it 'a strategic move' to bring Canadians into a discussion of North American values.[80] At their lunch meeting Underhill concurred with Marshall's proposal. In addition, both Underhill and Marshall agreed that one man in particular stood out as an ideal choice: Donald Creighton.[81]

What did Marshall mean by values that ought to be realized in the study of history? The Second World War, European fascism, and the collapse of France had precipitated a concern for western civilization and its attendant values. Democracy, the Foundation believed, hung in the balance. In his original letter to Creighton, Marshall explained his intent to release senior American scholars from their duties and to assign them the task of defining those values in history that historians might realize. He specifically mentioned his desire to include a Canadian: 'Feeling as strongly as I do about the place which Canada has and certainly is to have in North American life, I find myself drawn to the idea.'[82] Creighton was enthusiastic. After all, historians in Canada had begun to consider the question of values in history. This process, he explained, 'dates back probably to the summer of 1940 when the collapse of France forced us to undertake a reconsideration of [history] in the emerging world.'[83] In another letter, however, he expressed his confusion. The question of values in Canadian history was 'very general and inclusive.'

Such a study surely calls for both a mature historian and a mature philosopher. It seems to me to involve an examination of the political and social heritage of western civilization which we in Canada have derived, to a large extent, through the two main sources of France and Great Britain; and it involves further the question of how these more permanent values of western civilization have been modified or changed by our experience as colonial communities and, more recently, as a Canadian nation ... At all events, the subject is a huge one in which one could not get very far without a lot of hard thought.[84]

Besides, Creighton had already committed himself to teaching in the summer session. Yet Marshall was persistent. He also questioned Creighton's premise that there was a fundamental continuity between Europe and North America, followed by adaptation. According to Marshall, the North American tradition was different from that of western Europe,[85] but this was as far as Marshall ever went in defining either Creighton's project or his approach. Indeed, he knew that Creighton thought little of continental regionalism. In no uncertain terms, Creighton informed him that he doubted the 'validity' of North American regions, which 'break apart at the international boundary in more than one important way.'[86] The fact of the matter was that Marshall did not care. Creighton, however, remained non-committal. In addition to summer school, his general survey of Canadian history demanded his undivided attention.

With *Dominion of the North* at the printer in January 1944, Creighton turned his attention to Marshall's project. He was more convinced than ever of its importance. Historians must strive, he said, to help citizens to realize the 'fundamental values or objectives' in history.[87] Marshall was thrilled. Although Creighton had yet to decide on a specific research question, Marshall did not attempt to pressure him into selecting a particular topic. It was always understood to be entirely Creighton's decision. In March 1944 Marshall paid Creighton a visit. Over lunch the two men tossed around a few ideas – one possibility was a study in Canadian foreign policy; another was a study in the history of education – but still Creighton equivocated.[88] He wanted to pursue the question of values in Canadian history, but he did not see a definable, manageable means. Over the next few days he talked to various friends and colleagues, including Innis.[89] Everything seemed to point to a biography; a biography would provide a convenient frame through which to view what it meant to be Canadian, what values Canadians stood for and ought to continue to stand for. Of course, it could not be a biography of merely anybody; it had to be somebody of defining significance in Canadian history. If everything pointed to a biography, then everything also pointed to Sir John A. Macdonald: 'Unless there is no value in the study of British North American history, it must be conceded that Macdonald is a figure of central importance and interest.' The biography, he continued, would be not a purely factual reconstruction but an 'interpretive study of the man and of the whole generation to which he belonged.'[90] Marshall could not have been more pleased: 'I can say that this proposal recommends itself to us most highly, above all because it is the thing that you yourself came to after what I know to be full and mature deliberation.'[91] By the end of April the die was cast. Creighton would be released from his university duties on 1 July 1944 for a period of one year; the Foundation would pay his salary ($4,000) and provide him with a research budget ($2,500).[92] An ecstatic Creighton could not believe the opportunity now before him; in his own words, it was 'almost too good to be true' and he was a 'little dazzled' by it all.[93]

It was no accident that Creighton decided to write a biography. Not only did the decision reflect the concern over values that was animating the profession, it also reflected the concern over the fate of the individual in mass society. In a 1945 public talk at the University of New Brunswick Creighton offered his conception of history: 'History,' he said, 'is not made by inanimate forces and human automatons; it is made by living men and women, impelled by an endless variety of ideas and emotions, which can be best understood by that insight into character, that imaginative understanding of people, which is one of the great attributes of literary art.'[94] Carl Berger rightly observes that, within the historical profession at this time, 'Biography became a vehicle for reasserting the ability of men to make their own history. Fascism and the Communism were threats to the democratic importance of the individual, and these challenges may have contributed to a renewed concern with the single person in history.'[95] Creighton, however, was also attracted to Macdonald as Macdonald. Here was an opportunity to study the making of Canada, to define what Bartlet Brebner had termed 'Canadianism' in his 1940 CHA presidential address. Creighton's Macdonald embodied a vision of the country that was as relevant in the late nineteenth century as it was in the mid-twentieth century: a strong central government and a transcontinental economy would best protect Canada's British heritage and its autonomy in North America. A giant among men, Creighton's Macdonald understood that the greatest threat to Canada's independence came from the United States.[96]

Finally, Creighton's two-volume biography of Canada's first prime minister represented his commitment to reaching a wider audience. Historians had accomplished much in the past twenty-five years, he wrote in 1945, but they had tended to write for each other; they had neglected the obligation to write for the educated, reading public. The historian must strive to capture the Canadian soul and the Canadian imagination. Echoing W.D. Lighthall, the nineteenth-century historian, poet, and novelist and the founder of the Historic Landmarks Association, Creighton explained: 'The historian must have a feeling for design; but there are other literary qualities which he must seek just as earnestly to capture. He must try for pictorial vividness, for good characterization, for rapidity of action. It is only thus, for example, that he can bring out the real romance of the St. John River Valley – the excitements of the French period, the hard pioneering Loyalist days, the picturesque and strenuous life of the lumber trade.'[97] In this way history would become something more than a narrow, scientific, and professional pursuit while it reached a wider public.[98]

Creighton thus answered those questions animating the profession in the 1940s and early 1950s: What is history? What is the role of the historian? Has the profession become too private? Like Brebner, Lower, Underhill, Brown, Fieldhouse, Trotter, Morton, Simpson, Wilson, McInnis, Kenney, Innis, and Neatby, Creighton wanted to define Canada's values, to articulate Canada's myths, and to reach as large an audience as possible through his writing. As he explained in a 1959 interview, 'history is not a science. It is a humane study; and not merely its end-products, but its whole process has got to be made available to the lay reader.' The professional historian had forgotten this basic fact: history must be accessible and 'made available to the lay reader, so that the lay reader can really understand it.' The problem of history was the problem of professionalization. History had become a private conversation between professional historians when it should be a public conversation as well. The profession, Creighton believed, ignored this fact at its peril. 'History,' he said, 'cannot be too much professionalized.'[99]

The ongoing imperatives of professional history, however, would mean that Creighton's observation fell on deaf ears. In the 1950s and 1960s a new generation of historians emerged, and departments expanded very quickly to meet expanding post-war enrolments. By 1960 the University of Toronto had a permanent staff of twenty historians. The University of Saskatchewan increased its staff from four to six during the 1950s. Even in the small Maritimes universities history staffs doubled in size. By 1960 Acadia had four full-time professors; Dalhousie had five. Maurice Careless, Gerald Craig, Jack Saywell, Blair Neatby, Peter Waite, and Ramsay Cook now dominated the profession. It was not so much that this new generation deliberately ignored the general reader, but the continued growth of the profession meant its continued specialization. Fields like Canadian history were divided into sub-fields: political history, intellectual history, regional history, and economic history. Advancement through the ranks depended on learned monographs and scholarly articles in academic journals.

Yet specialization and academic writing continued to highlight the problematic nature of history's professionalization. Despite the books, the journals, the conferences, and the graduate students, professionalization was realized at a price: history's professionalization was also its privatization. It was this point that Western's W.K. Ferguson stressed in his 1961 presidential address to the Canadian Historical Association. History needed to recover its association with literature, it needed to be made readable, accessible, and enjoyable. But he was not particularly hopeful: 'Unfortunately, the doctoral dissertation frequently sets a pattern which the scholar will follow for the rest of his life, devoting such energies as he can spare from his academic duties to learning more and more about less and less.' As it must, specialized research led to specialized audiences. Specialized audiences led to smaller audiences. Smaller audiences led to one inescapable, unalterable fact: no one read what historians wrote. He reminded his colleages of their larger social function 'to put together the materials made by research into some larger synthesis, and interpret the facts so as to give them meaning for the interested but untrained reader.' If they did nothing else, Ferguson concluded, then at least they should disabuse their graduate students of the belief that 'it is the scholar's goal to leave behind him footnotes on the sands of time.'[100]

Conclusion

The focus of this book has been the professionalization of history in English Canada from the late nineteenth century to the middle of the twentieth century. History's professionalization should not be understood as a movement from darkness to light; rather, it should be seen as a transition from one way to another of organizing intellectual life.

Seen thus – as a transition, not as a rise – what came before history's professionalization is not necessarily inferior but different. To expect that men and women such as William Douw Lighthall, David Ross McCord, and Janet Carnochan could have written history as Donald Creighton, Alfred Bailey and Hilda Neatby did is unfair and ahistorical. Lighthall, McCord, and Canochan were what they were: late-nineteenth-century intellectuals interested in the past. Before the term came to mean someone who earned a living by writing and teaching history, these men and women were historians. They published books and articles; they built museums; and they founded local, provincial, and national historical societies. William Dawson LeSueur introduced 'a critical spirit' into Canadian intellectual life. Although not a professional historian, as that term is now understood, he articulated a modern approach to the writing of history in his 1912 presidential address to the Royal Society of Canada.[1]

Although the Lighthalls and the Carnochans should be not dismissed but studied on their own terms, the professionalization of history carried with it definite benefits. The *Canadian Historical Review*, the Canadian Historical Association, professorships, departments, scholarly monographs, multi–volume series, tenure, and academic freedom were – and are – obvious and tangible benefits. To see professionalization only as a project to monopolize social and economic rewards is to ignore the real gains associated with having a surgeon perform an appendectomy, a dentist fill a cavity, an engineer build a bridge, an architect design a building, and a professional historian write history.

For all the benefits of having professional historians write history, there also were costs. Professionalization was neither an inevitable nor a benign process. Professional historians deliberately, consistently, and favourably drew boundaries between what they did and what amateur historians did, and in doing so, they raised their status and authority. Protecting their status, authority, and access to the academic labour market, professional historians also excluded women from the professoriate. Whereas women were active in the historical community before its professionalization, they were conspicuous by their absence after its professionalization. Believed to be emotional and intuitive, women could not find a place in a profession defined by its commitments to reason and knowledge. In this sense, the professionalization of history was also its masculinization.

Conceptualizing the professionalization of history as a flat line as opposed to a rising curve draws our attention not only to the important changes brought by professionalization but to a fundamental continuity as well between intellectual life in the nineteenth century and intellectual life in the twentieth century. It was A.B. McKillop who first exposed and explained what he termed the moral imperative of English-Canadian intellectual life, the imperative to reconcile enquiry and affirmation.[2] Professional historians maintained a commitment to both fact and value, to the idea that facts amassed by social scientific means could be used for moral ends.

Hilda Neatby made precisely this point in the special study she prepared for the Royal Commission on National Development in the Arts, Letters and Sciences. History, she argued, is an art, not a science: 'The true appeal of history is philosophic, moral and aesthetic; it is killed by purely scientific dissection.' Neatby believed that history should offer moral instruction to society, not only an endless stream of Gradgrindian facts for professional historians. 'The professional historian,' she said, 'has not reached or touched the Canadian public.'[3] Neatby struck a resonant chord, one that has sounded across the decades: the professionalization of history has also meant its privatization. That is, in its academic incarnation history has become a private conversation between professional historians.

Another University of Saskatchewan historian would pick up this theme nearly fifty years later. In his 1997 presidential address to the

Canadian Historical Association, Jim Miller likens the profession to Lewis Carroll's Cheshire Cat. The profession, he says, 'seems alarmingly to be receding from prominence in public discourse, and even in the public's consciousness.' Against this backdrop, Miller urges historians to cultivate more alliances with non-professional historians, to make more use of new media in an effort to reach larger audiences, and to be more proactive and assertive in making claims about the importance of history. There are no magic solutions, Miller concludes, 'but with luck our efforts to reverse the fading of the historian to invisibility will turn out differently.'[4]

Miller is right: something is fading. But it is not the historical profession. After all, the profession is as strong now as it was in the salad days of Donald Creighton, Harold Innis, Frank Underhill, and Arthur Lower. Admittedly, some books, articles, and dissertations are narrowly conceived, but this situation is not new. W.S. Wallace made the same observation in the mid-1920s when he found himself 'filled with a sense of futility' at the tragically limited scope of the history dissertation.[5] In the early 1960s W.K. Ferguson similarly lamented the scholarly imperative to learn 'more and more about less and less.'[6] It is true, also, that the academic labour market cannot provide jobs for all of today's young PhDs. But it never could: to say nothing of the well-qualified women historians who were never hired by universities, the young Alfred Bailey and C.P. Stacey lived hand to mouth throughout the better part of the 1930s. If it is true that today's policy-makers do not pay attention to historians, it is also true that they never have done so. Arthur Lower once remarked that policy was made by politicians who, 'as a rule,' were blithely unaware of what academics talked about: 'We may conjure up great schemes and have great thoughts, but ... somebody sitting in a government office decides what is going to be done.'[7] Similarly, there is nothing new in the fact that Canadians do not read history. Writing in 1933, George Wrong observed that the influence of the historian had declined over the course of the previous half-century. In addition to the problem of historians' writing for other historians, not for the general reader, the simple fact remained, he explained, that women preferred to read gossip columns and advertisements while men preferred to read the sports section or listen to 'jazz and vulgar humour on the radio.'[8]

The problem is not a fading historical profession but the fading past. As Eric Hobsbawm writes, 'the destruction of the past ... is one of the most characteristic and eerie phenomena of the late twentieth century. Most young men and women at the century's end grow up in a permanent present lacking any organic relation to the public past of the times in which they live.'[9] In this context, historians would do well to remember that they are part of a larger intellectual and moral tradition in English Canada, one premised not on a separation of fact and value but on a recognition of their proximity.

Notes

Introduction

1 On the historical profession in Quebec see Serge Gagnon, *Quebec and Its Historians: 1840–1920* (Montreal: Harvest House, 1982); Serge Gagnon, *Quebec and its Historians: The Twentieth Century* (Montreal: Harvest House, 1985); Jean Lamarre, *Le Devenir de la nation québécoise, selon Maurice Séguin, Guy Frégault et Michel Brunet* (Sillery: Les éditions du Septentrion, 1993); and Ronald Rudin, *Making History in Twentieth-Century Quebec* (Toronto: University of Toronto Press, 1997). See also the articles dedicated to the theme of 'Les Pratiques de l'histoire de l'Amérique française depuis 50 ans' in *Revue d'histoire de l'Amerique française* 51, 2 (Autumn 1997).

2 See Carl Berger, *The Writing of Canadian History: Aspects of English-Canadian Historical Writing since 1900*, 2nd ed. (Toronto: University of Toronto Press, 1986); William Duncan Meikle, 'And Gladly Teach: G.M. Wrong and the Department of History at the University of Toronto,' PhD thesis, Michigan State University, 1977; Robert Bothwell, *Laying the Foundation: A Century of History at University of Toronto* (Toronto: Department of History, University of Toronto, 1991); and Paul T. Phillips, *Britain's Past in Canada: The Teaching and Writing of British History* (Vancouver: UBC Press, 1989).

3 Magali Sarfatti Larson, *The Rise of Professionalism: A Sociological Analysis* (Berkeley: University of California Press, 1977): xvi. See also Eliot Freidson, 'Are Professions Necessary?' in Thomas Haskell, ed., *The Authority of Experts: Studies in History and Theory* (Bloomington: Indiana University Press, 1984).

4 See Anne Witz, *Professions and Patriarchy* (London: Routledge, 1992).

5 Tracey Adams, *A Dentist and a Gentleman: Gender and the Rise of Dentistry in Ontario* (Toronto: University of Toronto Press, 2000): viii, 167

6 Thomas Bender, *Intellect and Public Life: Essays on the Social History of Academic*

Intellectuals in the United States (Baltimore, Md.: Johns Hopkins University Press, 1993): xiii–xiv. See also Rudin, *Making History,* 10.

7 See Doug Owram, *The Government Generation: Canadian Intellectuals and the State, 1900–1945* (Toronto: University of Toronto Press, 1986).

8 See Robin S. Harris, *A History of Higher Education in Canada, 1663–1960* (Toronto: University of Toronto Press, 1976); and A.B. McKillop, *Matters of Mind: The University in Ontario, 1791–1951* (Toronto: University of Toronto Press, 1994).

9 S.E.D. Shortt, *The Search for an Ideal: Six Canadian Intellectuals and Their Convictions in an Age of Transition, 1890–1930* (Toronto: University of Toronto Press, 1976); A.B. McKillop, *A Disciplined Intelligence: Critical Inquiry and Canadian Thought in the Victorian Era* (Montreal and Kingston: McGill-Queen's University Press, 1979, 2001); McKillop, 'Science, Humanism, and the Ontario University,' in McKillop, *Contours of Canadian Thought* (Toronto: University of Toronto Press, 1987); Ramsay Cook, *The Regenerators: Social Criticism in Late Victorian English Canada* (Toronto: University of Toronto Press, 1985); and Marlene Shore, *The Science of Social Redemption: McGill, the Chicago School, and the Origins of Social Research in Canada* (Toronto: University of Toronto Press, 1987).

10 Cook, *The Regenerators,* 5

11 McKillop, *Matters of Mind,* 178–9

12 Michael Gauvreau, 'Baptist Religion and the Social Science of Harold Innis,' *Canadian Historical Review* 76, 2 (June 1995): 163

13 McKillop, *A Disciplined Intelligence,* 230–1. See also McKillop, 'Moralists and Moderns,' *Journal of Canadian Studies* 14, 4 (Winter 1979–80): 144–50.

14 See Donald Fisher, *The Social Sciences in Canada: 50 Years of National Activity by the Social Science Federation of Canada* (Waterloo, Ont.: Wilfrid Laurier University Press, 1991); Barry Ferguson and Doug Owram, 'Social Scientists and Public Policy from the 1920s through World War II,' *Journal of Canadian Studies* 15, 4 (Winter 1981): 3–17.

15 See Watson Kirkconnell and A.J.P. Woodhouse, *The Humanities in Canada,* 2 vols. (Ottawa: Humanities Research Council, 1946); n.a., *Humanities Research Council of Canada, Canadian Federation for the Humanities, 1943–1983: A Short History* (Ottawa: Canadian Federation for the Humanities, 1983)

16 National Archives, Royal Commission on National Development in the Arts, Letters and Sciences Fonds, RG 33, 28, vol. 13, Minutes of Proceedings and Evidence, Canadian Historical Association, 19 August 1949

17 Frank Underhill, 'The University and Politics,' reprinted in Underhill, *In Search of Canadian Liberalism* (Toronto: Macmillan, 1960): 268

18 Peter Novick, *That Noble Dream: The Objectivity Question and the American Histor-*

ical Profession (Cambridge: Cambridge University Press, 1988)
19 See McKillop, *A Disciplined Intelligence;* and Philip Massolin, *Canadian Intellectuals, the Tory Tradition, and the Challenge of Modernity, 1939–1970* (Toronto: University of Toronto Press, 2001).

Chapter 1

1 It is difficult to determine the precise number of associations and societies. There are no central records, and some societies had a tendency to decline, only to be revived a few years later. See 'Canadian Historical Societies,' *Canadian Historical Review* 12, 4 (December 1931): 356–63.
2 See Carl Berger, *The Writing of Canadian History: Aspects of English-Canadian Historical Writing since 1900,* 2nd ed. (Toronto: University of Toronto Press, 1986): 1; Norman Knowles, *Inventing the Loyalists: The Ontario Loyalist Tradition and the Creation of Usable Pasts* (Toronto: University of Toronto Press, 1997): 111.
3 See Carl Berger, *Sense of Power: Studies in the Ideas of Canadian Imperialism* (Toronto: University of Toronto Press, 1970).
4 See W.D. Lighthall, *An Account of the Battle of Chateauguay* (Montreal: W. Drysdale, 1889).
5 The use of history in fiction in nineteenth-century English Canada was common. See Diane Hallman, 'Cultivating a Love of Canada through History: Agnes Maule Machar, 1837–1927,' in Beverly Boutilier and Alison Prentice, eds, *Creating Historical Memory: English-Canadian Women and the Work of History* (Vancouver: UBC Press, 1997).
6 See W.D. Lighthall, *The Young Seigneur, or Nation Making* (Montreal: Wm Drysdale, 1888).
7 W.D. Lighthall, *The Master of Life: A Romance of the Five Nations and of Prehistoric Montreal* (Toronto: Musson, 1908): v. See also Donald Wright, 'W.D. Lighthall and David Ross McCord: Antimodernism and English-Canadian Imperialism, 1880s-1918,' *Journal of Canadian Studies* 32, 2 (Summer 1997): 134–53.
8 See Linda Orr, 'The Revenge of Literature: A History of History,' *New Literary History* 18, 1 (Autumn, 1986): 1–22.
9 Dennis Duffy, *A Tale of Sad Reality: John Richardson's Wacousta* (Toronto: ECW Press, 1993): 31. See also Duffy, *Sounding the Iceberg: An Essay on Canadian Historical Novels* (Toronto: ECW Press, 1986).
10 On the development of anthropology in Canada see Douglas Cole, 'The Origins of Canadian Anthropology, 1850–1910,' *Journal of Canadian Studies* 8, 1 (February 1973): 33–45.

11 See W.D. Lighthall, *A New Hochelagan Burying-Ground discovered at Westmount on the Western Spur of Mont Royal, Montreal, July-September 1898* (Montreal: n.p., 1898); 'Hochelagans and Mohawks: A Link in Iroquois History,' *Proceedings and Transactions of the Royal Society of Canada*, 2nd series, 5 (1899): 199–211; 'The Westmount Stone-Lined Grave Race,' *Proceedings and Transactions of the Royal Society of Canada*, 3rd series, 16 (1922): 73–5; 'Hochelaga and the "Hill of Hochelaga,"' *Proceedings and Transactions of the Royal Society of Canada*, 3rd series, 18 (1924): 91–106; 'The False Plan of Hochelaga,' *Proceedings and Transactions of the Royal Society of Canada*, 3rd series, 26 (1932): 181–92; 'New Hochelaga Finds in 1933,' *Proceedings and Transactions of the Royal Society of Canada*, 3rd series, 28 (1934): 103–108.

12 For a consideration of Lighthall's contribution to the debate over Hochelaga see Bruce Trigger, 'Hochelaga: History and Ethnohistory,' in Bruce Trigger and J.F. Pendergast, *Cartier's Hochelaga and the Dawson Site* (Montreal and Kingston: McGill-Queen's University Press, 1972).

13 Lighthall, 'A New Hochelagan Burying-Ground,' 4

14 For a history of the McCord family see Donald Fyson and Brian Young, 'Origins, Wealth and Work,' in Pamela Miller et al., *The McCord Family: A Passionate Vision* (Montreal: McCord Museum of Canadian History, 1992). See also Brian Young, *The Making and Unmaking of a University Museum: The McCord, 1921–1996* (Montreal and Kingston: McGill-Queen's University Press, 2000).

15 Moira T. McCaffrey, '*Rononshonni* – the Builder: McCord's Collection of Ethnographic Objects,' in Miller et al., *The McCord Family*, 111

16 Of William Kingsford, McCord believed that 'He never could have done anything without the Archives. What I mean is, he was not one who went to the Archives, as we all must, after long years of previous reading & ripening. He went there for the reading and ripening as well as the special knowledge for which archives are created.' McCord Museum of Canadian History, McCord Family Papers, file no. 2024, Canadian Note Book no. 3, 282–3

17 For an analysis of McCord's military collection see Donald Wright, 'Remembering War in Imperial Canada: David Ross McCord and the McCord National Museum,' *Fontanus: From the Collections of McGill* 9 (1996): 97–104.

18 *Review of Historical Publications Relating to Canada* 1 (1896): 11. According to M. Brook Taylor, Kingsford 'approached the [the writing of history] as would an engineer: he surveyed the existing material, excavated the relevant information, and hammered it into shape.' Taylor, 'Kingsford, William,' *Dictionary of Canadian Biography*, vol. 12: 1891–1900 (Toronto: University of Toronto Press, 1990): 495

19 See Margaret Banks, *Sir John George Bourinot, Victorian Canadian: His Life, Times, and Legacy* (Montreal and Kingston: McGill-Queen's University Press,

2001); and Carl Berger, 'Race and Liberty: The Historical Ideas of Sir John George Bourinot,' *Annual Report of the Canadian Historical Association* (1965): 87–104.

20 See Hugh Alexander Stevenson, 'James H. Coyne: His Life and Contributions to Canadian History,' MA thesis, University of Western Ontario, 1960.

21 See Heather MacDougall, 'Canniff, William,' *Dictionary of Canadian Biography*, vol. 13: 1901–1910 (Toronto: University of Toronto Press, 1994): 156–8. There was no contradiction between Canniff's medical career, on the one hand, and his writing of history, on the other. David Boyle, secretary of the Ontario Historical Society, wrote to Canniff to tell him how pleased he was to learn 'that you are ... in the historical as well as the medical field.' David Boyle to William Canniff, 2 October 1899, Archives of Ontario (AO), William Canniff Papers, MS 768, Reel 1, Series F, Historical Societies

22 See David McConnell, 'E.A. Cruikshank: His Life and Work,' MA thesis, University of Toronto, 1965. For a quick summary of Cruikshank's career see Ernest Green, 'In Memoriam: Ernest Alexander Cruikshank,' Ontario Historical Society, *Papers and Records*, 33 (1939): 5–9. Cruikshank's first wife wrote a book on their time in Niagara in which she makes various references to her husband's distractions with 'battles long ago.' Julia Cruikshank, *Whirlpool Heights: The Dream-House on the Niagara River* (London: George Allen & Unwin 1915), 40. The Dalhousie historian D.C. Harvey once wondered if the 'old general' 'kept the book before his poor second wife as an example or a warning.' D.C. Harvey to Fred Landon, 11 August 1945, University of Western Ontario, J.J. Talman Regional Collection, Fred Landon Papers, Box 4209, file 28

23 See Terry Crowley, *Marriage of Minds: Isabel and Oscar Skelton Reinventing Canada* (Toronto: University of Toronto Press, 2003); Cecilia Morgan, 'History, Nation, and Empire: Gender and Southern Ontario Historical Societies, 1890–1920s,' *Canadian Historical Review* 82, 3 (September 2001): 491–528; Janet Guildford, 'Elizabeth Murdoch Frame: A Nova Scotian Historian,' *Collections of the Royal Nova Scotia Historical Society* 44 (1996): 15–25; Anne Innis Dagg, 'Canadian Voices of Authority: Non-Fiction and Early Women Writers,' *Journal of Canadian Studies* 27, 2 (Summer 1992): 107–22; and Hallman, 'Cultivating a Love of Canada.'

24 Sarah Curzon, 'Historical Societies,' *Journal and Transactions of the Wentworth Historical Society* 1 (1892): 105, 106

25 See Stella Cook, 'The Women's Canadian Historical Society of Toronto, 1895–1970,' Women's Canadian Historical Society of Toronto, *Transaction*, No. 29 (1970).

26 In its report, the Ontario Historical Society stated that the success of the Vic-

toria University historical exhibition was owed 'to the labours of the
Women's Canadian Historical Society.' David Boyle, Report of the Ontario
Historical Society, in *Proceedings and Transactions of the Royal Society of Canada*,
2nd series, 6 (1900): Appendix C, iv

27 In 1951 the Bytown Museum was moved to its present location, the former
Commissariat Building at the entrance to the Rideau Canal. In 1956 the
WHSO became the Historical Society of Ottawa. The latter's mandate was
similar: 'To carry on the work of the Women's Canadian Historical Society of
Ottawa and the Bytown Historical Museum and Reference Library ... and to
foster Canadian Loyalty and Patriotism.' See Constitution and By-laws of the
Historical Society of Ottawa,' Bytown Museum Archives, Women's Canadian
Historical Society of Ottawa Fonds, Box 67, 1/4

28 Beverly Boutilier, 'Women's Rights and Duties: Sarah Anne Curzon and the
Politics of Canadian History,' in Boutilier and Prentice, *Creating Historical
Memory*, 51–2. See also Knowles, *Inventing the Loyalists*, 125–6, 137.

29 Boutilier, 'Women's Rights and Duties,' 66. The Literary and Historical Society of Quebec was exclusively male; the Antiquarian and Numismatic Society
of Montreal had a ladies auxiliary, the Women's Antiquarian Society.

30 Boutilier, 'Women's Rights and Duties,' 66

31 See WHS 'Annual Reports,' printed in *Proceedings and Transactions of the Royal
Society of Canada.*

32 See EHSI 'Annual Reports,' printed in *Proceedings and Transactions of the Royal
Society of Canada.*

33 William Douw Lighthall to Mary FitzGibbon, 21 May 1896, AO, Women's
Canadian Historical Society of Toronto Fonds, Series A, MU 7837, Correspondence 1890–1896

34 James S. Coyne to Mary FitzGibbon, 1 September 1896, ibid.

35 Charles Mair to Mary FitzGibbon, 8 May 1896, ibid.

36 William Kirby to Emma Currie, Women's Literary Club of St Catharines,
Brock University Special Collections, RG 18, Women's Literary Club of St
Catharines Fonds, Box 9, Scrapbook 'Memories'

37 Boutilier, 'Women's Rights and Duties,' 69

38 See AO, Ontario Historical Society Fonds, Series D, MU 5440, Scrapbook,
Janet Carnochan.

39 Janet Carnochan, 'Report of the Niagara Historical Society,' in *Proceedings
and Transactions of the Royal Society of Canada*, 3rd series, 7 (1913): Appendix G

40 T.A.S. Hay, Report of the Peterborough Historical Society, in *Proceedings and
Transactions of the Royal Society of Canada*, 2nd series, 6 (1900): Appendix C

41 See Ontario Historical Society, *Papers and Records*, 3 (1901): 4.

42 For a description of the Kingston Historical Society see Louis J. Flynn, 'The Early Years of the Kingston Historical Society, 1893–1906,' *Historic Kingston* 11 (March 1963): 35–46.

43 AO, Ontario Historical Society Fonds, Series B, MS 249, Minutes, 30 March 1898

44 Terry Crowley, '*Ontario History* at 100,' *Ontario Historical Society Bulletin* 114 (May 1998): 7

45 Between 1899 and 1923 twenty different women published thirty-two papers in *Papers and Records*. See 'Index of Authors and Subjects,' Ontario Historical Society, *Papers and Records* 20 (1922): 149–84.

46 See Marjorie J.F. Fraser, 'Feudalism in Upper Canada,' Ontario Historical Society, *Papers and Records* 12 (1914): 142–52.

47 Crowley, '*Ontario History* at 100,' 7. See also AO, Niagara Historical Society Fonds, Reel 15, H IV.1, Clementina Fessenden Papers.

48 Only E.A. Cruikshank, who published eight essays, and W.R. Riddell, who published nine, had as many papers printed. See papers by Janet Carnochan in Ontario Historical Society, *Papers and Records*, 3 (1901); 5 (1904); 7 (1906); 8 (1907); 13 (1915); 15 (1917); 17 (1919); 19 (1922).

49 See 'Report of the Women's Canadian Historical Society of Ottawa,' *Proceedings and Transactions of the Royal Society of Canada*, 2nd series, 9 (1903): Appendix D.

50 See Matilda Edgar, *Ten Years of Upper Canada in Peace and War, 1805–1815* (Toronto: William Briggs, 1890; reprinted as *Ten Years of Upper Canada in Peace and War [The Thomas Ridout Captivity]* [New York: Garland, 1977]); Edgar, *General Brock* (Toronto: Morang, 1904); and Edgar, *A Colonial Governor in Maryland: Horatio Sharpe and His Time, 1753–1773* (London: Longmans, Green, 1912).

51 See, 'Fessenden, Mrs. Clementina,' in H.J. Morgan, ed., *The Canadian Men and Women of the Time*, 2nd ed. (Toronto: William Briggs, 1912): 392. See also Molly Puvar Ungar, 'Trenholme, Clementina (Fessenden),' *Dictionary of Canadian Biography*, vol. 14: *1911–1920* (Toronto: University of Toronto Press, 1998): 1008–9.

52 Boutilier, 'Women's Rights and Duties,' 69

53 Morgan, 'History, Nation, and Empire,' 494

54 W.D. Lighthall to Mayor Willett, 30 August 1905, McGill University Rare Books and Special Collections (MURBSC), W.D. Lighthall Papers, Box 17, file 16

55 W.D. Lighthall to Major William Wood, 1 September 1905, ibid.

56 Carl Berger, *Honour and the Search for Influence: A History of the Royal Society of Canada* (Toronto: University of Toronto Press, 1996): 30, 31

57 *Proceedings and Transactions of the Royal Society of Canada*, 2nd series, 11 (1905): Appendix E, cxviii
58 See F.C. Wurtele to W.D. Lighthall, 16 September 1905; William Wood to W.D. Lighthall, 17 October 1906; and William Wood to W.D Lighthall, 5 April 1907, MURBSC, W.D. Lighthall Papers, Box 17, file 16.
59 Historic Landmarks Association, Circular, 1908, NA, Historic Landmarks Association Fonds, MG 28 I 52, vol. 1
60 Régimbald reported that in 1919 the HLA became the Historic Sites and Monuments Board, and that in 1922 the HSMB became the Canadian Historical Association. He was wrong: the HSMB was a government body created in 1919. It still exists. In 1922 the HLA became the CHA. See Patrice Régimbald, 'La Disciplinarisation de l'histoire au Canada français,' *Revue d'histoire de l'Amérique française* 51, 2 (Autumn 1997): 163–200.
61 Historic Landmarks Association, pamphlet, 1908, NA, Historic Landmarks Association Fonds, MG 28 I 52, vol. 1.
62 Historic Landmarks Association, Minutes of Annual Meeting, ibid. It is not unreasonable to assume that Lighthall was the author, because he often employed such optimistic, ebullient language.
63 G. Durnford, Treasurer's Report, 27 May 1914, NA, W.D. Lighthall Papers, MG 29 D 93, vol. 1, file 26
64 Pemberton Smith, 'President's Address,' Historic Landmarks Association, *Annual Report* (1915): 8
65 Historic Landmarks Association, Minutes of the Annual Meeting, 19 May 1920, NA, Historic Landmarks Association Fonds, MG 28 I 52, vol. 1
66 Lawrence Burpee, 'Presidential Address,' Historic Landmarks Association, *Annual Report* (1921): 12
67 Edgar, 'Introduction,' *Ten Years of Upper Canada*
68 John G. Bourinot, *Canada under British Rule, 1760–1900* (Cambridge: Cambridge University Press, 1900): viii
69 William Kingsford, *The History of Canada*, vol. 1: *1608–1682* (Toronto: Rowsell & Hutchison, 1887): 2
70 Janet Carnochan, 'Some Mistakes in History,' Ontario Historical Society, *Papers and Records* 13 (1915): 28
71 E.A. Cruikshank, 'The Study of History and the Interpretation of Documents,' *Proceedings and Transactions of the Royal Society of Canada*, 3rd series, 15 (1921): Section II, 13
72 W.D. LeSueur, 'The Scientific Spirit,' 1879; reprinted in A.B. McKillop, ed., *A Critical Spirit: The Thought of William Dawson LeSueur* (Toronto: McClelland and Stewart, 1977): 111
73 According to A.B. McKillop, 'The place of W.D. LeSueur within the history

of the Anglo-Canadian moral imagination, and Canadian history in general, is an important one, for it was he who first introduced the spirit of modern criticism into Canadian life.' Ibid., xx

74 Ibid., 248

75 See ibid., 247–67. See also Daniel Francis, *National Dreams: Myth, Memory, and Canadian History* (Vancouver: Arsenal Pulp Press, 1997): 114–19.

76 See W.D. LeSueur, *Count Frontenac* (Toronto: Morang, 1906).

77 Quotation in McKillop, *A Critical Spirit*, 249.

78 W.D. LeSueur, *William Lyon Mackenzie: A Reinterpretation*, ed. A.B. McKillop (Toronto: Macmillan, 1979): xxxiii

79 George Morang to W.D. LeSueur, 6 May 1908; reprinted in McKillop, *A Critical Spirit*, 273–5

80 A.B. McKillop, 'Editor's Introduction,' in LeSueur, *William Lyon Mackenzie*, xxi–xxii

81 W.D. LeSueur to George Morang, 11 May 1908; reprinted in McKillop, *A Critical Spirit*, 276

82 W.D. LeSueur to Isabella Hay Stitt, 27 January 1913, NA, W.D. LeSueur Papers, MG 30 D 51, vol. 2, file Correspondence Isabella Hay Stitt

83 W.D. LeSueur, 'History: Its Nature and Methods,' *Proceedings and Transactions of the Royal Society of Canada*, 3rd series, 7 (1913): Appendix A, lxii, lxv–lxvi, lxii, lxxxiii

84 Doug Owram, *The Government Generation: Canadian Intellectuals and the State, 1900–1945* (Toronto: University of Toronto Press, 1986): 14. See A.B. McKillop, *Matters of Mind: The University in Ontario* (Toronto: University of Toronto Press, 1994), chaps 7 and 8.

85 James Loudon, 'The Universities in Relation to Research,' *Proceedings and Transactions of the Royal Society of Canada*, 2nd series, 8 (1902): Appendix A

86 See A.B. McKillop, 'The Research Ideal and the University of Toronto,' in A.B. McKillop, *Contours of Canadian Thought* (Toronto: University of Toronto Press, 1987).

87 See W.L. Morton, *One University: A History of the University of Manitoba, 1877–1952* (Toronto: McClelland and Stewart, 1957).

88 H.M. Tory to A.C. Rutherford, 6 March 1906, NA, H.M. Tory Papers, MG 30 D 115, vol. 2, file 21. See Mario Creet, 'H.M. Tory and the Secularization of Canadian Universities,' *Queen's Quarterly* 88, 4 (Winter 1981): 718–36; and E.A. Corbett, *Henry Marshall Tory: A Biography* (Toronto: Ryerson Press, 1954; reprinted with an introduction by Doug Owram [Edmonton: University of Alberta Press, 1992]).

89 See Michael Hayden, *Seeking a Balance: The University of Saskatchewan, 1907–1982* (Vancouver: University of British Columbia Press, 1983).

90 Paul Axelrod, *Making a Middle Class: Student Life in English Canada during the Thirties* (Montreal and Kingston: McGill-Queen's University Press, 1990): 10

91 M. Brook Taylor, *Promoters, Patriots, and Partisans: Historiography in Nineteenth-Century English Canada* (Toronto: University of Toronto Press, 1989): 265

92 George Wrong to W.D. Lighthall, 9 July 1907, MURBSC, W.D. Lighthall Papers, Box 1, file 19; Alfred Bailey to W.D. Lighthall, June 1933; W.D. Lighthall to Alfred Bailey, 19 June 1933, University of New Brunswick Archives (UNBA), RG 80, A.G. Bailey Papers, Series 12, Case 60, file 3. Lighthall advised Bailey to investigate 'the Hochelagan pottery collections in the McCord Museum & the Chateau de Ramezay Museum in Montreal – the only ones in the world.' In the preface to his book, Bailey thanked Lighthall, John Clarence Webster, and W.F. Ganong for their assistance. See Alfred Bailey, *The Conflict of European and Eastern Algonkian Cultures, 1504–1700* (Saint John: New Brunswick Museum, 1937).

93 Founded in 1905, the Champlain Society publishes primary documents relating to the history of Canada.

94 Adam Shortt to Janet Carnochan, 27 September 1924, Queen's University Archives, Adam Shortt Papers, Box 6, file Correspondence 1924

95 Leon Harvey to William Wood, 30 October 1924, NA, William Wood Papers, MG 30 C 60, vol.1, file 1923–1933

96 Stevenson, 'James H. Coyne,' 197

97 University of Saskatchewan Archives, President's Office Fonds, Walter Murray, RG 1, series 1, B38: Annual Reports, 36: History, 1926–1927. See also Donald Wright, 'History at the University of Saskatchewan from E.H. Oliver to Hilda Neatby,' *Essays: University of Saskatchewan* 1, 1 (1999): 1–47.

98 These three men contributed dozens of reviews to the *Canadian Historical Review*. For a complete list see *Canadian Historical Review, Index, Volumes I–X, 1920–1929* (Toronto: University of Toronto Press, 1930); *Canadian Historical Review, Index, Volumes XI–XX, 1930–1939* (Toronto: University of Toronto Press, 1944); *Canadian Historical Review, Index, Volumes XXI–XXX, 1939–1949* (Toronto: University of Toronto Press, 1959).

99 James Shotwell to H.F. Angus, 5 January 1934, Columbia University, Rare Book and Manuscript Library, James Shotwell Papers, Box 284, file Can-American Relations, H.F. Angus

Chapter 2

1 David Ross McCord to Sir Wilfrid Laurier, 8 August 1905, McCord Museum of Canadian History, McCord Family Papers, file 1803, Application for Beit Professorship

2 Justice Loranger to David Ross McCord, 31 July 1905, ibid.

3 George Murray to David Ross McCord, 3 August 1905, ibid.

4 William Duncan Meikle, 'And Gladly Teach: G.M. Wrong and the Department of History at the University of Toronto,' PhD thesis, Michigan State University, 1977: 37 See also Robert Bothwell, *Laying the Foundation: A Century of History at University of Toronto* (Toronto: Department of History, University of Toronto, 1991).

5 Quotation in W.S. Wallace, 'The Life and Work of George M. Wrong,' *Canadian Historical Review* 29, 3 (June 1948): 229

6 See Elizabeth Hulse, ed., *Thinking with Both Hands: Sir Daniel Wilson in the Old World and the New* (Toronto: University of Toronto Press, 1999).

7 H.H. Langton, *Sir Daniel Wilson: A Memoir* (Toronto: Thomas Nelson and Sons, 1929): 92–3

8 Alan Bowker, 'Truly Useful Men: Maurice Hutton, George Wrong, James Mavor and the University of Toronto, 1880–1927,' PhD thesis, University of Toronto, 1975: 194

9 George Wrong, *Application and Testimonials of George M. Wrong, BA, for the post of Professor of History in the University of Toronto* (Toronto, 1894)

10 See Martin Friedland, *The University of Toronto: A History* (Toronto: University of Toronto Press, 2002): 160–4

11 George Wrong, *Historical Study in the University: An Inaugural Lecture* (Toronto: Bryant Press, 1895)

12 See Doris Goldstein, 'History at Oxford and Cambridge: Professionalization and the Influence of Ranke,' in Georg Iggers and James Powell, eds, *Leopold von Ranke and the Shaping of the Historical Discipline* (Syracuse, N.Y.: Syracuse University Press, 1990); Peter Novick, *That Noble Dream: The 'Objectivity Question' and the American Historical Profession* (Cambridge: Cambridge University Press, 1988): 21–46.

13 George Wrong, 'The Beginnings of Historical Criticism in Canada: A Retrospect, 1896–1936,' *Canadian Historical Review* 17, 1 (March 1936): 2–8

14 *Review of Historical Publications Relating to Canada* 1 (1896): 167. Review authors are not identified in the *RHPRC*.

15 'Organization Plans for Women's Canadian Historical Society of Ottawa,' 3 June 1898, Bytown Museum Archives, Women's Canadian Historical Society of Ottawa Fonds, Box 66, HSOT 1/3

16 'Report of our Delegate, Mrs. J.B. Simpson to the American Historical Convention,' WCHSO, *Annual Report*, 1909–10, 17. See Albert Bushnell Hart, 'Imagination in History,' *American Historical Review* 15, 2 (January 1910): 227–51.

17 'Report of our Delegate, Mrs. G.M. Bayly to the Twenty-Seventh Annual

Meeting of the American Historical Society,' WCHSO, *Annual Report*, 1911–1912, 19. See William Sloane, 'The Substance and Vision of History,' *American Historical Review* 17, 2 (January 1912): 235–51.

18 WCHSO, *Annual Report*, 1914–15

19 *Review of Historical Publications Relating to Canada* 6 (1902): 78

20 Ibid., 15 (1911): 63

21 Ibid., 18 (1914): 121–2

22 Ibid., 20 (1916): 63

23 Ibid., 22 (1919): 106

24 Ibid., 20 (1915): 109

25 For a discussion of the socially constructed and gendered boundary between experience and knowledge see Jean Barman '"I walk my own track in life & no mere male can bump me off it": Constance Lindsay Skinner and the Work of History,' in Beverly Boutilier and Alison Prentice, eds, *Creating Historical Memory: English-Canadian Women and the Work of History* (Vancouver: UBC Press, 1998).

26 *Review of Historical Publications Relating to Canada* 5 (1900): 122

27 Ibid., 15 (1910): 105

28 Ibid., 20 (1915): 103

29 Quotation in Gerald Killan, *Preserving Ontario's Heritage: A History of the Ontario Historical Society* (Ottawa: Ontario Historical Society, 1976): 107.

30 George Parkin to George Wrong, 15 January 1905, National Archives (NA), George Parkin Papers, MG 30 D 77, vol. 7, file 'G. Parkin–Prof. George Wrong, 1904–1915.' McGill's Charles Colby also considered applying, but his father's poor health prevented him from leaving Canada. See George Wrong to Charles Colby, 16 July 1905; and George Wrong to Charles Colby, 12 August 1905, Stanstead Historical Society Archives, Colby Fonds, C.W. Colby, Series 2, Subseries A, Box 2, file 4.

31 See George Wrong, 'Louisbourg in 1745: The Anonymous Letter d'un Habitant de Louisbourg,' *University of Toronto Studies: History and Economics* 1, 1 (1897); Wrong, *The British Nation: A History* (Toronto: Appleton, 1903); Wrong, *The Earl of Elgin* (London: Methuen, 1905).

32 George Wrong to George Parkin, 18 January 1905, NA, George Parkin Papers, MG 30 D 77 vol. 7, file 'G. Parkin-Prof. George Wrong, 1904–1915.' Hugh Egerton received the Beit Professorship. He was assisted by a Canadian, W.L. Grant. For letters pertaining to the Beit Professorship see William Ashley to George Wrong, 5 July 1905, Thomas Fisher Rare Book Room, University of Toronto (TFRBR-UT), George Wrong Papers, MS Coll. 36, Box 1, file 4; Hugh Egerton to George Wrong, 29 April 1906, ibid., Box 1, file 69; George Parkin to Sir William Osler, 16 August 1905, ibid., Box 2, file 84

33 George Wrong, Notes prepared at the suggestion of George Smith, 1944, University of Toronto Archives (UTA), University of Toronto Press, CHR Files, A86-0044, Box 5, file CHR, 25th Anniversary Letters, no. 1

34 The following list indicates the name, degrees, and length of tenure of Wrong's early appointments: E.J. Kylie, BA (Toronto), BA (Oxon.), 1904–16; A.G. Brown, BA (Toronto), BA (Oxon.), 1905–14; K.G. Feiling, BA (Oxon.), 1907–9; K.N. Bell, BA (Oxon.), 1909–11; W.S. Wallace, BA (Toronto), BA (Oxon.), 1910–24, 1927–29; J.J. Bell, BA (Oxon.), 1911–12; W. Harvey, BA (Toronto), MA (Toronto), 1911–12; R. Hodder-Williams, BA (Oxon.) 1912–23; G.M. Smith, BA (Toronto), BA (Oxon.), 1912–29; H. McMurchie, BA (Toronto), MA (Toronto), 1912–19; Vincent Massey, BA (Toronto), BA (Oxon.), 1913–19; W.P.M. Kennedy, BA (Dublin), MA (Dublin), 1914–16; Margaret Wrong, BA (Oxon.), MA (Toronto), 1915–21; S.H. Hooke, BA (Oxon.), 1916–23; Marjorie Reid, BA (Toronto), BA (Oxon.), 1918–20, 1922–26.

35 Quotation in Bowker, 'Truly Useful Men,' 307. For a description of Wrong's Anglophilia, elitism, and Oxford obsession see Arthur Lower, 'Once They Were Alive, Our Betters – My Instructors, George Wrong,' Queen's University Archives (QUA), Arthur Lower Papers, Box 42, B 977.

36 Bothwell, *Laying the Foundation*, 41–2. For a strong endorsement of the tutorial method see R. Hodder Williams, 'The Tutorial Experiment,' *University of Toronto Monthly* 15, 4 (February 1915): 195–203.

37 Bothwell, *Laying the Foundation*, 51–6

38 Keith Feiling to George Wrong, 27 November 1909, TFRBR-UT, George Wrong Papers, MS Coll. 36, Box 1, file 76

39 Bowker, 'Truly Useful Men,' 105

40 See Reba Soffer, 'Nation, Duty, Character and Confidence: History at Oxford, 1850–1914,' *Historical Journal* 30, 1 (1987): 77–104

41 Quotation in Bowker, 'Truly Useful Men,' 302. See also Ramsay Cook, 'Kylie, Edward Joseph,' *Dictionary of Canadian Biography*, Vol. 14: 1911–1920 (Toronto: University of Toronto Press, 1998): 565–6.

42 Frank Underhill to George Wrong, 2 February 1912, TFRBR-UT, George Wrong Papers, MS Coll. 36, Box 3 file 59. According to J.M.S. Careless, Underhill grew to be sentimental about his Oxford days. 'Even Frank Underhill, who was very down on things imperial, used to get starry eyed about Balliol and about Oxford,' he recalled. Interview with J.M.S. Careless, 13 July 1983, UTA, B86-0038, Tape 4

43 George Wrong to Frank Underhill, 14 March 1912, NA, Frank Underhill Papers, MG 30 D 204, vol. 2, file G.M. Wrong 1907–1927

44 Ronald Longley, 'History at Acadia,' Acadia University Archives (AUA), Ronald Longley Papers, Box 10, file 'Centennial'

45 Ibid.
46 AUA, Acadia University Calendar, 1879
47 Longley, 'History at Acadia'
48 See Peter Waite, *The Lives of Dalhousie University*, vol. 1: 1818–1925 (Montreal and Kingston: McGill-Queen's University Press, 1994).
49 George Wrong, Notes prepared at the suggestion of George Smith, 1944, UTA, University of Toronto Press, CHR Files, A86–0044, Box 5, file CHR, 25th Anniversary Letters, no. 1
50 A. Stanley Mackenzie to D.C. Harvey, 7 January 1913, Public Archives of Nova Scotia (PANS), D.C. Harvey Papers, MG 1, vol. 1200, file 1
51 Ibid.
52 A. Stanley Mackenzie to James Todd, 1 August 1916, Dalhousie University Archives (DUA), President's Office, MS-1-3 A-538, History Department 1913–60
53 Quotation in Michael Perceval-Maxwell, 'The History of History at McGill,' unpublished paper, McGill University Archives
54 Hilda Neatby, *Queen's University*, vol. 1: *1841–1917* (Montreal and Kingston: McGill-Queen's University Press, 1978): 135
55 Quotation in Katherine Ferguson, 'George Dalrymple Ferguson: First Professor of History at Queen's University,' *Historic Kingston* 14 (January 1966): 51
56 See W.L. Morton, *One University: A History of the University of Manitoba, 1877–1952* (Toronto: McClelland and Stewart, 1957).
57 For a detailed history of the Saskatchewan History Department see Donald Wright, 'History at the University of Saskatchewan from E.H. Oliver to Hilda Neatby,' *Essays: University of Saskatchewan* 1, 1 (1999): 1–47.
58 Diary of Edmund H. Oliver, 22 September 1909, University of Saskatchewan Archives (USA), Jean Murray Papers, MG 61, E. IV. Name and Subject Files, N. Oliver, E.H., 2. Diary. Oliver taught economics until a separate appointment was made in 1913.
59 James T. Shotwell, *The Autobiography of James T. Shotwell* (New York: Bobbs-Merrill, 1961): 42. See also Peter Novick, *That Noble Dream: The 'Objectivity Question' and the American Historical Profession* (Cambridge: Cambridge University Press, 1988): 104
60 J.H. Robinson to E.H. Oliver, 14 August 1909, USA, E.H. Oliver Papers, MG 6, S 1, A. Correspondence, II. Miscellaneous Correspondence
61 USA, President's Office Fonds, Walter Murray, RG 1, Series 1, B38: Annual Reports, 36: History, 1913–1914
62 USA, University of Saskatchewan Calendar, 1915–16
63 George Wrong, Diary, 5 June 1912, TFRBR-UT, George Wrong Papers, MS Coll. 36, Box 6, file 45

64 Diary of Edmund H. Oliver, 22 September 1909, USA, Jean Murray Papers, MG 61, E. IV. Name and Subject Files, N. Oliver, E.H., 2. Diary

65 George Wrong, Diary, 27 June 1916, TFRBR-UT, George Wrong Papers, MS Coll. 36, Box 6, file 58

66 QUA, Adam Shortt Papers, The Adam Shortt Diaries, 11 May 1909

67 See S.E.D. Shortt, *The Search for an Ideal: Six Canadian Intellectuals and Their Convictions in an Age of Transition, 1890–1930* (Toronto: University of Toronto Press, 1976), chap. 6; Carl Berger, *The Writing of Canadian History: Aspects of English-Canadian Historical Writing since 1900*, 2nd ed. (Toronto: University of Toronto Press, 1986): 21–2; and Barry Ferguson, *Remaking Liberalism: The Intellectual Legacy of Adam Shortt, O.D. Skelton, W.C. Clark and W.A. Mackintosh, 1890–1925* (Montreal and Kingston: McGill-Queen's University Press, 1993): 53–61.

68 Danielle Lacasse and Antonio Lechasseur, *The National Archives of Canada, 1872–1997*, Historical Booklet (Ottawa: Canadian Historical Association, 1998): 6

69 For a detailed summary of the respective careers of Shortt and Doughty see Ian Wilson, 'Shortt and Doughty: The Cultural Role of the Public Archives, 1904–1935,' MA thesis, Queen's University, 1973.

70 QUA, Adam Shortt Papers, The Adam Shortt Diaries, 11 May 1909; 24 June 1909; 14 July 1909; 24 July 1909; 30 July 1909; 5 September 1909; 9 September 1909; 10 September 1909; 11 September 1909; 14 September 1909; 26 September 1909; 3 October 1909; 7 October 1909; 7 December 1909; 14 December 1909; 24 February 1910; 13 March 1910; 17 March 1910; 22 March 1910; 23 April 1910; 16 June 1910; 5 August 1910; 4 September 1910; 8 December 1910; 10 January 1911; 16 January 1911; 18 January 1911; 25 January 1911; 26 January 1911; 7 February 1911; 16 February 1911; 26 February 1911; 2 March 1911; 6 March 1911; 5 April 1911; 7 April 1911; 8 April 1911; 14 April 1911; 19 April 1911; 18 May 1911; 24 May 1911; 28 May 1911; 31 May 1911; 6 June 1911; 16 June 1911; 19 June 1911; 21 June 1911; 23 June 1911; 2 January 1912; 14 January 1912; 13 February 1912; 18 March 1912; 18 November 1912. Shortt's diaries for the period end at this point.

71 W.A. Mackintosh, 'Adam Shortt, 1859–1931,' *Canadian Journal of Economics and Political Science* 4, 2 (May 1938): 173

72 Arthur Lower, 'Adam Shortt, Founder,' *Historic Kingston* 17 (January 1969): 6

73 Donald Creighton, *Harold Adams Innis: Portrait of a Scholar* (Toronto: University of Toronto Press, 1957): 78

74 Lacasse and Lechasseur, *The National Archives*, 8

75 See D.C. Scott, Pelham Edgar, and W.D. LeSueur, eds, *The Makers of Canada*, 20 vols (Toronto: Morang, 1906–8); and G.M. Wrong and H.H. Langton, eds, *Chronicles of Canada*, 32 vols (Toronto: Glasgow, Brook, 1914–16).

76 Adam Shortt and Arthur Doughty, eds, *Canada and Its Provinces*. 23 vols
   (Toronto: Publishers' Association of Canada, 1913): Vol. 1, ix
77 Berger, *The Writing of Canadian History*, 28. On the need for specialists in the
   series see Robert Glasgow to Adam Shortt, 5 December 1911, QUA, Adam
   Shortt Papers, Box 3, file Correspondence Sept.–Dec. 1911.
78 E.H. Oliver to George Wrong, 27 February 1911, TFRBR-UT, George Wrong
   Papers, MS Coll. 36, Box 2, file 83
79 USA, President's Office Fonds, Walter Murray, RG1, Series 1, President's
   Report, 1909–1910, 12–13
80 See Thomas Haskell, ed., *The Authority of Experts: Studies in History and Theory*
   (Bloomington: Indiana University Press, 1984); and Doug Owram, *The Gov-
   ernment Generation: Canadian Intellectuals and the State, 1900–1945* (Toronto:
   University of Toronto Press, 1986).
81 See E.H. Oliver, *The Canadian Northwest, Its Early Development and Legislative
   Records, 1870–1912* (Ottawa: Government Printing Bureau, 1914); and
   Oliver, 'Saskatchewan and Alberta: General History, 1870–1912,' in Shortt
   and Doughty, *Canada and Its Provinces*, Vol. 19.
82 W.D. Lighthall to Arthur Doughty, 25 September 1910, NA, W.D. Lighthall
   Papers, MG 29 D 93, vol. 1, file 23
83 W.D. Lighthall, 'English Settlement in Quebec,' in Shortt and Doughty, *Canada and Its Provinces*, Vol. 15, 121
84 Shortt and Doughty, *Canada and Its Provinces*, Vol. 1, viii
85 QUA, Adam Shortt Papers, The Adam Shortt Diaries, 5 September 1909; 14
   December 1909
86 Berger, *The Writing of Canadian History*, 181
87 QUA, Adam Shortt Papers, The Adam Shortt Diaries, 24 May 1911
88 George Wrong, 'The Historian's Problem,' *Annual Report of the Canadian Historical Association* (1927): 5–7
89 George Wrong, 'The Historian's Duty to Society,' paper presented at American Historical Association Annual Meeting, 1932. Printed as 'The Historian
   and Society,' *Canadian Historical Review* 14, 1 (March 1933): 4–8.
90 Berger, *The Writing of Canadian History*, 31
91 Albert Henry Newman to John Castle, 6 June 1881. Quotation in Jerry Brea-
   zeate, 'Albert Henry Newman: Historian and Theologian,' Doctor of Theology thesis, New Orleans Baptist Theological Seminary, 1960: 21. See Albert
   Henry Newman, *A History of the Baptist Churches in the United States* (New York:
   Christian Literature, 1894).
92 In his history of McMaster, Charles Johnston wrote: 'Baptist educators
   pressed ahead with new fields of instruction at McMaster. Steps were taken
   before the first convocation to add to the store of "modern" subjects by

introducing political history, as distinct from the purely ecclesiastical history that had long been the staple of institutions developed under denominational auspices ... By 1895 both constitutional history and ancient history were being offered, along with considerable work in the old course in church history, by Professor Newman, the first occupant of the history chair at the university.' Charles Johnston, *McMaster University*, vol. 1: *The Toronto Years* (Toronto: University of Toronto Press, 1976): 62

93 Albert Henry Newman, *A Manual of Church History*, vol. 1 (Philadelphia: American Baptist Society, 1900): 3, 4

94 Albert Henry Newman, Annual Report, 24 April 1901, Canadian Baptist Archives, McMaster University (CBA), Box McMaster University, Chancellor's Reports and Reports to Him, 1901–1909, file McMaster University Annual Reports – Departmental, 1900–1907. See also Albert Henry Newman, Annual Report, 5 April 1900, CBA, Box McMaster University, Chancellor's Reports and Reports to Him, 1901–9, file McMaster University Annual Reports – Woodstock College, Departmental 1899–1900; and Albert Henry Newman, Annual Report, 5 April 1899, CBA, Box McMaster University Chancellor's Reports 1891–1892, 1895–1900, file McMaster University, Annual Reports – Chancellor's Report to Senate, Moulton College, Woodstock College, Departmental, 1898–1899

95 Newman, *A Manual of Church History*, 5. For a similar conception of Church history see John Dall, 'The Study of History,' *Queen's Quarterly* 19, 3 (January 1912): 253–68

96 Charles Colby, 'History and Patriotism,' *Proceedings of the Canadian Club, 1904–1905* (Toronto, 1905): 108, 110, 115

97 Charles Colby, 'The Modern Historian,' n.d., Stanstead Historical Society Archives, Colby Fonds, C.W. Colby, Series 2, Subseries C, Box 5, file 59

98 Charles Colby, *Canadian Types of the Old Régime, 1608–1698* (New York: Holt, 1910): 3–4, 313–21

99 Charles Colby, 'The Teaching of History,' n.d., Stanstead Historical Society Archives, Colby Fonds, C.W. Colby, Series 2, Subseries C, Box 5, file 73

100 J.L. Morison, 'Some Recent Historical Literature: European and British,' *Queen's Quarterly* 19, 3 (January 1912): 269–73

101 W.L. Grant, 'The Study of History in Ontario,' *Canadian Magazine* 22, 5 (March 1904): 431–6

102 W.L. Grant, 'The Teaching of Colonial History,' *Queen's Quarterly* 18, 3 (January 1911): 186

103 Diary of Edmund H. Oliver, 18 September 1909, USA, Jean Murray Papers, MG 61, E. IV. Name and Subject Files, N. Oliver, E.H., 2. Diary. Oliver had been moved and inspired by Milner. In a 1904 letter to George Wrong,

Oliver said that he intended to dedicate his Columbia thesis to Milner: 'Further, in carrying out this [thesis] I have come more and more to appreciate the learning and ability, and to admire the personality of Mr. Milner. I have come to respect and love him, as I do few men.' E.H. Oliver to Wrong, 18 December 1904, TFRBL-UT, George Wrong Papers, MS Coll. 36, Box 2, file 83

104 Diary of Edmund H. Oliver, 23 September 1909, USA, Jean Murray Papers, MG 61, E. IV. Name and Subject Files, N. Oliver, E.H., 2. Diary; 7 November 1909; 15 January 1912

105 Oliver enjoyed a long career with the Theological College, renamed St Andrew's College in 1924. In the 1920s he was a leader in the movement for Church unification; in 1930 he was selected moderator of the United Church. He died in 1935.

106 Diary of Edmund H. Oliver, 18 September 1909, USA, Jean Murray Papers, MG 61, E. IV. Name and Subject Files, N. Oliver, E.H., 2, Diary; 15 January 1912

107 James Loudon, 'The Universities in Relation to Research,' *Proceedings and Transactions of the Royal Society of Canada*, 2nd series, 8 (1902): Appendix A. See also Norman Nicholson, 'The Evolution of Graduate Studies in the Universities of Ontario, 1841–1971,' PhD thesis, University of Toronto, 1975: 65–71.

108 See Marlene Shore, *The Science of Social Redemption: McGill, the Chicago School, and the Origins of Social Research in Canada* (Toronto: University of Toronto Press, 1987); Ferguson, *Remaking Liberalism*; and Owram, *The Government Generation*.

109 A.B. McKillop, *Matters of Mind: The University in Ontario, 1791–1951* (Toronto: University of Toronto Press, 1994): 292 See also McKillop, 'Science, Authority, the American Empire,' in McKillop, *Contours of Canadian Thought* (Toronto: University of Toronto Press, 1987).

110 USA, President's Office Fonds, Walter Murray, RG1, Series 1, President's Report, 1916–17, 4–5

111 Patricia Jasen, 'The English Canadian Liberal Arts Curriculum: An Intellectual History, 1800–1950,' PhD thesis, University of Manitoba, 1987: 189

112 See McKillop, *Matters of Mind*, 474–5; McKillop, 'Introduction to the Carleton Library Edition,' in *A Disciplined Intelligence: Critical Inquiry and Canadian Thought in the Victorian Era* (Montreal and Kingston: McGill-Queen's University Press, 2001); Michael Gauvreau, 'Baptist Religion and the Social Science of Harold Innis,' *Canadian Historical Review* 76, 2 (1995): 161–204; and Philip Massolin, *Canadian Intellectuals, the Tory Tradition, and the Challenge of Modernity, 1939–1970* (Toronto: University of Toronto Press, 2001).

113 QUA, Reginald Trotter Papers, Box 26, file Correspondence Queen's, D. McArthur

Chapter 3

1 A.L. Burt, Preface, *The Old Province of Quebec* (Minneapolis: University of Minnesota Press; Toronto: Ryerson Press, 1933). See also Burt, 'The Need for a Wider Study of Canadian History,' Department of Extension of the University of Alberta, *Press Bulletin* 9, 5 (23 November 1923): 2.

2 Burt was not the only historian to observe the activity at the Public Archives. Frank Underhill also commented on the Archives as a summer meeting place: 'we have a very agreeable crowd in Ottawa for the summer – Burt of Alberta, Harvey of Manitoba, three or four men from Toronto, Morton and myself from Sask.' Frank Underhill to Monica McQueen, 27 June 1926, National Archives (NA), Frank Underhill Papers, MG 30 D 204, vol. 1, file Monica McQueen 1907–1927. In a letter to a colleague in New York, Reginald Trotter remarked: 'I am delighted to learn that you will be at Ottawa this summer, joining the growing circle of history men who gather there seasonally.' Reginald Trotter to Prof. Bonham, 27 February 1929, Queen's University Archives (QUA), Reginald Trotter Papers, Box 26, file Summer School of Historical Research, 1922–1933. In his biography of Harold Innis Donald Creighton captured something of the summer of 1925 spent at the archives in Ottawa: 'Arthur Morton from Saskatchewan, Chester Martin from Manitoba, Ross Livingston and Duncan McArthur were all in Ottawa for part of that summer. There were picnics, sails on the lake, fishing trips, and visits with the Lowers and Marshalls; and in August Mary Innis arrived, with Donald, now over a year old, and they rented an apartment for the rest of the summer.' Donald Creighton, *Harold Adams Innis: Portrait of a Scholar* (Toronto: University of Toronto Press, 1957): 65. See also Interview with Charles Perry Stacey (1977), NA, R9079.

3 A.L. Burt to Dorrie Burt, 13 July 1926, NA, A.L. Burt Papers, MG 30 D 103, vol. 1, file 1

4 E.R. Adair presented a scathing indictment of Canadian insularity in 1943; he even considered Chester New to be a Canadianist. See E.R. Adair, 'The Canadian Contribution to Historical Science,' *Culture* 4, 1 (March 1943): 63–83.

5 A.L. Burt to Donald Creighton, 26 May 1948, NA, Donald Creighton Papers, MG 31 D 77, vol. 2, file General Correspondence 1948

6 W.A. Kerr to H.M. Tory, 4 May 1918, NA, H.M. Tory Papers, MG 30 D 115, vol. 2, file 5

7 For a list of who was appointed where, when they were appointed, and their qualifications see Donald Wright, 'The Professionalization of History in English Canada to the 1950s,' PhD thesis, University of Ottawa, 1999: 108–114

8 In an autobiographical essay written late in his life, Dalhousie's George Wilson remarked: 'Outside the classroom, I was completely free. There was no demand for publication. If I wished to write that was my own affair. If I did not wish to write the University was quite unconcerned. "Publish or perish" was a threat that had never reached this part of the world.' Although Wilson may not have felt pressure to publish at Dalhousie, that pressure existed at other universities. See George Earle Wilson, *All for Nothing?* (1972): 43. A copy of this self-published memoir is located in The Dalhousie University Archives (DUA), MS-1-Ref.

9 Sir Arthur Currie to Basil Williams, 11 August 1921, McGill University Archives (MUA), RG 2, Box 61, file History: Prof. Basil Williams, 1921–1925

10 Basil Williams left McGill in 1925 to take a position at the University of Edinburgh. He was replaced by E.R. Adair in 1926.

11 Basil Williams, Report on History Department of McGill University, 31 December 1921, MUA, RG 2, Box 61, file Department of History, 1920–1925

12 Basil Williams to Sir Arthur Currie, 10 March 1924, ibid.

13 Arthur Lower, *My First Seventy-five Years* (Toronto: Macmillan, 1967): 130

14 Ralph Flenely to C.P. Stacey, 26 January 1929, University of Toronto Archives (UTA), Charles Stacey Papers, B90-0020, Box 8, file Princeton, Correspondence

15 Lester Pearson, *Mike: The Memoirs of the Rt. Hon. Lester B. Pearson*, vol. 1: *1897–1948* (Toronto: University of Toronto Press, 1972): 51–2

16 John English, *Shadow of Heaven: The Life of Lester Pearson*, vol. 1: *1897–1948* (Toronto: Lester & Orpen Dennys, 1989): 127

17 George Wrong to Frank Underhill, 21 March 1923, NA, Frank Underhill Papers, MG 30 D 204, vol. 1, file G.M. Wrong 1907–1927; emphasis mine

18 A.L. Burt to Dorrie Burt, 9 July 1926 and 25 July 1926, NA, A.L. Burt Papers, MG 30 D 103, vol. 1, file 1

19 C.P. Stacey, *A Date with History* (Ottawa: Deneau, 1982): 15

20 English, *Shadow of Heaven*, vol. 1, 133

21 W.J. Goode, 'Encroachment, Charlatanism and the Emerging Profession: Psychology, Sociology and Medicine,' *American Sociological Review* 25 (1960): 903

22 See Norman Nicholson, 'The Evolution of Graduate Studies in the Universities of Ontario, 1841–1971,' PhD thesis, University of Toronto, 1975, chap. iv,

'Prelude to the PhD' and chap. v, 'Developing the Graduate Curriculum, 1895–1945.'

23 William Duncan Meikle, 'And Gladly Teach: G.M. Wrong and the Department of History at the University of Toronto,' PhD thesis, Michigan State University, 1977: 184

24 Robert Bothwell, *Laying the Foundations: A Century of History at University of Toronto* (Toronto: Department of History, University of Toronto, 1991): 67

25 UTA, University of Toronto Calendar, 1897

26 P.N. Ross, 'The Origins and Development of the PhD at the University of Toronto, 1871–1932,' PhD thesis, Ontario Institute for Studies in Education, 1972: 278

27 J. Playfair McMurrich, Report of the Chairman of the Board of Graduate Studies, UTA, University of Toronto President's Report, 1921–1922

28 George Wrong to Adam Shortt, 29 November 1922, QUA, Adam Shortt Papers, Box 6, file Correspondence July–Dec. 1922

29 Lower, *My First Seventy-five Years,* 130

30 UTA, University of Toronto Calendar, 1924–1925

31 George Wrong to Frank Underhill, 17 March 1924; George Wrong to Frank Underhill, 23 April 1924, NA, Frank Underhill Papers, MG 30 D 204, vol. 1, file G.M. Wrong, 1907–1927

32 UTA, University of Toronto Calendar, 1915–1916

33 President Falconer to A.B. Corey, 6 February 1924, UTA, University Historian, A83–0036, Box 6, file Department of History

34 George Wrong to President Falconer, 19 May 1923, ibid. In his 1927 presidential address to the Canadian Historical Association, Wrong complained about the 'dull chronicle' and the 'mere record of a succession of facts' in historical writing. See George M. Wrong, 'The Historian's Problem,' Canadian Historical Association, *Annual Report* (1927): 6. Similarly, in his review of Innis's monumental work on the fur trade, George Wilson noted that 'it would not injure the fur trade in any way if the facts of its history were presented with somewhat more ease and grace.' Indeed, Wilson continued, 'The present work savours too much of a PhD thesis.' Although he also had a PhD, Wilson continually worried that history had become too technical at the expense of its essentially philosophical nature. See George Wilson, *Dalhousie Review* 10 (1930–1): 575; and 'Why Teach History?' *Queen's Quarterly* 40, 3 (August 1933): 406–13.

35 UTA, University of Toronto Calendar, 1928–1929. J.J. Talman, who completed his PhD in 1930, recounted his experiences in Toronto's graduate program in a lengthy letter to Robin S. Harris. See J.J. Talman to Robin S.

Harris, J.J. Talman Regional Collection, University of Western Ontario (JJTRC-UWO), J.J. Talman Papers, Box 11, file 19

36 See Stanley Brice Frost, *McGill University: For the Advancement of Learning*, vol. II: *1895–1971* (Montreal and Kingston: McGill-Queen's University Press, 1984): 80–2, 177–81.

37 Basil Williams, Report on History Department of McGill University, 31 December 1921, MUA, RG 2, Box 61, file Department of History, 1920–1925

38 Basil Williams to Principal Arthur Currie, 10 March 1924, ibid., file History: Prof. Basil Williams

39 Frank D. Adams to Charles Colby, 21 May 1923; W.T. Waugh to Dean of the Faculty of the Graduate School, n.d.; and Charles Colby, 'Memorandum Re: Thesis on the Imperial Federation Movement with Special Reference to Canada,' 24 May 1923, Stanstead Historical Society Archives, Colby Fonds, C.W. Colby, Series 2, Subseries A, Box 3, file 4.

40 See E.R. Adair, 'The Study of History at McGill University,' *Culture* 2, 1 (March 1941).

41 MUA, McGill University Calendar, 1934–1935

42 Hilda Neatby, *Queen's University*, vol. 1: *1841–1917* (Montreal and Kingston: McGill-Queen's University Press, 1978): 185

43 Frederick W. Gibson, *Queen's University*, vol. 2: *1917–1961* (Montreal and Kingston: McGill-Queen's University Press, 1983): 318

44 Reginald Trotter to Edith Ware, 26 April 1933, QUA, Reginald Trotter Papers, Box 1, file 6

45 'Queen's University Summer School of Historical Research,' 1929, ibid., Box 26, file Summer School of Historical Research, 1922–1933. The Summer School continued to 1939, when it was terminated because of the war in Europe.

46 However, W.N. Sage did not think much of a Toronto PhD. As he explained to Grant, 'my dream is to get an English doctorate, preferably from London, but in the meantime I should be glad to obtain a Toronto PhD.' W.N. Sage to W.L. Grant, 16 October 1921, NA, W.L. Grant Papers, MG 30 D 59, vol. 9, file Sa-Si.

47 Lower, *My First Seventy-five Years*, 131

48 Ibid., 158. See also Arthur Lower, 'Once They Were Alive, Our Betters – My Instructors, George Wrong,' QUA, Arthur Lower Papers, Box 42, B 977.

49 Gerald Graham to W.L. Grant, 12 October 1926, NA, W.L. Grant Papers, MG 30 D 59, vol. 11, file Correspondence Parkin Travelling Scholarship, 1924–1929

50 Gerald Graham, Report of Progress at Harvard, n.d., c. April 1927, copy in ibid.

51 W.L. Grant to Gerald Graham, 5 May 1927, ibid. See also Paul T. Phillips, *Britain's Past in Canada: The Teaching and Writing of British History* (Vancouver: UBC Press, 1989), chap. 6, 'An Interview with Gerald S. Graham.'

52 Stacey, *A Date with History,* 39–40. Toronto's Ralph Flenley advised him to pick a large topic. 'So many of the PhD subjects are too microscopic,' he said. Ralph Flenley to C.P. Stacey, 26 January 1929, UTA, Charles Stacey Papers, B90–0020, Box 8, file Princeton, Correspondence

53 W.S. Wallace, 'Some Vices of Clio,' *Canadian Historical Review* 7, 2 (June 1926): 201–3. Chester Martin agreed. Although he welcomed graduate work, he also wanted history to be alive: 'The task of Canadian history ... can never be completed by the technique of "graduate schools." Professional research may discover the truth, and inspire the teacher, and illumine the textbook. But it requires a coal off the altar to make Canadian history live for the Canadian people. Trevelyan in a moment of exasperation at the mechanics of research once claimed that Sir Walter Scott had done more for British history than all the professional historians.' Martin, 'Fifty Years of Canadian History,' in *Royal Society of Canada: Fifty Years Retrospect* (Ottawa: RSC, 1932): 69. See also Charles W. Colby, 'The Craftsmanship of the Historian,' in Jean Jules Jusserand et al., *The Writing of History* (New York: Charles Scribner's Sons, 1926).

54 W.S. Wallace to President Falconer, 15 August 1928, UTA, University Historian, A83-0036, Box 6, file Department of History

55 Goode, 'Encroachment, Charlatanism and the Emerging Profession,' 903

56 Burton Bledstein, *The Culture of Professionalism: The Middle Class and the Development of Higher Education in America* (New York: W.W. Norton, 1976): 94

57 See QUA, Reginald Trotter Papers, Box 23, file Correspondence, Pritchett, J.P. (i); file Correspondence, Pritchett, J.P. (ii); and file Correspondence, Pritchett, J.P. (iii).

58 John Pritchett to Reginald Trotter, 2 April 1937, ibid., file Correspondence, Pritchett, J.P. (iii)

59 Reginald Trotter to John Pritchett, 5 April 1937, ibid.

60 George Brown to Reginald Trotter, 5 April 1941, ibid., Box 24, file CHR 1934–1950. In the offending review Pritchett had stated that Wrong lacked objectivity because he relied on the premise of superior 'races, classes, political devices, religious creeds [and] economic tendencies.' See John Pritchett, *Mississippi Valley Historical Review* 27, 4 (March 1941): 663–4.

61 Reginald Trotter to George Brown, 10 April 1941, QUA, Reginald Trotter Papers, Box 24, file CHR 1934–1950

62 Reginald Trotter to George Brown, 30 April 1941, ibid.

63 Samuel Mack Eastman to President Klinck, 7 October 1922, University of

British Columbia Archives (UBCA), President's Office Collection, Microfilm Roll 323

64 UBCA, University of British Columbia Calendar, 1927–1928

65 D.C. Harvey, 'The Department of History: University of British Columbia,' 22 July 1931, UBCA, W.N. Sage Papers, Box 4–21

66 University of Manitoba Archives (UMA), University of Manitoba Calendar, 1931–1932. When he was at the University of Manitoba, Chester Martin pleaded for an expanded departmental library for teaching purposes. 'It cannot be too strongly emphasized,' he argued, '… that the subject of history is pursuing precisely the methods employed by scientific departments in their lectures and laboratory work – with books for our apparatus and reagents, with written instead of visual evidence for the basis of reasoning, and with the existence of observation and judgment as the chief requisite for sound work. On a subject like history – unlike a subject in which theory or purely literary taste predominates – a reliance upon lectures alone would be to put a premium upon credulity and to stultify sound historical methods at the very outset.' See Chester Martin, 'Memorandum on Departmental Libraries,' n.d., c. 1920s, copy in Public Archives of Nova Scotia (PANS), D.C. Harvey Papers, MG 1, vol. 441, folder 101

67 UMA, University of Manitoba Calendar, 1933–1934

68 UMA, Annual Reports, Department of History, 1933–1934. In his memoirs, Ernest Sirluck recalled that as a teacher Fieldhouse 'made much of the need to use primary source material.' At the same time, Sirluck questioned Fieldhouse's capacity as a scholar. Ernest Sirluck, *First Generation: An Autobiography* (Toronto: University of Toronto Press, 1996): 41.

69 QUA, Queen's University Calendar, 1935–1936

70 See George Wrong, *Historical Study in the University: An Inaugural Lecture* (Toronto: Bryant Press, 1895).

71 UTA, University of Toronto Calendar, 1919–1920

72 Frank Underhill to Walter Murray, 4 January 1926, NA, Frank Underhill Papers, MG 30 D 204, vol. 1, file W.C. Murray 1907–1927

73 n.t., 2 November 1929, NA, Donald Creighton Papers, MG 30 D 77, vol. 24, file History Dept. 1928–1938

74 'The Course in Modern History,' UTA, A70-0025, Box 9, file 85. The document is dated 5 December 1938.

75 Interview with J.M.S. Careless, 13 July 1983, UTA, B86-0038, Tape I

76 Adair, 'The Study of History at McGill,' 56–7

77 University of Alberta Archives (UAA), University of Alberta Calendar, 1932–1933

78 Canadian Baptist Archives, McMaster University (CBA), Box: McMaster University Annual Reports, 1934–1938, file Reports to Chancellor, 1937–1938
79 George Stanley to John Clarence Webster, 23 January 1944, New Brunswick Museum Archives (NBMA), J.C. Webster Papers, F302
80 University of New Brunswick Archives (UNBA), University of New Brunswick Calendar, 1939–1940
81 A.G. Bailey, 'Origins of the Study of History in UNB,' (1972), UNBA, A.G. Bailey Papers, MS4.7.1.10
82 W.S. Wallace, 'The Establishment of the *Canadian Historical Review*,' *Canadian Historical Review* 26, 1 (March 1945): 101
83 Notes and Comments, *Canadian Historical Review* 1, 1 (March 1920): 1–2. For a history of the *CHR* see Marlene Shore, 'Remember the Future: The *Canadian Historical Review* and the Discipline of History, 1920–95,' *Canadian Historical Review* 76, 3 (September 1995): 410–63; Marlene Shore, ed., *The Contested Past: Reading Canada's History, Selections from the Canadian Historical Review* (Toronto: University of Toronto Press, 2002).
84 See Thomas Haskell, *The Emergence of Professional Social Science: The American Social Science Association and the Nineteenth-Century Crisis of Authority* (Urbana: University of Illinois Press, 1977): 19
85 Lower, *My First Seventy-five Years*, 49
86 For a history of the CHA from its beginnings to the present see Donald Wright, *The Canadian Historical Association: A History* (Ottawa: CHA, 2003).
87 As he explained, the CHA would 'continue the activities of the Landmarks Association, and also attempt to cover for Canada somewhat the same field as the American Historical Association does in the United States.' Lawrence Burpee to Col. Dennis, 27 July 1922, McGill University, Department of Rare Books and Special Collections (MURBSC), W.D. Lighthall Papers, Box 5, file 2. See also Lawrence Burpee, 'Presidential Address,' Canadian Historical Association, *Annual Report* (1923): 9
88 'Constitution,' Canadian Historical Association, *Annual Report* (1922): 20–1
89 'Minutes of the Annual Meeting,' ibid., 18
90 The following is a list of the first executive: Lawrence Burpee, president; W.D. Lighthall, vice-president; C. Marius Barbeau, secretary-treasurer; J.F. Kenney, editor of *Annual Report*. The first council, 1922–5, consisted of Arthur Doughty, Pierre-Georges Roy, George Wrong, Chester Martin, Archibald MacMechan, and Frederic Howay. Burpee, Lighthall, and Howay were non-academics; Wrong, Martin, and MacMechan were academics. Kenney, Doughty, and Roy were archivists, and Barbeau worked at the Victoria Museum in Ottawa.

91 Lawrence Burpee, 'Presidential Address,' Canadian Historical Association, *Annual Report* (1922): 8

92 Alfred Burt to Dorrie Burt, 15 July 1923, NA, A.L. Burt Papers, MG 30 D 103, vol. 1, file 1

93 Lawrence Burpee, 'Co-operation in Historical Research,' *University Magazine* 7, 3 (October 1908): 360. Burpee also understood that history never can achieve finality. Disagreeing with another author's interpretation, he stated that two men, 'studying the same documents from somewhat different angles, can arrive at surprisingly different conclusions.' Lawrence Burpee, 'Professor Morton and La Vérendrye,' *Canadian Historical Review* 10, 1 (March 1929): 55.

94 See Lawrence Burpee, *Pathfinders of the Great Plains: A Chronicle of La Vérendrye and his Sons* (Toronto: Glasgow, Brook, 1915); *Sandford Fleming: Empire Builder* (London: Oxford University Press, 1915); *The Search for the Western Sea: The Story of the Exploration of North-Western America*, 2 vols (Toronto: Macmillan, 1935; originally published 1907).

95 See D. Mack Eastman, 'Report of the Assembly of the International Committee of Historical Sciences,' Canadian Historical Association, *Annual Report* (1929): 17–19; Reginald Trotter, 'Report of the Assembly of the International Committee of Historical Sciences,' Canadian Historical Association, *Annual Report* (1930): 13–15.

96 Burpee took the idea from the relationship between the American Historical Association and the *American Historical Review*. Lawrence Burpee, 'Presidential Address,' Canadian Historical Association, *Annual Report* (1923): 12; 'Minutes of the Annual Meeting at Montreal, May 21–23, 1925,' Canadian Historical Association, *Annual Report* (1925): 16

97 'Minutes of the Annual Meeting at Montreal, May 21–23, 1925,' Canadian Historical Association, *Annual Report* (1925): 17

98 Lawrence Burpee to W.D. Lighthall, 23 April 1923, MURBSC, W.D. Lighthall Papers, Box 5, file 3. Burpee likewise pleaded with Charles Colby to attend: 'Do you think you could put together a short paper for the Canadian Historical Association this year. As this is really the first meeting of the new organization, it is rather important that we should have a good programme, and I should very much appreciate it if you could help us out. It does not matter what the subject is, as long as it falls within the wide boundaries of history, and it is equally unimportant whether you have a formal paper or give us an informal talk.' Lawrence Burpee to Charles Colby, 17 April 1923, Stanstead Historical Society Archives, Colby Fonds, C.W. Colby, Series 2, Subseries A, Box 3, file 2

99 Lawrence Burpee to A.S. Morton, 11 June 1924, University of Saskatchewan

Archives (USA), A.S. Morton Papers, MG 2 I.1 General Corr., 1918–1944. See also C. Marius Barbeau, 'Report of the Secretary-Treasurer,' Canadian Historical Association, *Annual Report* (1925): 11.

100 'Notes and Comments,' *Canadian Historical Review* 8, 2 (June 1927): 94

101 Haskell, *The Emergence of Professional Social Science*, 19

102 Robert Craig Brown, *Robert Laird Borden: A Biography*, Vol. II (Toronto: Macmillan, 1980): 186, 203, 202

103 Robert Laird Borden, Personal Diary, 26 May 1931, NA, Robert Laird Borden Papers, Personal Diary, microfilm no. c-1866

104 Canadian Historical Association, *Annual Report* (1926): 13

105 Aegidius Fauteux to Gustave Lanctôt, 30 mars 1927, NA, Gustave Lanctôt Fonds, MG 30 D 95, vol. 6, file Correspondence-les Archives, l'histoire 1927

106 Reginald Trotter to Norman Fee, 5 April 1935, QUA, Reginald Trotter Papers, Box 24, file Canadian Historical Association, 1934–35

107 Arthur Maheux, 'A Dilemma for Our Culture,' Canadian Historical Association, *Annual Report* (1949): 6

108 Patrice Régimbald, 'La Disciplinarisation de l'histoire au Canada français,' *Revue d'histoire de l'Amérique française* 51, 2 (Autumn 1997): 182

109 W.H. Atherton, 'The Study of Local History,' Canadian Historical Association, *Annual Report* (1924): 46

110 Frank Underhill to Charles Cochrane, 29 May 1926; Charles Cochrane to Frank Underhill, 22 November 1926, NA, Frank Underhill Papers, MG 30 D 204, vol. 1, file C.N. Cochrane, 1907–1927

111 Frank Underhill, 'What, Then, Is the Manitoban? Or This Almost Chosen People,' *Historical Papers* (1970): 38. Actually, Underhill could not present the paper in person; it was read for him.

112 Excerpt from diary of Harold Innis, NA, Donald Creighton Papers, MG 31 D 77, vol. 15, file Harold Adams Innis, 1924–54

113 George Brown to D.C. Harvey, May 1928, PANS, D.C. Harvey Papers, MG 1, vol. 1200, no. 53. See also George Brown, 'Annual Meeting of the Canadian Historical Association,' *Canadian Historical Review* 9, 2 (June 1928): 101

114 Frank Underhill to Fred Landon, 8 May 1929, JJTRC-UWO, J.J. Talman Papers, Box 11, file 19

115 For an amusing account of contemporary annual meetings of the American Historical Association see Theodore S. Hamerow, *Reflections of History and Historians* (Madison: University of Wisconsin Press, 1987): 72–5.

116 Emile Durkheim, *Professional Ethics and Civic Morals* (Glencoe, Ill.: Free Press, 1958): 25

117 Lower, *My First Seventy-five Years*, 181

118 Susan Mann Trofimenkoff, 'Gossip in History,' *Historical Papers* (1985): 3

119 See Jörg R. Bergman, *Discreet Indiscretions: The Social Organization of Gossip* (New York: Aldine de Gruyter, 1993).

120 Donald Creighton, CBC Radio, Obituary of Harold Innis, 28 November 1952, NA, Donald Creighton Papers, MG 31 D 77, vol. 15, file Harold Adams Innis, 1924–1954. In a 1978 appraisal of Innis's career, Creighton recalled an Innis visit to his Muskoka cottage and the 'endless academic gossip.' Donald Creighton, 'Harold Adams Innis: A Special and Unique Brilliance,' in Donald Creighton, *The Passionate Observer: Selected Writings* (Toronto: McClelland and Stewart, 1980): 147.

121 Michael Bliss, *Right Honourable Men: The Descent of Canadian Politics from Macdonald to Mulroney* (Toronto: Harper Collins, 1994): 123

122 Charles Cochrane to Frank Underhill, 11 September 1913, NA, Frank Underhill Papers, MG 30 D 204, vol. 1, file C.N. Cochrane, 1907–1927

123 Chester Martin to A.S. Morton, 2 May 1926, USA, A.S. Morton Papers, MG 2 S I.1 Subject Files, 9, Other Universities, 1921–1943

124 Harold Innis to Arthur Lower, 13 May 1931, QUA, Arthur Lower Papers, Box 7, A 127

125 Bartlet Brebner to C.P. Stacey, 27 May 1941, UTA, Charles Stacey Papers, B90–0020, Box 42, file Carnegie Endowment for International Peace, 1934–46; 1971

126 George Glazebrook to Donald Creighton, 19 December 1940, NA, Donald Creighton Papers, MG 31 D 77, vol. 1, file General Correspondence 1941

127 A.L. Burt to Dorrie Burt, 21 June 1927, NA, A.L. Burt Papers, MG 30 D 103, vol. 1 file 1

128 Fred Landon to Frank Underhill, 25 September 1950, NA, Frank Underhill Papers, MG 30 D 204, vol. 5, file Fred Landon, 1928–1956

129 A.L. Burt to Dorrie Burt, 2 July 1923, NA, A.L. Burt Papers, MG 30 D 103, vol. 1, file 1

130 Harold Innis to Arthur Lower, 20 March 1931, QUA, Arthur Lower Papers, Box 7, A 127. For the correspondence between John Clarence Webster, George Brown

131 Harold Innis to Arthur Lower, 13 May 1931, ibid. For the correspondence between John Clarence Webster, George Brown, and the president of Dalhousie dated November 1930 to April 1931 see NBMA, J.C. Webster Papers, F263

132 A.L. Burt to A.S. Morton, 22 February 1935; A.S. Morton to A.L. Burt, 1 March 1935, USA, A.S. Morton Papers, MG 2, I.11 Personal-General, 1908–1946

133 Arthur Lower to R.O. MacFarlane, 6 June 1938, QUA, Arthur Lower Papers, Box 1, file A 10

134 R.O. MacFarlane to Arthur Lower, 7 June 1938, ibid.

135 See Arthur Lower to R.O. MacFarlane, 11 June 1938, ibid.

136 Quotation in Arthur Lower to W.A. Mackintosh, 28 June 1938, ibid.

137 Harold Innis to Arthur Lower, n.d., ibid., Box 1, file A 11

138 W.A. Mackintosh to Arthur Lower, 2 July 1938, ibid. John Pritchett, a doctoral candidate at Queen's, complained about the gossiping among historians at the Public Archives: 'The petty jealousies that exist between a number of the Canadian history professors are surprising and disgusting to me. Nasty and dirty insinuations about this man and that man are not at all uncommon among some men here. Inferiority and superiority complexes appear to be basic causes.' John Pritchett to Reginald Trotter, 11 July 1928, QUA, Reginald Trotter Papers, Box 23, file Correspondence, Pritchett, J.P. (i)

139 Arthur Lower to H.N. Fieldhouse, 28 June 1938, ibid.

140 Ronald Longley, n.d., UTA, University of Toronto Press, CHR Files, A86–0044, Box 5, file CHR, 25th Anniversary Letters, no. 1

141 Fred Soward, 19 October 1944, ibid.

142 Sherwood Fox, Fred Landon, J.J. Talman, and M.A. Garland, 6 November 1944, ibid. Fred Landon had requested in 1922 that the *CHR* contain a 'News' section, which would keep historians abreast the comings and goings of other historians. The editor, W.S. Wallace, agreed that such a section would be desirable, but that the *CHR* lacked the necessary 'machinery' for gathering information. See W.S. Wallace to Fred Landon, 13 January 1922, JJTRT-UWO, Fred Landon Papers, Box 4208, file 4. For the editors' summary and analysis of the survey results see George Brown and Donald Creighton, 'Canadian History in Retrospect and Prospect,' *Canadian Historical Review* 25, 4 (December 1944): 357–75.

143 From 1926 to 1932 the Public Archives paid for the printing costs of the CHA *Annual Report.*

144 Minutes of the Council Meeting, 27 October 1934, NA, Canadian Historical Association, MG 28 I 4, vol. 1, Minutes 1924–43

145 Fee had requested that Trotter 'destroy' this letter. Norman Fee to Reginald Trotter, 5 June 1935, QUA, Reginald Trotter Papers, Box 24, file Canadian Historical Association, 1934–35

146 Bartlet Brebner to James Shotwell, 10 November 1939, Columbia University, Rare Book and Manuscript Library, James Shotwell Papers, Box 284, file Can-American Relations, J.B. Brebner

147 Minutes of the Council Meeting, 4 November 1939, NA, Canadian Historical Association, MG 28 I 4, vol. 1, Minutes 1924–1943

148 Reginald Trotter to Bartlet Brebner, 30 November 1939, QUA, Reginald Trotter Papers, Box 24, file Canadian Historical Association, 1939–1940

149 Report of Committee appointed by the President under instructions from the Council to report on proposals advanced by the Royal Society of Canada for the closer affiliation between that Society and the Canadian Historical Association, 22 May 1940, NA, Canadian Historical Association, MG 28 I 4, vol. 1, Minutes 1924–1943

150 George Wrong, 'History in Canadian Secondary Schools,' American Historical Association, *Annual Report* (1898): 551–5. In his 1895 inaugural lecture at the University of Toronto, Wrong reported that, 'on high authority,' there was no other subject so 'ill-taught in our schools' as history. See Wrong, *Historical Study in the University,* 8.

151 On historians and the debate over history teaching see Ken Osborne, '"Our History Syllabus Has Us Gasping": History in Canadian Schools – Past, Present, and Future,' *Canadian Historical Review* 81, 3 (September 2000): 404–35.

152 Quotation in W.D. LeSueur, 'The Teaching of History,' 1912; reprinted in A.B. McKillop, ed., *A Critical Spirit: The Thought of William Dawson LeSueur* (Toronto: McClelland and Stewart, 1977): 283.

153 George Wrong to Frank Underhill, 15 September 1921, NA, Frank Underhill Papers, MG 30 D 204, vol. 1, file G.M. Wrong 1907–1927

154 See Canadian Historical Association, *Annual Report* (1923): 20

155 Duncan McArthur, 'The Teaching of Canadian History,' Ontario Historical Society, *Papers and Records* 21 (1924): 206

156 'Rather Startling Commentary as to History Teaching,' *Ottawa Citizen,* 15 June 1929, 5

157 Arthur Lower, *Colony to Nation: A History of Canada* (Toronto: Longmans, Green, 1946): x. In 1960 C.P. Stacey commented on how poorly the schools taught history; the end result was that history had failed to have the desired effect on national life. C.P. Stacey, 'The Historian's Craft,' Speech before the Library and History Sections of the OEA [Ontario Education Association], 20 April 1960, UTA, Charles Stacey Papers, B90-0020, Box 45, file 1960-040-20

158 Canadian Historical Association, *Annual Report* (1923): 21; (1926): 15

159 Canadian Historical Association, *Annual Report* (1924): 11. See Lawrence Burpee, *An Historical Atlas of Canada* (Toronto: Thomas Nelson and Sons, 1927).

160 Canadian Historical Association, *Annual Report* (Ottawa: CHA 1937): 50

161 George Brown, 25 March 1937, UTA, University of Toronto Press, CHR Files, A86-0044, Box 5, file Durham Report June CHR

162 Minutes of Council Meeting, 4 November 1939, NA, Canadian Historical Association, MG 28 I 4 vol. 1, Minutes 1924–1943

163 Minutes of Council Meeting, 23 May 1946, ibid., vol. 2, Minutes 1944–1953

164 Minutes of Council Meeting, 20 October 1951, ibid.

165 C.P. Stacey to Morden Long, 6 January 1954, ibid., vol. 8, 26

166 R.A. Preston to David Farr, 1 February 1954, ibid.

167 Bledstein, *The Culture of Professionalism*, 100

168 Meikle, 'And Gladly Teach,' appendix E.

169 Forty years later, Wrong recalled the writing of this particular book. 'Messrs. Appleton of New York asked me to write a textbook on the history of England. During four years I spent what time I could on "The British Nation," which came out in 1903 [sic]. I took great care with the illustrations and in my judgment it is a very good piece of work. It was used for some years in both the United States and Canada. A textbook, however, rarely lasts for more than about ten years.' See George Wrong, unpublished document, c. 1940s, UTA, University of Toronto Press, CHR Files, A86-0044, Box 5, file CHR, 25th Anniversary Letters, no. 2

170 Anxious to see his book approved for use in New Brunswick, Brown arranged for his publisher to send a copy to the prominent New Brunswicker and past president of the Canadian Historical Association, John Clarence Webster, in the hope that he might have some influence. See George Brown to John Clarence Webster, 20 May 1945, NBMA, J.C. Webster Papers, F296

171 Lower, *My First Seventy-five Years*, 358

172 A.L. Burt to C.K. Burt, 11 April 1937, NA, A.L. Burt Papers, MG 30 D 103, vol. 4, file 9. On Burt's textbooks see, 'Professor A.L. Burt's Publications with W.J. Gage Limited,' 12 July 1971, UAA, Lewis H. Thomas Collection, Acc. no. 75-42, Box 1, file 4.

173 This figure is taken from Meikle, 'And Gladly Teach,' appendix E

174 See financial statements in Thomas Fisher Rare Book Room, University of Toronto, W.S. Wallace Papers, MS Coll. 31, Box 24, file Accounts with Publishers

175 Magali Sarfatti Larson, *The Rise of Professionalism: A Sociological Analysis* (Berkeley: University of California Press, 1977): xvii

176 Lower, *My First Seventy-five Years*, 131

Chapter 4

1 W.J. Eccles, Review of *Company of Adventurers*, by Peter C. Newman, *Canadian Historical Review* 67, 3 (September 1986): 399–400

2 Quotation in Jennifer Brown, 'Newman's *Company of Adventurers* in Two Soli-

tudes: A Look at Reviews and Responses,' *Canadian Historical Review* 67, 4 (December 1986): 562

3 Ibid., 563, 570

4 Peter C. Newman, 'Response by Peter C. Newman to Jennifer Brown,' ibid., 573, 577, 578

5 Thomas Gieryn, 'Boundary-Work and the Demarcation of Science from Non-Science: Strains and Interests in Professional Ideologies of Scientists,' *American Sociological Review* 48 (December 1983): 781–2

6 Robert Berkhofer has argued: 'In setting boundaries between their own and other disciplines, historians carefully divide the nature of proper history from the similar or contiguous subject matter of other disciplines, such as historical sociology and philosophy of history, in order to set disciplinary bounds. Likewise, most historians distinguish between professional histories and lay histories, between formal and folk histories, between historical sources, source books, and "proper" histories as such to promote the authority of the profession and themselves.' Robert F. Berkhofer, *Beyond the Great Story: History as Text and Discourse* (Cambridge: Harvard University Press, 1995): 228

7 Lady Tweedsmuir, 'The Amateur Historian,' *Canadian Historical Review* 20, 1 (March 1939): 1

8 See David Regéczi, 'Stop Telling Stories: The Splintering of History into Academic and Non-Academic Discourses in the United States from 1870,' MA thesis, Queen's University, 1999; and Regéczi, 'Tired Conventions: A Historical and Rhetorical Analysis of the Academic Historian's Relationship with Non-Academic History,' paper presented to the annual meeting of the Canadian Historical Association, 2000.

9 George Wrong, 'The Beginnings of Historical Criticism in Canada: A Retrospect, 1896–1936,' *Canadian Historical Review* 17, 1 (March 1936): 3

10 George Wrong, *Historical Study in the University: An Inaugural Lecture* (Toronto: Bryant Press, 1895): 6

11 Charles Colby, 'The Teaching of History' n.d., Stanstead Historical Society Archives, Colby Fonds, C.W. Colby, Series 2, Subseries C, Box 5, file 73

12 Adam Shortt, 'The Aims of the Canadian Political Science Association,' *Proceedings, Canadian Political Science Association* (1913): 10

13 Mack Eastman to W.L. Grant, 29 May 1921, National Archives (NA), W.L. Grant Papers, MG 30 D 59, vol. 3, file E. See also letters from W.N. Sage to W.L. Grant, ibid., vol. 9, file Sa-Si

14 See Charles W. Humphries, 'The Banning of a Book in British Columbia,' *BC Studies* 1, 1 (Winter 1968–9): 1–12.

15 Mack Eastman, 'Teachers and Textbooks,' address delivered at Teachers'

Convention, King Edward High School, Easter 1922, University of British Columbia Archives (UBCA), S. Mack Eastman Papers, Box 1, file 17

16 Reginald Trotter, 'The Character of Clio,' address delivered at the Saturday Club, 13 October 1928, Queen's University Archives (QUA), Reginald Trotter Papers, Box 27, file The Character of Clio, Saturday Club, 1928

17 A.G. Bailey, 'Dramatic Incidents in New Brunswick's History and the Historical Solution of our Problems,' unrevised notes for address to Saint John Vocational School, 1937, University of New Brunswick Archives (UNBA), A.G. Bailey Papers, Series 3, Case 89, file 1

18 Notes and Comments, *Canadian Historical Review* 1, 2 (June 1920): 134–5. The author is not identified; however, it was more likely than not W.S. Wallace, the managing editor.

19 A.S. Morton, 'La Vérendrye: Commandant, Fur-Trader, and Explorer,' *Canadian Historical Review* 9, 4 (December 1928): 1

20 Lawrence J. Burpee, 'Professor Morton and La Vérendrye,' *Canadian Historical Review* 10, 1 (March 1929): 54

21 Morton, 'La Vérendrye,' 1

22 Carl Berger included A.S. Morton among an earlier generation of fact finders and footnote chasers 'for whom history was an avocation.' Making a gentle jab, Berger declared that 'Morton excelled in establishing the precise locations of trading posts in the West.' Carl Berger, *Honour and the Search for Influence: A History of the Royal Society of Canada* (Toronto: University of Toronto Press, 1996): 30. Yet Morton considered himself a professional historian; history was his vocation. In 1941 he received the highest award available to Canadian historians, the J.B. Tyrrell Gold Medal from the Royal Society of Canada. In no uncertain terms, W.J. Eccles referred to Morton as 'that francophobe Presbyterian historian' (Eccles, Review of *Company of Adventurers*). Morton might have been a francophobe. The point is not that he achieved a dispassionate objectivity, but that he presented himself as a dispassionate, objective, professional historian. For a consideration of Morton's career, see Donald Wright, 'History at the University of Saskatchewan from E.H. Oliver to Hilda Neatby,' *Essays: University of Saskatchewan* 1, 1 (1999): 1–47.

23 For example, see William Wood, *The Fight for Canada* (Toronto: Musson, 1906).

24 David Ross McCord to W.D. Lighthall, 13 December 1909, NA, W.D. Lighthall Papers, MG 29 D 93, vol. 1, file 28

25 W.T. Waugh, *James Wolfe: Man and Soldier* (Montreal and New York: Louis Carrier, 1928): 25, 116

26 See Donald Wright, 'Remembering War in Imperial Canada: David Ross

McCord and the McCord National Museum' *Fontanus: from the Collections of McGill* 9 (1996): 97–104.

27 Waugh, *James Wolfe*, 121, 255

28 George Wrong, Review of *James Wolfe: Man and Soldier*, by W.T. Waugh, *Canadian Historical Review* 9, 4 (December 1928): 341–5

29 George Brown to Aegidius Fauteux, 7 June 1932, University of Toronto Archives (UTA), University of Toronto Press, CHR Files, A86-0044, Box 5, file The Canadian Historical Association and the Canadian Historical Review

30 E.R. Adair, 'The Military Reputation of Major-General James Wolfe,' Canadian Historical Association, *Annual Report* (1936): 31

31 'Gen. Wolfe No Hero Speaker Declares,' *Montreal Gazette*, 18 November 1938

32 Barbara J. Whitely, 'Professor Adair: The Iconoclast,' in E.A. Collard, ed., *The McGill You Knew: An Anthology of Memories, 1920–1960* (Don Mills, Ont.: Longman, 1975): 74

33 E.R. Adair, 'Dollard des Ormeaux and the Fight at the Long Sault,' *Canadian Historical Review* 13, 2 (June 1932): 128–38. For a reconstruction of the battle from an Amerindian perspective see John Dickinson, 'Annaotaha and Dollard Seen from the Other Side of the Palisade,' in Terry Crowley, ed., *Clio's Craft: A Primer of Historical Methods* (Toronto: Copp Clark Pitman, 1988).

34 Aegidius Fauteux to George Brown, 10 May 1932, UTA, University of Toronto Press, CHR Files, A86-0044, Box 5, file The Canadian Historical Association and the Canadian Historical Review. Brown agreed that Adair could be very outspoken and that he was capable of too much 'debunking.' As editor, he had toned down Adair's manuscript and invited Gustave Lanctôt to write a response. George Brown to Aegidius Fauteux, 13 May 1932 and 7 June 1932, ibid. See Gustave Lanctôt, 'Was Dollard the Saviour of New France?' *Canadian Historical Review* 13, 2 (June 1932): 138–46.

35 For an expanded discussion of Adair on Dollard see Patrice Groulx, *Pièges de la mémoire : Dollard des Ormeaux, les Amérindiens et nous* (Hull, Que.: Vents d'Ouest, 1998): 249–56; Colin Coates and Cecilia Morgan, *Heroines and History: Representations of Madeleine de Verchères and Laura Secord* (Toronto: University of Toronto Press, 2002): 97–8.

36 W. Stewart Wallace, *The Story of Laura Secord: A Study in Historical Evidence* (Toronto: Macmillan, 1932): 3, 4, 17, 25, 25

37 Coates and Morgan, *Heroines and History*, 159

38 Ibid., 160

39 'Historical Question Debated,' *Saturday Night* 47, 10 (16 January 1932): 1. Charlesworth clearly sided with Wallace. In a private letter to Wallace he offered the following: 'As a matter of fact I was trying to vindicate you by

irony in the Laura Secord editorial. The most amusing by-product of the controversy relates to the pretensions of the Fitzgibbon family a shabby genteel outfit who for decades have been exploiting Grandfather's military reputation. It now appears that he and Laura were equally out of it.' Hector Charlesworth, Managing Editor, to W.S. Wallace, 14 January 1932, Thomas Fisher Rare Book Room, University of Toronto (TFRBR-UT), W.S. Wallace Papers, MC 31, Box 37, file Correspondence 1932, A–J.

40 W.S. Wallace to G.F. Rogers, 14 January 1932, ibid., Box 37, file Correspondence 1932, P–Z

41 See also Rosemary Jann, 'From Amateur to Professional: The Case of the Oxbridge Historians,' *Journal of British Studies* 22, 2 (Spring 1983): 122.

42 Waugh, *James Wolfe*, 12

43 In a 1931 article in the *CHR* 'local' and 'general' were also used to mean amateur and professional. See 'Canadian Historical Societies,' *Canadian Historical Review* 12, 4 (December 1931): 356–63.

44 D.C. Harvey, 'The Importance of Local History in the Writing of General History,' *Canadian Historical Review* 13, 3 (September 1932): 244–51. For a similar depiction of the genealogist, the antiquarian, and the professional historian in the Maritimes, see John Bartlet Brebner, 'Uses and Abuses of History,' *Dalhousie Review* 24 (1944–5): 34–7.

45 J.J. Talman, 'History Must Be More Than An Adornment,' n.d., c. 1940s, J.J. Talman Regional Collection, University of Western Ontario, J.J. Talman Papers, Box 11, file 8

46 C.P. Stacey to George Stanley, 30 November 1951, UTA, Charles Stacey Papers, B91–0013, Box 3, file CHA 1946–1952

47 Charles Stacey to Jean Bruchési, 22 December 1951, ibid.

48 Hilda Neatby, 'The Canadian Historical Association, The Canadian Historical Review, and Local History: A Symposium,' Canadian Historical Association, *Annual Report* (1952): 46–50

49 Jim Conacher, ibid., 50–3. The *CHR* began its Notes on Historical Societies in 1932.

50 R.A. Preston, ibid., 53–6. See also Richard Preston, 'Is Local History Really History?' *Saskatchewan History* 10, 3 (1957): 97–103. Preston acknowledged the weakness of much local history, but he urged his colleagues to take local history seriously and to assist local historians when and where possible. Local history, he believed, was essential to the health and growth of civic pride and, ultimately, citizenship.

51 Lewis Thomas, 'The Canadian Historical Association, The Canadian Historical Review, and Local History: A Symposium,' Canadian Historical Association, *Annual Report* (1952): 56–9

52 Linda Ambrose, 'Ontario Women's Institutes and the Work of Local History,' in Boutilier and Prentice, eds., *Creating Historical Memory*, 89
53 Neatby, 'Symposium,' 50
54 Charles Stacey, 'Symposium,' 65
55 See Margaret Ormsby, 'Report of the Local History Section,' Canadian Historical Association, *Annual Report* (1960): 120–2.
56 Arthur Lower to Chester New, 15 December 1936, QUA, Arthur Lower Papers, Box 1, file A8
57 Robert Bothwell, *Laying the Foundation: A Century of History at University of Toronto* (Toronto: Department of History, University of Toronto, 1991): 48. However, George Wrong thought Jewish history should be a topic of research for MA students. He told Adam Shortt that he wanted to increase the research component of the MA degree and that, among other topics, 'some work might be done on the Jew in both Toronto and Montreal.' George Wrong to Adam Shortt, 29 November 1922, QUA, Adam Shortt Papers, Box 6, file Correspondence July–December 1922.
58 Frank Underhill to Ontario Selection Committee, Rhodes Scholarship Trust, 23 November 1938, NA, Frank Underhill Papers, MG 30 D 204, vol. 7, file Rhodes Scholarship Trust, 1928–1956
59 Frank Underhill to Herbert Heaton, 25 January 1939, ibid., file Albert Rose, 1928–1956
60 In 1945 McGill sought candidates for the Kingsford Chair in History. As part of the search process it solicited names from scholars in England. One responded with two names, one a German, the other a Jew. Of the Jew he said, 'The only possible "out" about him, which, however, may not be an objection to you, is that he is a Jew. But he has none of the undesirable characteristics which people sometime associate with his race.' [Name deleted] to Principal Cyril James, 18 June 1945, McGill University Archives (MUA), RG 2, Container 690, file History Selection Committee, Kingsford Chair. Principal James responded that, all things being equal, 'we should probably like to appoint a Protestant from North America or Great Britain.' Principal Cyril James to [name deleted], 6 July 1945, ibid.
61 Author's interview with Jill Ker Conway, Boston, Mass., 9 June 1998. See also Kenneth McNaught, *Conscience and History: A Memoir* (Toronto: University of Toronto Press, 1999): 144.
62 Jean Burnet, 'Minorities I Have Belonged To,' *Canadian Ethnic Studies* 13, 1 (1981): 30
63 Arthur Lower to Gordon Rothney, 1 May 1947, QUA, Arthur Lower Papers, Box 26, file B691

64 Ernest Sirluck, *First Generation: An Autobiography* (Toronto: University of Toronto Press, 1996): 42

65 W.L. Grant to O.D. Skelton, 2 February 1934, NA, W.L. Grant Papers, MG 30 D 59, vol. 9, file Skelton, O.D.

66 Frank Underhill to Arthur Lower, 28 February 1939, QUA, Arthur Lower Papers, Box 1, file A-12. The American historian C.C. Tansill did not want Gelber to review his book in the *Canadian Historical Review*. As he told George Brown, 'in the United States we regard Lionel Gelber as a bumptious Jew with much talk but with little real learning.' George Brown refused to consider Tansill's request and he forwarded his letter to the American Historical Association. C.C. Tansill to George Brown, 7 January 1944, copy in Columbia University, Rare Book and Manuscript Library, John Bartlet Brebner Papers, Box 10, file Bartlet, John Brebner.

67 Speculating about anti-Semitism and the historical profession in the United States in the interwar years, Peter Novick writes: 'The number of Jews within the profession who were discriminated against in this period was probably smaller than the number of those who, knowing what they were in for, stayed out of it.' Peter Novick, *That Noble Dream: The 'Objectivity' Question and the American Historical Profession* (Cambridge: Cambridge University Press, 1988): 173, 367

Chapter 5

1 George Wrong, 'A College for Women,' *University of Toronto Monthly* 10, 1 (November 1909): 7

2 George Wrong, *The Rise and Fall of New France*, Vol. 1 (Toronto: Macmillan, 1928): 226

3 Beverly Boutilier and Alison Prentice also refer to the masculinization of history. See their 'Introduction: Locating Women in the Work of History,' in Boutilier and Prentice, eds, *Creating Historical Memory: English-Canadian Women and the Work of History* (Vancouver: UBC Press, 1997).

4 Lorraine Code, *What Can She Know? Feminist Theory and the Construction of Knowledge* (Ithaca, N.Y.: Cornell University Press, 1991): xi; emphasis in original

5 Ibid., 181; emphasis in original. See also Elizabeth Fee, 'Women's Nature and Scientific Objectivity,' in M. Lowe and R. Hubbard, eds, *Women's Nature: Rationalizations of Inequality* (New York: Pergamon Press, 1981); Genevieve Lloyd, *The Man of Reason: 'Male' and 'Female' in Western Philosophy* (Minneapolis: University of Minnesota Press, 1984); Bonnie Smith, 'Gender, Objectivity, and the Rise of Scientific History,' in Wolfgang Natter, Theodore R. Schatzki,

and John Paul Jones, eds, *Objectivity and Its Other* (New York: Guildford Press, 1995); and E. Doyle McCarthy, *Knowledge as Culture: The New Sociology of Knowledge* (London: Routledge, 1996).

6 Feminist scholars have documented the tension between the socially constructed categories of 'woman' and 'professional.' See Nancy Cott, *The Grounding of Modern Feminism* (New Haven, Conn.: Yale University Press, 1987), chap. 7, 'Professionalism and Feminism'; Anne Witz, *Professions and Patriarchy* (London: Routledge, 1992); and Tracey Adams, *A Dentist and a Gentleman: Gender and the Rise of Dentistry in Ontario* (Toronto: University of Toronto Press, 2000). For the tension between 'woman' and 'professional scientist' see Margaret W. Rossiter, *Woman Scientists in America: Struggles and Strategies to 1940* (Baltimore: Johns Hopkins University Press, 1982), chap. 4, 'A Manly Profession.'

7 On women in higher education in English Canada see Veronica Strong-Boag, *The New Day Recalled: Lives of Girls and Women in English Canada, 1919– 1939* (Toronto: Copp Clark Pitman, 1988): 23–6; the essays on women in Paul Axelrod and John G. Reid, eds, *Youth, University and Canadian Society: Essays in the Social History of Higher Education* (Montreal and Kingston: McGill-Queen's University Press, 1989); Paul Axelrod, *Making a Middle Class: Student Life in English Canada during the Thirties* (Montreal and Kingston: McGill-Queen's University Press, 1990); and A.B. McKillop, *Matters of Mind: The University in Ontario, 1791–1951* (Toronto: Ontario Historical Studies Series, University of Toronto Press, 1994), 124–46, 420–37. On women in the professoriate see Judith Fingard, 'Gender and Inequality at Dalhousie: Faculty Women before 1950,' *Dalhousie Review* 64, 4 (Winter 1984–5): 687–703; Alison Prentice, 'Bluestockings, Feminists, or Women Workers? A Preliminary Look at Women's Employment at the University of Toronto,' *Journal of the Canadian Historical Association* 2 (1991): 231–61; and Mary Kinnear, *In Subordination: Professional Women in Manitoba, 1870–1970* (Montreal and Kingston: McGill-Queen's University Press, 1995), chap. 2, 'Discourse by Default: Women University Teachers.'

8 On women in history in English Canada see Boutilier and Prentice, *Creating Historical Memory*. In their very useful introduction, Boutilier and Prentice place the experiences of women in history in English Canada in the larger contexts of women in history in Europe and the United States. See also Michael Hayden, ed., *So Much to Do, So Little Time: The Writings of Hilda Neatby* (Vancouver: University of British Columbia Press, 1983); and Chad Reimer, 'The Making of British Columbia History: Historical Writing and Institutions, 1784–1958,' PhD thesis, York University, 1995, chap. 8, 'Margaret Ormsby and a First Generation of British Columbia Historians.' For informa-

tion on women in history in the United States see Joan Wallach Scott, *Gender and the Politics of History* (New York: Columbia University Press, 1988), chap. 9, 'American Women Historians, 1884–1984'; and Jacqueline Goggin, 'Challenging Sexual Discrimination in the Historical Profession: Women Historians and the American Historical Association, 1890–1940,' *American Historical Review* 97, 3 (June 1992): 769–802.

9 Alison Prentice, 'Laying Siege to the History Professoriate,' in Boutilier and Prentice, *Creating Historical Memory*.

10 Ibid., 203–4. See also Sara Z. Burke, *Seeking the Highest Good: Social Service and Gender at the University of Toronto, 1888–1937* (Toronto: University of Toronto Press 1996): 80.

11 Lloyd, *The Man of Reason*, 104

12 Vicki Schultz, 'Sex Is the Least of It,' *The Nation*, 25 May 1998: 11

13 Vicki Schultz, 'Reconceptualizing Sexual Harassment,' *Yale Law Journal* 107, 6 (April 1998): 1687, 1691

14 Prentice, 'Laying Siege,' 200. Prentice studied UBC, Saskatchewan, Toronto, Queen's, McGill, and Dalhousie.

15 R. Douglas Francis, *Frank H. Underhill: Intellectual Provocateur* (Toronto: University of Toronto Press, 1986): 36

16 Quotation in Axelrod, *Making a Middle Class*, 91

17 Arthur Lower, *My First Seventy-five Years* (Toronto: Macmillan, 1967): 327

18 Robert Bothwell, *Laying the Foundation: A Century History at University of Toronto* (Toronto: University of Toronto, Department of History, 1991): 86

19 A.L. Burt to Dorrie Burt, 12 March 1919, National Archives (NA), A.L. Burt Papers, MG 30 D 103, vol. 4, file 2

20 A.L. Burt to E. Boyd, 21 November 1949, University of Alberta Archives (UAA), History Club, Acc. no. 75-42, Box 1, file 3

21 Author's interview with Sylvia Van Kirk, St John's, Newfoundland, 5 June 1997. See also Sylvia Van Kirk, 'Ladies in the History Club,' 22 March 1969, UAA, History Club, Acc. no. 74-153, item 7.

22 McGill University Archives (MUA), *Old McGill*, 1924, 1925, 1921

23 Frank Underhill to Secretary, J.S. McLean Scholarship Committee, 30 March 1937, NA, Frank Underhill Papers, MG 30 D 204, vol. 7, file S-General no. 4

24 In 1939 Toronto students created a second history club open to both men and women, the Modern History Club. However, it did not enjoy the same status as the older Historical Club.

25 Lower, *My First Seventy-five Years*, 48

26 A.L. Burt to E. Boyd, 21 November 1949, UAA, History Club, Acc. no. 75-42, Box 1, file 3

27 Bothwell, *Laying the Foundation*, 54

28 Interview with J.M.S. Careless, 13 July 1983, University of Toronto Archives (UTA), B86-0038, Tape II

29 Kenneth McNaught, *Conscience and History: A Memoir* (Toronto: University of Toronto Press, 1999): 28

30 C.P. Stacey, *A Date with History* (Ottawa: Deneau, 1982): 26

31 Lower, *My First Seventy-five Years*, 53

32 That message could take the form of sexist jokes. H.N. Fieldhouse was reputed to have cracked such jokes in his class. In his memoirs, H.S. Ferns recalls that in a lecture on some English aristocratic politician Fieldhouse remarked, 'And he admired and appreciated equally the beautiful limbs of horses and women.' At this point, 'Fieldhouse paused momentarily and without the suggestion of a leer or of any feeling at all he allowed his eyes to scan the form of the most beautiful girl in the class sitting with her wonderfully attractive legs crossed in the front row. She blushed, and Fieldhouse went on as coolly as ever.' See H.S. Ferns, *Reading from Left to Right: One Man's Political History* (Toronto: University of Toronto Press, 1983): 37.

33 W.L. Grant to Marian Buck, 11 November 1925, NA, W.L. Grant Papers, MG 30 D 59, vol. 11, file Correspondence Parkin Traveling Scholarship, 1924–1929. Marian Buck provided the money for the scholarship.

34 Frank Underhill to Margaret Cameron, University Women's Federation, 29 January 1937, NA, Frank Underhill Papers, MG 30 D 204, vol. 6, file Margaret MacLaren

35 Prentice, 'Laying Siege,' 201–2

36 W.J. Eccles, 'Forty Years Back,' *William and Mary Quarterly* 41, 3 (July 1984): 411

37 This quotation is taken from a summary of the candidates prepared for jury member W.S. Wallace. Thomas Fisher Rare Book Room, University of Toronto, W.S. Wallace Papers, MC 31, Box 32, file Royal Society, Section II (1936)

38 A.L. Burt to Dorrie Burt, 23 October 1918, NA, A.L. Burt Papers, MG 30 D 103, vol. 4, file 1

39 A.L. Burt to Dorrie Burt, 25 December 1918 and 27 July 1926, ibid., vol. 1, file 1

40 A.L. Burt to Frank Underhill, 28 November 1922, NA, Frank Underhill Papers, MG 30 D 204, vol. 1, file A.L. Burt, 1907–27. George Wrong also wrote well of Dunham: 'Miss Dunham has remarkable industry and a spirit of thoroughness which guarantees that her work will be of high character. She has an original mind and the promise of an admirable literary style.' George Wrong, 28 January 1924, UTA, Department of History, A70-0025, Box 8, file 52

41 Lewis Thomas, *The Renaissance of Canadian History: A Biography of A.L. Burt* (Toronto: University of Toronto Press 1975): 14

42 Katharine MacNaughton to Alfred Bailey, 3 June 1943, University of New Brunswick Archives (UNBA), A.G. Bailey Papers, RG 80, Series 8, case 36, file 6

43 Alfred Bailey to Katharine MacNaughton, 8 June 1943, ibid.

44 See Katherine MacNaughton, *The Development of the Theory and Practice of Education in New Brunswick, 1794–1900: A Study in Historical Background,* (Fredericton: University of New Brunswick, 1947).

45 Alfred Bailey to Katharine MacNaughton, 4 March 1947, UNBA, A.G. Bailey Papers, RG 80, Series 8, case 36, file 6

46 Katharine MacNaughton to Alfred Bailey, 30 May 1949, ibid.

47 Frank Underhill to Registrar, University College, 3 March 1938, NA, Frank Underhill Papers, MG 30 D 204, vol. 6, file L-General, 1928–1956

48 Frank Underhill to David Owen, Chair, Dept of History, Harvard, 9 February 1948, ibid., vol. 8, file Universities-Harvard, 1928–1956,

49 Arthur Lower to J.E. Reid, Dept. of External Affairs, 14 March 1942, Queen's University Archives (QUA), Arthur Lower Papers, Box 1, A 18

50 Fred Landon to Frank Underhill, 25 September 1950, NA, Frank Underhill Papers, MG 30 D 204, vol. 5, file Fred Landon, 1928–1956,

51 In two separate letters for the same student, Bailey referred to her as 'one of the most brilliant students now enrolled at the University' and as 'the most brilliant student that we have here this year.' UNBA, A.G. Bailey Papers, RG 80, Series 5, case 50, file 2, 6 April 1949; 14 March 1950

52 Ibid., 14 February 1948; 19 February 1949

53 Report of W. Aiken, Lecturer in History, 1940, McMaster University, Canadian Baptist Archives, Box McMaster University Chancellor's Reports, Annual Reports, 1938–1942, file Reports to Chancellor 1939–40

54 Frank Underhill to Registrar, University College, 3 March 1938, NA, Frank Underhill Papers, MG 30 D 204, vol. 5, file L-General, 1928–1956

55 Frank Underhill to Dean, School of Graduate Studies, University of Michigan, 9 February 1948, ibid., vol. 6, file McLaughlin to McVannel, 1928–1956

56 Frank Underhill to David Owen, Chair, Dept. of History, Harvard University, 9 February 1948, ibid., vol. 8, file Universities-Harvard, 1928–1956

57 Arthur Lower to National Research Council, 10 December 1952, QUA, Arthur Lower Papers, Box 52, D34

58 History was not the only academic labour market to exclude women: 'The proportion of women university teachers in Canada changed little between the 1920s and the 1970s, when the Royal Commission on the Status of Women found that the number of men was "roughly six times greater than

number of women" and that the women were concentrated in the lower ranks.' Kinnear, *In Subordination*, 30–1

59 J.H. Riddell to Acting Head, Toronto, 28 February 1919, UTA, Department of History, A70-0025, Box 7, file 2,

60 A.L. Burt to Frank Underhill, 17 December 1927, NA, Frank Underhill Papers, MG 30 D 204, vol. 1, file A.L. Burt, 1907–1928

61 Arthur Lower to W.C. Abbott, 4 May 1937, QUA, Arthur Lower Papers, Box 51, D1

62 Arthur Lower to Frank Underhill, 10 January 1939, NA, Frank Underhill Papers, MG 30 D 204, vol. 5, file A.R.M. Lower, 1928–1956

63 James S. Thomson to Frank Underhill, 8 December 1939, ibid., vol. 8, file Universities-Saskatchewan

64 James S. Thomson to Reginald Trotter, 8 December 1939, QUA, Reginald Trotter Papers, Box 26, file Correspondence, Queen's, Lockhart, A.D.

65 Arthur Lower to Frank Underhill, 22 February 1946, NA, Frank Underhill Papers, MG 30 D 204, vol. 5, file A.R.M. Lower, 1928–1956

66 'Evidence of administrative ability' ranked seventh, while the capacity for independent research and the desire to publish ranked ninth. J.J. Talman to Frank Underhill, 9 June 1952, ibid., vol. 8, file J.J. Talman, 1928–1956

67 L.H. Schaus to Department of History, Toronto, 18 June 1953, ibid., vol. 8, file Universities-General

68 Noel Fieldhouse to Sir Lewis Namier, 17 February 1955, MUA, RG 2, Box 179, file History Department, 6236

69 Wallace K. Ferguson to D.G.G. Kerr, 14 February 1958, J.J. Talman Regional Collection, University of Western Ontario, Wallace K. Ferguson Papers, Box 5641–2, file Correspondence 1958, 1959, 1960

70 Hilda Oakeley, *My Adventures in Education* (London: Williams and Norgate, 1939): 88

71 C.E. Fryer to Charles Colby, 20 January 1920, MUA, RG 2, Box 61, file Department of History, 1920–1925

72 Charles Colby to F.D. Adams, 31 March 1920, ibid.

73 Sir Arthur Currie to Sir Campbell Stuart, 11 August 1921, ibid., file History: Prof. Basil Williams, 1921–1925

74 [Name deleted] to Principal Currie, 17 March 1924, ibid., file History Applications 1920–25

75 N.a. to Miss Mackenzie, School of Graduate Studies, Toronto, 23 March 1942, UTA, Department of History, A70-0025, Box 8, file 68. Anna Wright taught at Queen's from 1943 to 1946 as a replacement for Eric Harrison, who was in the Army. In 1946 she went to the University of London on a British Council Scholarship. According to Reginald Trotter, she wanted to

return to teach in Canada. Reginald Trotter to Arthur Lower, 24 March 1947, QUA, Reginald Trotter Papers, Box 1, file 27. She eventually married and remained in England. In 1950 she delivered the Neil Matheson McWharrie Lecture at the Royal Society of Arts in London on the subject of education in Canada. See *Queen's Review* 24, 1 (January 1950).

76 The William Ready Division of Archives and Research Collections, McMaster University, Minutes, Board Of Governors, McMaster University, vol. 3, 176. Gwendolen Carter went to the United States; she taught at Smith University from 1943 to 1964. In 1964 she went to Northwestern University, where she worked for the remainder of her career.

77 George Wrong, 'What Has Befallen Us,' *University of Toronto Quarterly* 4, 1 (1934–5): 44

78 See Theresa Corcoran, SC, *Mount Saint Vincent University: A Vision Unfolding, 1873–1988* (Lanham, MD.: University Press of America, 1999).

79 Elizabeth Smyth, 'Writing Teaches Us Our Mysteries: Women Religious Recording and Writing History,' in Boutilier and Prentice, *Creating Historical Memory*, 123

80 D. Pelleut to Reginald Trotter, 25 July 1947, QUA, Reginald Trotter Papers, Box 26, file History Dept., Applications 1946–1950. For a brief discussion of Pelleut's career at Dalhousie see Fingard, 'Gender and Inequality at Dalhousie,' 695–7.

81 Quotation in Prentice, 'Laying Siege,' 212

82 Hilda Neatby to Frank Underhill, 27 October 1930, NA, Frank Underhill Papers, MG 30 D 204, vol. 6, Hilda Neatby 1928–1956; Hilda Neatby to Frank Underhill, 19 November 1930, ibid.

83 See Hayden, *So Much to Do, So Little Time*, 136, 142.

84 At the College of Wooster there is today an Aileen Dunham Chair in history.

85 MUA, RG 2, Box 61, file History Applications Junior, 1928–1933, n.a., n.d.

86 Prentice, 'Laying Siege,' 216

87 D.C. Harvey to John Clarence Webster, 15 September 1946, New Brunswick Museum Archives (NBMA), J.C. Webster Papers, F-266

88 George Stanley to John Clarence Webster, 16 April 1946, ibid., F-353

89 Reimer, 'Making of British Columbia History,' 381–2. Both Reimer and Prentice report that Thrupp eventually went to Chicago and became a leading medievalist in North America.

90 A.S. Morton wrote a personal letter to Toronto's chair of history, George Wrong, asking that he give 'Miss Jean Murray, the daughter of our President ... such guidance as she may need.' A.S. Morton to George Wrong, 8 October 1923, University of Saskatchwan Archives (USA), A.S. Morton Papers, MG 2 I.30, Students – General, 1917–23. In a letter to the dean of the School of

Graduate Studies at the University of Toronto, George Wrong wrote: 'The only case which I wish to particularly mention is that of Miss Murray. At first she seemed to have difficulty in dealing with Historical material, and, until recently, I thought it would be impossible for her to take the degree this year. Her time was extended a little and now she has submitted a thesis which Professor Flenley and I agree in thinking worth the degree. We have also given her an examination which she passed satisfactorily. I am gratified at this result because her case gave me considerable cause for thought, *and the fact that she was the daughter of the President of a University made one feel it important that we should do her full justice*' (italics mine). George Wrong to J.P. McMurrich, 30 May 1924, UTA, Department of History, A70-0025, Box 2, file 52. See also George Wrong to Frank Underhill, 17 March 1924 and 23 April 1924, NA, Frank Underhill Papers, MG 30 D 204, vol. 1, file G.M. Wrong, 1907–1927.

91 Kate (Neatby) Nicoll to Michael Hayden, 18 February 1981, Saskatchewan Archives Board, Saskatoon (SABS), J.M. Hayden Papers, A-493

92 Walter Murray explained the situation to the premier as follows. 'I am bringing to your attention a personal matter since it is possible that a question may be raised about the remuneration which I am receiving from the University. As you will notice in the Estimates my salary has been reduced $2,000. My daughter, Jean, is giving instruction in History. For this she receives no salary from the University. Her predecessor in this position last year received $2100 from the University. I am giving my daughter an allowance out of my salary. The impropriety of the President recommending his daughter for a salaried position in the University is obvious.' Walter Murray to J.T.M. Anderson, 28 December 1931, USA, President's Office Fonds, Walter Murray, RG 1, Series 1, B6, Anderson, J.T.M. Murray also hired his daughter Lucy Murray to teach English at Regina College

93 Kate (Neatby) Nicoll to Michael Hayden, 18 February 1981, SABS, J.M. Hayden Papers, A-493

94 USA, President's Office Fonds, Walter Murray, RG 1, Series 1, B.38: Annual Reports, 36: History, 1923–1924

95 Burt 'has told me that he has had only one other student ... the equal of Miss Neatby.' A.S. Morton to Secretary, Royal Society of Canada, 28 January 1933 USA, A.S. Morton Papers, MG 2, I.32, Students-Rec., 1919–1942

96 Frank Underhill to The Dean, School of Graduate Studies, University of Minnesota, 1 March 1931, NA, Frank Underhill Papers, MG 30 D 204, vol. 6, file Neatby, Hilda 1928–1956

97 Departmental Minutes, 16 September 1944, UTA, Department of History, A90-0023, Box 29, file Minutes 1928–45

98 James Thomson to W.P. Thompson, 23 May 1946, USA, J.M. Hayden Papers, MG 72, F. So Much to Do, 6. Neatby, U of S, 1919–1967

99 See Michael Taft, *Inside These Greystone Walls: An Anecdotal History of the University of Saskatchewan* (Saskatoon: University of Saskatchewan, 1984): 174–90.

100 Hilda Neatby to her mother, 11 January 1924, SABS, Hilda Neatby Papers, A-139, I.3 (2)

101 Hayden, *So Much to Do, So Little Time*, 25

102 Wilson was referring to Louise Thompson Welch, a Dalhousie psychology professor. Quotation in Fingard, 'Gender and Inequality at Dalhousie,' 699.

103 Irene Spry, interviewed by David Cayley, 'The Legacy of Harold Innis,' part 3, CBC Radio, *Ideas*, 20 December 1994

104 Donald Creighton, *Harold Adams Innis: Portrait of a Scholar* (Toronto: University of Toronto Press, 1957): 61

105 Burnet, 'Minorities I Have Belonged To,' 30. Innis hired Burnet in 1945: 'Because of the grave need for faculty to meet the great demand from students, there had to be a few [women], but they were kept few.' Interview with Jean Burnet, 23 November 1979, UTA, B92-0014.

106 Bridget Moran, *A Little Rebellion* (Vancouver: Arsenal Pulp Press, 1992): 11–12

107 Schultz, 'Sex Is the Least of It,' 12

108 W. Peterson to George Wrong, 25 January 1915, MUA, Information file, History Department, no. 2

109 Marjorie Reid to Frank Underhill, 13 July 1925, NA, Frank Underhill Papers, MG 30 D 204, vol. 1, file R-General, 1907–1927

110 W.P.M. Kennedy to Dean Sellery, 14 May 1925, UTA, Department of History, A70–0025, Box 5, file 150

111 W.P.M. Kennedy to Dean Sellery, 9 May 1925, ibid. In a letter to Mack Eastman, Kennedy also tried to secure something for Reid at UBC: 'She has been with us a for a couple of years as a junior, but, as you know, there is not much chance of promotion for a woman here. I was just wondering if your developments would allow you to take on another junior. If so, I wonder if you could make a place for the fall of this year? An immediate appointment such as that would be very welcome.' W.P.M. Kennedy to Mack Eastman, 9 May 1925, ibid. In a third letter, Kennedy again was explicit: 'Our departmental organization ... does not permit for anything like prospects especially for a woman, and Miss Reid has decided to seek another appointment. If it were at all possible, I should like if she could obtain this in the fall of 1925.' W.P.M. Kennedy to King, 9 May 1925, ibid.

112 A.L. Burt to Reginald Trotter, 11 February 1936, QUA, Reginald Trotter Papers, Box 26, file History Dept. Applications, 1933–43

113 One clear example of discrimination from the 1940s cannot be recounted because of restrictions imposed by the Mount Allison University Archives. See Mount Allison University Archives, Accession no. 7804, A. Administrative Records, Subject Correspondence, file 1A/173. Toronto had an unofficial policy of not hiring women to full-time positions until the 1960s. Even then, Toronto was not particularly welcoming. For a description of Toronto's anti-female culture in the 1960s see Jill Ker Conway, *True North* (Toronto: Vintage Canada, 1995): 148–66. For a discussion of women historians and women's history in Canada in the 1970s see Deborah Gorham, 'Making History: Women's History in Canadian Universities in the 1970s,' in Boutilier and Prentice, *Creating Historical Memory*. Finally, there have been three separate studies on the status of women in the profession of history, each confirming that women continue to confront sexism and that they are under-represented in the professoriate. See Judith Fingard, 'Women Historians in Canada / Les Historiennes au Canada,' *CHA Bulletin* 3, 3 (Summer 1977): 2–3; Linda Kealey, 'The Status of Women in the Historical Profession in Canada, 1989 Survey,' *Canadian Historical Review* 72, 3 (September 1991): 370–88; Working Group on the Status of Women Graduate Students in History, 'Highlights of the Preliminary Report on the Status of Women as Graduate Students in History in Canada,' *CHA Bulletin* 17, 1 (Winter 1991): 1, 8. Ruby Heap completed a fourth study on the status of women in 1999. Although the situation for women has improved since Kealey's 1989 study, Heap cautions historians not to dismiss 'the problems which remain and the belief shared by many of our female respondents that sexism still exists within academia and that the "ideal," "serious," or "model" historian is still associated with the male sex.' Ruby Heap, 'Status of Women in the Historical Profession in Canada: Results of Survey Conducted in 1998 with Female and Male Professors in Canadian Departments of History,' *CHA Bulletin* 25, 3 (1999): 8–9.

114 Author's interview with Margaret Banks, London, Ontario, 15 October 1997

115 As MacNutt said, 'In September we shall have a vacancy for a third man in the Department.' W.S. MacNutt to Frank Underhill, 4 January 1952, UNBA, A.G. Bailey Papers, RG 80, Series 2, case 7, file 1

116 Personal Diary of Dr Margaret Banks, 22 January 1952. I would like to thank Dr Banks for sharing some of her personal papers with me.

117 Frank Underhill to W.S. MacNutt, 29 January 1952, NA, Frank Underhill Papers, MG 30 D 204, vol. 8, file Universities – New Brunswick, 1928–1956

118 Author's interview with Margaret Banks, London, Ontario, 15 October 1997. See also Banks, 'Response from a Mouse,' *CHA Bulletin* 24, 1 (Winter 1998): 6.

119 Margaret Banks to Alfred Bailey, 15 January 1953, UNBA, A.G. Bailey
    Papers, RG 80, Series 2, case 7, file 1; Margaret Banks to Alfred Bailey,
    9 March 1954, ibid., case 2, file 5
120 Alfred Bailey to Margaret Banks, 1 May 1954, ibid., case 7, file 1; Alfred
    Bailey to Margaret Banks, 21 January 1953; ibid., case 2, file 5
121 Donald Creighton to Alfred Bailey, 25 January 1954, ibid., case 2, file 5
122 Author's interview with Margaret Banks, London, Ontario, 15 October
    1997
123 'Lack Cash for Top Men, Fear Crisis at U of T As Enrollment Mounts,' *Globe
    and Mail* 18 January 1955
124 Margaret Banks to Sidney Smith, 19 January 1955. Letter in possession of
    Margaret Banks.
125 Hilda Neatby to Frank Underhill, 13 March 1958, NA, Frank Underhill
    Papers, MG 30 D 204, vol. 13, file H. Neatby 1957–71. Neatby was referring
    to Margaret Prang. In 1959 Prang received a part-time position at UBC; she
    was offered a full-time position in the 1960s. Like Murray, Neatby, and
    Ormsby, Prang did not marry.
126 Hilda Neatby to J.H. Stewart Reid, Executive Secretary, CAUT, 14 April
    1961, SABS, Hilda Neatby Papers, A-139, V-151
127 Margaret Banks to Ogden Glass, 1 December 1960. Letter in possession of
    Margaret Banks
128 Rose Coser. Quotation in Patricia Albjerg Graham, 'Expansion and Exclu-
    sion: A History of Women in American Higher Education,' *Signs* 3, 4 (Sum-
    mer 1978): 767

Chapter 6

1 Quotation in R. Douglas Francis, *Frank H. Underhill: Intellectual Provocateur*
    (Toronto: University of Toronto Press, 1986): 110. Frank Underhill's battles
    with the University of Toronto administration have been well documented.
    See Michiel Horn, *Academic Freedom in Canada: A History* (Toronto: University
    of Toronto Press, 1999): 118–22, 154–64; A.B. McKillop, *Matters of Mind: The
    University in Ontario, 1791–1951* (Toronto: University of Toronto Press,
    1994): 377–98, 541–3; and Carl Berger, *The Writing of Canadian History:
    Aspects of English-Canadian Historical Writing since 1900*, 2nd ed. (Toronto:
    University of Toronto Press, 1986): 79–84.
2 Record of telephone call, n.a., n.d.; the call was received in the principal's
    office on 23 November 1939. McGill University Archives (MUA), RG 2, Box
    61, file Dept. of History, Morgan and Douglas, 1935–1939
3 Frank Underhill to George Ferguson, 21 April 1939, National Archives (NA),

Frank Underhill Papers, MG 30 D 204, vol. 4, file G.V. Ferguson, 1928–1956

4 Francis, *Frank H. Underhill,* 113

5 Frank Underhill to George Ferguson, 21 April 1939, NA, Frank Underhill Papers, MG 30 D 204, vol. 4, file G.V. Ferguson, 1928–56. Although Innis and Underhill had 'crossed swords' in the past, Innis was prepared to lose his position in defence of Underhill. Donald Creighton, *Harold Adams Innis: Portrait of a Scholar* (Toronto: University of Toronto Press, 1957): 109. See also Arthur Lower, 'Harold Innis As I Remember Him,' *Journal of Canadian Studies* 20, 4 (Winter 1985–6): 9.

6 Quotation and *Telegram* reference in Francis, *Frank H. Underhill,* 115

7 Frank Underhill to Donald Creighton, 24 September 1940, NA, Donald Creighton Papers, MG 31 D 77, vol. 1, file General Correspondence 1940

8 Frank Underhill to D. Bruce Macdonald, Chairman, Board of Governors, University of Toronto, 8 January 1941, NA, Frank Underhill Papers, MG 30 D 204, vol. 8, file Universities, Toronto, no. 1

9 It was not only the hard line taken by the Toronto faculty that saved Underhill. Hugh Keenleyside and Jack Pickersgill used their considerable influence in Ottawa to persuade Mitch Hepburn to ease his attack. See Jack Pickersgill, 'The Decisive Battle for Academic Freedom in Canada,' University of Toronto Archives (UTA), Robert Bothwell Papers, B90-0034, Box 7, file Article, Pickersgill

10 In addition to Harold Innis, Underhill's colleagues in the Department of History stood by him: they included Chester Martin, George Brown, Bertie Wilkinson, and Ralph Flenley. See Robert Bothwell, *Laying the Foundation: A Century of History at University of Toronto* (Toronto, 1991): 99.

11 Donald Creighton to Frank Underhill, 9 January 1941, NA, Frank Underhill Papers, MG 30 D 204, vol. 3, file D.G. Creighton, 1928–1956

12 W.J. Goode, 'Encroachment, Charlatanism and the Emerging Profession: Psychology, Sociology and Medicine,' *American Sociological Review* 25 (1960): 903

13 M. Brook Taylor, 'Kingsford, William,' *Dictionary of Canadian Biography,* vol. 12: *1891–1900* (Toronto: University of Toronto Press, 1990): 495

14 Although it had been a recommendation of the 1951 Royal Commission on National Development in the Arts, Letters and Sciences, it was not until 18 January 1957 that Prime Minister Louis St Laurent stood in the House of Commons to announce the creation of the Canada Council. As a federally funded agency, the Canada Council would at long last make money available to Canadian artists, writers and scholars. For too long, St Laurent explained, 'Our scholars and our students have had to rely mainly on foreign sources

for grants-in-aid and for scholarships.' The 'exclusive reliance on the generosity of others,' he continued, 'is not worthy of our real power and does not exemplify our real sense of values.' Besides, 'it is generally felt that more financial assistance is now urgently needed if our nation is to continue to make progress in the arts, the humanities and the social sciences.' Canada, House of Commons, *Debates*, 18 January 1957, 393–4

15 W. Stewart Wallace, *A Sketch of the History of the Champlain Society* (Toronto, 1937): 3

16 George Wrong to John Clarence Webster, 11 July 1924, New Brunswick Museum Archives (NBMA), J.C. Webster Papers, F304

17 W. Stewart Wallace to Adam Shortt, 22 June 1920, Queen's University Archives (QUA), Adam Shortt Papers, Box 5, file Correspondence 1920

18 A.L. Burt to Dorrie Burt, 29 July 1923, NA, A.L. Burt Papers, MG 30 D 103, vol. 1, file 1. Frank Underhill was only half joking when he called upon someone among Canada's 'intelligent millionaires' to provide Canadian historians with copies of S.E. Morison's *History of American Life* and Charles Beard's *Rise of American Civilization*. These books, he believed, should serve as models for the writing of Canadian history. Frank Underhill, 'Canadian and American History – And Historians,' *Canadian Forum* 8, 93 (June 1928): 685

19 Arthur Lower, 'Some Neglected Aspects of Canadian History,' Canadian Historical Association, *Annual Report* (1929): 71

20 Chester Martin, 'Memorandum on the Claims of History Upon the National Research Council,' University of Saskatchewan Archives (USA), A.S. Morton Papers, MG 2 I.9 Other Universities, 1921–1943. In 1940 the Royal Commission on Dominion-Provincial Relations recommended the creation of a funding agency for the social sciences similar to the National Research Council. The recommendation fell on deaf ears. *Report of the Royal Commission on Dominion-Provincial Relations*, Book 2: *Recommendations* (Ottawa, 1940): 52

21 Donald Creighton, 'Harold Adams Innis: A Special and Unique Brilliance,' in Donald Creighton, *The Passionate Observer: Selected Writings* (Toronto: McClelland and Stewart, 1980): 152

22 Quotation in Charles Taylor, *Radical Tories: The Conservative Tradition in Canada* (Toronto: Anansi, 1982): 28

23 'Grants in Canada of the Carnegie Corporation of New York,' Rockefeller Archive Center (RAC), Rockefeller Foundation (RF), RG 2-1949, 427, Box 480, file 3089

24 'The Rockefeller Foundation and Canada,' 1 December 1955, RAC, RF, RG 2, 427, Box 5, file 321. For a more complete picture of the relationship between American philanthropy and Canadian arts and letters see Jeffrey

Brison, 'Cultural Interventions: American Corporate Philanthropy and the Construction of the Arts and Letters in Canada, 1900–1957,' PhD thesis, Queen's University, 1998. See also Maria Tippett, *Making Culture: English-Canadian Institutions and Arts before the Massey Commission* (Toronto: University of Toronto Press, 1990); and Robin Harris, *A History of Higher Education in Canada, 1663–1960* (Toronto: University of Toronto Press, 1976).

25 Lewis Coser, *Men of Ideas: A Sociologist's View* (New York: Free Press, 1965): 339

26 Donald Fisher, *Fundamental Development of the Social Sciences: Rockefeller Philanthropy and the United States Social Science Research Council* (Ann Arbor: University of Michigan Press, 1993): 232. See also Donald Fisher, 'The Role of Philanthropic Foundations in the Reproduction and Production of Hegemony: Rockefeller Foundations and the Social Sciences,' *Sociology* 17, 2 (May 1983): 206–33; Robert Arnove, ed., *Philanthropy and Cultural Imperialism: The Foundations at Home and Abroad* (Bloomington: Indiana University Press, 1982); and Edward Berman, *The Influence of Carnegie, Ford, and Rockefeller Foundations on American Foreign Policy: Ideology and Philanthropy* (Albany: State University of New York Press, 1984).

27 Brison, 'Cultural Interventions,' 20, 360

28 Stanley Ryerson to Edward Stanley and Tessie Ryerson, 13 April 1934, in Andrée Lévesque, 'Les années de formation du militant' in R. Comeau and R. Tremblay, eds, *Stanley Bréhault Ryerson, un intellectual de combat* (Hull: Éditions Vents d'Ouest, 1996): 39. See also Interview with Stanley Ryerson, n.d., c. 1990s, in UQAM, Service des archives et du gestion des documents, Fonds Stanley Bréhaut Ryerson, 27P-010/4.

29 Theodore S. Hamerow, *Reflections on History and Historians* (Madison: University of Wisconsin Press, 1987): 71 and appendix A, 'The Philanthropic Foundations and Historical Scholarship'

30 Marlene Shore, *The Science of Social Redemption: McGill, the Chicago School, and the Origins of Social Research in Canada* (Toronto: University of Toronto Press, 1987): 162

31 On the importance of interdisciplinary work with specific reference to the Frontiers of Settlement Series see R.C. Wallace, 'Co-operation in the Natural and Human Sciences,' *Canadian Historical Review* 14, 4 (December 1933): 371–4.

32 'Committee on Pioneer Belts, Memorandum for March 27, 1926,' RAC, Social Science Research Council (SSRC), RG 1, Series I, subseries 19, Box 188, file 1116: Committee on Pioneer Belts Minutes, 31 December 1925 to 1934

33 Italics in original. Isaiah Bowman, 'The Scientific Study of Settlement,' *Geographical Review* 16, 4 (October 1926): 653

34 Shore, *The Science of Social Redemption*, 166
35 O.E. Baker, 'Memorandum for Dr. Bowman, Chairman, Committee on Pioneer Belts,' 31 July 1926, RAC, SSRC, RG 1, Series I, subseries 19, Box 188, file 1116: Committee on Pioneer Belts Minutes. 31 December 1925 to 1934; Committee of Pioneer Belts, Minutes of Meeting, 12 August 1926, ibid.
36 Shore, *The Science of Social Redemption*, 170. In a foreword to the first volume, Isaiah Bowman states, 'A committee, composed exclusively of Canadians, was set up and given virtually complete liberty of action.' W.A. Mackintosh, *Prairie Settlement: The Geographical Setting* (Toronto: Macmillan, 1934): x.
37 'Memorandum Concerning the Social Sciences in Canada, with special reference to the present need of Canadian Graduate Scholarships,' 31 January 1930, RAC, SSRC, RG 1, Series I, subseries 19, Box 188, file 1116: Committee on Pioneer Belts Minutes. 31 December 1925 to 1934. No author is listed, although presumably it was W.A. Mackintosh. See also Mackintosh, *Prairie Settlement*, xv; and Shore, *Science of Social Redemption*, 172.
38 See 'Notes and Comments,' *Canadian Historical Review* 7, 1 (March 1926): 1–2
39 William Mackintosh to Hugh Eayrs, President, Macmillan of Canada, 28 July 1932, William Ready Division Archives and Research Collections, McMaster University, Macmillan Company of Canada Fonds, Box 82, file 2
40 Hugh Eayrs to W.A. Mackintosh, 13 August 1932, ibid.
41 W.A. Mackintosh to Hugh Eayrs, 28 January 1933, ibid., file 3
42 Hugh Eayrs to W.A. Mackintosh, 4 May 1935, ibid., file 4
43 W.A. Mackintosh to Hugh Eayrs, 20 May 1935, ibid.
44 Ellen Elliott, Macmillan, to W.A. Mackintosh, 2 May 1944, ibid., file 6
45 Chester Martin, *'Dominion Lands' Policy.* Introduction by Lewis Thomas (Toronto: McClelland and Stewart, 1973): xi
46 Arthur Lower, 'Foreword,' in Welf H. Heick, ed., *Arthur Lower and the Making of Canadian Nationalism* (Vancouver: University of British Columbia Press, 1975): xiii
47 Arthur Lower, *Settlement and the Forest Frontier in Eastern Canada* (Toronto: Macmillan, 1936): 146
48 Harold Innis, 'Canadian Frontiers of Settlement: A Review,' *Geographical Review* 25, 1 (January 1935): 106. In his review of Mackintosh's volume D.C. Harvey commented on the importance of the series: 'In a word, these studies are assembling a vast amount of authoritative information for the use of provincial and Canadian statesmen.' Review of W.A. Mackintosh, *Prairie Settlement: The Geographical Setting, Dalhousie Review* 14 (1934): 261
49 See Carl Berger, 'The Conferences of Canadian-American Affairs, 1935–1941: An Overview,' in Frederick W. Gibson and Jonathon G. Rossie, eds, *The*

Road to Ogdensburg: The Queen's/St. Lawrence Conferences on Canadian-American Affairs, 1935–1941 (East Lansing: Michigan State University Press, 1993).

50 After endowment grants, general operating grants, and medical school grants, it was the single largest grant the Carnegie Corporation, through the Carnegie Endowment, made to higher education in Canada.

51 James T. Shotwell, *The Autobiography of James T. Shotwell* (New York: Bobbs-Merrill, 1961): 1, 17, 18, 20, 19, 27

52 James T. Shotwell, 'A Personal Note on the Theme of Canadian-American Relations,' *Canadian Historical Review* 28, 1 (March 1947): 42–3

53 See James H. Robinson, *The New History* (New York, 1912).

54 Richard Hofstadter, *The Progressive Historians: Turner, Beard, Parrington* (New York: Alfred A. Knopf, 1968): 185

55 See Harold Josephson, 'History for Victory: The National Board for Historical Service,' *Mid-America* 52, 3 (July 1970): 205–24. See also Harold Josephson, *James T. Shotwell and the Rise of Internationalism in America* (Rutherford, N.J.: Fairleigh Dickinson University Press, 1975), chap. 3, 'The Historians Mobilize.'

56 See Samuel Haber, *Efficiency and Uplift: Scientific Management in the Progressive Era* (Chicago: University of Chicago Press, 1964); Robert Weibe, *The Search for Order, 1877–1920* (New York: Hill and Wang, 1967). See also Charles DeBenedetti, 'James T. Shotwell and the Science of International Politics,' *Political Science Quarterly* 89, 2 (June 1974).

57 'Scientific Method in Research and Discussion in International Relations, A Proposal for Institutes of International Relations,' Columbia University, Rare Book and Manuscript Library (CUL), Carnegie Endowment for International Peace (CEIP), Box 144, item no. 41230

58 'Memorandum for Dr. Crane on Canadian-American Relations,' 8 April 1932, CUL, James Shotwell Papers, Box 286, file Can-American Relations, H.A. Innis

59 Minutes of the Annual Meeting of the Board of Trustees, Carnegie Endowment for International Peace, 5 May 1932, CUL, CEIP, Box 22, item no. 1256

60 'Survey of the Economic, Social and Political Relations of Canada and the United States,' 6 October 1932, CUL, CEIP, Box 144, item no. 41236

61 Ibid. In July 1932 Canada and the United States signed a treaty to build a St Lawrence seaway. The U.S. Senate refused to ratify the treaty, however, and a seaway was not built until the 1950s.

62 James Shotwell to Nicholas Butler, 11 October 1932, CUL, CEIP, Box 142, item no. 40622

63 Executive Committee Resolution, 1 May 1933, ibid., Box 142, item no. 40635

64 'Canadian-American Conference on Research,' 28–9 October 1933, ibid., Box 525, item no. 114891

65 James Shotwell to Frederick Keppel, 15 February 1934, CUL, James Shotwell Papers, Box 286, file Can-American Relations, K-General

66 James T. Shotwell, 'Annual Report for 1938 of the Division of Economics and History,' CUL, CEIP, Box 2, item no. 237

67 Harold Innis to James Shotwell, 20 March 1931, CUL, James Shotwell Papers, Box 286, file Can-American Relations, H.A. Innis

68 Harold Innis to James Shotwell, 6 May 1932, ibid.

69 Quotation in Creighton, *Harold Adams Innis*, 79. Carl Berger refers to Innis as a 'jealous guardian of the independence of Canadian scholarship.' Berger, 'Internationalism, Continentalism, and the Writing of History: Comments on the Carnegie Series on the Relations of Canada and the United States,' in Richard Preston, ed., *The Influence of the United States on Canadian Development: Eleven Case Studies* (Durham, N.C.: Duke University Press, 1972): 52.

70 Quotation in Shore, *Science of Social Redemption*, 306

71 James Shotwell to Harold Innis, 27 July 1932, UTA, Harold Innis Papers, B72–0025, Box 11, file 14

72 James Shotwell to Harold Innis, 6 October 1932. Quotation in McKillop, *Matters of Mind*, 479.

73 Harold Innis to James Shotwell, 11 August 1932, CUL, James Shotwell Papers, Box 286, file Can-American Relations, H.A. Innis

74 'Canadian-American Relations Conference on Research,' 12 November 1933, CUL, CEIP, Box 525. In the introduction to a collection of essays on the Canadian economy published in 1934, Innis elaborated: 'we lack vital information on which to base prospective policies.' Harold Innis, 'Introduction,' in Harold Innis and A.F.W. Plumptre, eds, *The Canadian Economy and Its Problems* (Toronto: Canadian Institute of International Affairs, 1934): 17–18.

75 Harold Innis to James Shotwell, 15 November 1933, CUL, James Shotwell Papers, Box 286, file Can-American Relations, H.A. Innis

76 For a discussion of Brebner's career see Paul T. Phillips, *Britain's Past in Canada: The Teaching and Writing of British History* (Vancouver: UBC Press, 1989), chap. 5, 'The View from Morningside Heights.'

77 J. Bartlet Brebner to James Shotwell, n.d., c. November 1933, CUL, James Shotwell Papers, Box 286, file Can-American Relations, H.A. Innis

78 J. Bartlet Brebner, 'Memorandum on the Innis Budget,' 23 January 1934, ibid., Box 284, file Can-American Relations, J.B. Brebner

79 Harold Innis to James Shotwell, 15 November 1933, CUL, James Shotwell Papers, Box 286, file Can-American Relations, H.A. Innis

80 'A Survey of Canadian-American Relations,' June 1935, CUL, CEIP, Box 525, item no. 114931

81 James Shotwell to Harold Innis, 20 February 1935, CUL, John Bartlet Brebner Papers, Box 10, file Sept. 1933 – Mar. 1937. As it turned out, Spry did not complete the research and the volume was never published. She married Graham Spry.

82 'A Survey of Canadian-American Relations,' February 1935, ibid.

83 George Glazebrook to J. Bartlet Brebner, 26 April 1935, ibid.

84 Harold Innis to James Shotwell, 21 February 1935, CUL, James Shotwell Papers, Box 286, file Can-American Relations, H.A. Innis

85 James Shotwell to Harold Innis, 25 February 1935, ibid.

86 Harold Innis to James Shotwell, 26 February 1935, ibid.

87 J. Bartlet Brebner to Harold Innis, 15 March 1935, CUL, John Bartlet Brebner Papers, Box 10, file Sept. 1933 – Mar. 1937

88 James Shotwell to Harold Innis, 20 March 1935, CUL, James Shotwell Papers, Box 286, file Can-American Relations, H.A. Innis

89 'Memorandum re. The Canadian-American Research Project,' 7 May 1935, QUA, Lorne Pierce Papers, Box 6, file 3, no. 42

90 Sandra Campbell, 'From Romantic History to Communications Theory: Lorne Pierce as Publisher of C.W. Jefferys and Harold Innis,' *Journal of Canadian Studies* 30, 3 (Fall 1995): 109

91 Arthur Lower to Lorne Pierce, 18 October 1937, QUA, Arthur Lower Papers, Box 25, B 669. See also Arthur Lower to Harold Innis, 16 November 1937, ibid.

92 James Shotwell to George Finch, 12 November 1937, CUL, CEIP, Box 525, item no. 115007

93 Harold Innis to James Shotwell, 6 December 1937, CUL, James Shotwell Papers, Box 286, file Can-American Relations, G. de T. Glazebrook

94 James Shotwell to George Glazebrook, 17 December 1937, ibid.

95 Harold Innis to James Shotwell, March 1938, ibid., file Can-American Relations, H.A. Innis

96 James Shotwell to Harold Innis, 31 March 1938, ibid.

97 Harold Innis to James Shotwell, 2 April 1938, ibid.

98 James Shotwell to George Finch [CEIP], 28 April 1939, CUL, CEIP, Box 525, item no. 115010

99 Norman Donaldson to Lorne Pierce, 2 May 1939, QUA, Lorne Pierce Papers, Box 7, file 5, no. 60

100 Lorne Pierce to Norman Donaldson, 1 June 1939, ibid., Box 7, file 5, no. 62.

101 Campbell stated that together Innis and Pierce protested to save the contract for Ryerson. (See Campbell, 'From Romantic History to Communica-

tions Theory,' 109.) This is not true. Innis was happy to leave Ryerson. As he explained to Shotwell after Donaldson's notice of termination, Ryerson was not marketing the series, it was charging too high a price, and it was using the series to subsidize its greater interest in popular books. 'There is little point in arguing with [Pierce] on many matters,' he told Shotwell, 'because he cannot grasp our point of view.' Harold Innis to James Shotwell, n.d., c. May 1939, CUL, James Shotwell Papers, Box 286, file Can-American Relations, H.A. Innis

102 Harold Innis to J. Bartlet Brebner, 23 September 1939, CUL, John Bartlet Brebner Papers, Box 10, file August 1937 to August 1940

103 Memo, by J. Bartlet Brebner, 4 October 1939, ibid.

104 Harold Innis to J. Bartlet Brebner, 6 October 1939, ibid.

105 Fred Landon, *Western Ontario and the American Frontier*; F.W. Howay, W.N. Sage, and H.F. Angus, *British Coumbia and the United States*; R.H. Coats and M.C. MacLean, *The American Born in Canada: A Statistical Interpretation*; and Gustave Lanctôt, ed., *Les Canadiens français et leurs voisin du sud*. Lanctôt's volume, however, was not printed by Ryerson but by M. Valiquette of Montreal. Although Sandra Campbell found no evidence that UTP ever became involved in the series, see the letters between UTP and Brebner in CUL, J. Bartlet Brebner Papers, Box 10, file August 1937 to August 1940 and file Bartlet, John Brebner. See also James Shotwell to Lorne Pierce, 8 August 1941, QUA, Lorne Pierce Papers, Box 8, file 6, item 36.

106 Harold Innis, 'The Role of Intelligence: Some Further Notes,' *Canadian Journal of Economics and Political Science* 1, 2 (May 1935): 280–6

107 Campbell, 'From Romantic History to Communications Theory,' 91

108 If Arthur Lower remembered his friend with fondness, he also recalled their disagreement on accountability. Lower believed a grant recipient ought to be held accountable for the grant. Innis would have none of it: 'He seemed to think that this cut into academic freedom.' Lower, 'Harold Innis As I Remember Him,' 9.

109 Harold Innis, 'A Note on Universities and the Social Sciences,' *Canadian Journal of Economics and Political Science* 1, 2 (May 1935): 286

110 Donald Creighton, 'Presidential Address,' Canadian Historical Association, *Annual Report* (1957): 3

111 Harvey, Trotter, McArthur, Brown, Underhill, Martin, and Whitelaw never completed their volumes.

112 Arthur Lower to Harold Innis, 2 December 1933, QUA, Arthur Lower Papers, Box 7, A 127

113 Arthur Lower to Harold Innis, 19 November 1933, UTA, Harold Innis Papers, B72-0025, Box 11, file 13

114 Donald Creighton to James Shotwell, 6 June 1934 and 17 July 1934, CUL, James Shotwell Papers, Box 285, file Can-American Relations, D.G. Creighton

115 C.P. Stacey to his mother, 22 January 1934, UTA, Charles Stacey Papers, B93-0021, Box 1, file 2

116 C.P. Stacey to George Throop, Chancellor, Washington University, 13 December 1935, UTA, Charles Stacey Papers, B90-0020, Box 1, file Applications for positions

117 Reginald Trotter to John Pritchett, 28 May 1934, QUA Reginald Trotter Papers, Box 23, file Correspondence, Pritchett, J.P. (iii). Not surprisingly, Pritchett dedicated his volume in the series to Trotter.

118 Donald Creighton to James Shotwell, 3 November 1937, CUL, James Shotwell Papers, Box 285, file Can-American Relations, D.G. Creighton

119 When a Brown University historian asked Shotwell if the series had room for a book on Canadian land colonization policies, Shotwell responded negatively but conceded the Canadian focus of the series: 'I have already interpreted the scope of our enterprise in a way which, as you say, almost seems to imply a general interest in Canadian things. This, however, was a somewhat special bit of cooperation with Canadian economists and historians on which we were attempting to build a larger synthesis. But in granting this interpretation of our purpose for the completion of these works, I made it a matter of principle not to extend beyond the program which the Canadians had presented.' James Shotwell to James B. Hedges, 8 August 1938, ibid., Box 286, file Can-American Relations, H – General

120 James Shotwell to H.F. Angus, 10 May 1937, ibid., Box 284, file Can-American Relations, H.F. Angus

121 James Shotwell to Lorne Pierce, 28 November 1938, ibid., Box 285, file Can-American Relations, D.G. Creighton

122 J. Bartlet Brebner to James Shotwell, 7 February 1940, ibid., Box 287, file Can-American Relations, F. Landon

123 James Shotwell to Frank Flemington, Ryerson Press, 4 March 1944, QUA, Lorne Pierce Papers, Box 11, file 4, item no. 39

124 John Pritchett, *The Red River Valley, 1811–1849* (New Haven, Conn.: Yale University Press, 1942): xvi

125 James Shotwell to Arthur Lower, 10 December 1937, QUA, Arthur Lower Papers, Box 25, B 669

126 Arthur Lower to James Shotwell, 26 December 1937, ibid.

127 James Shotwell to Harold Innis, 9 January 1938, CUL, James Shotwell Papers, Box 287, file Can-American Relations, A.R.M. Lower – W.A. Carrothers – S.A. Saunders

128 In reference to a November 1933 conference of those Canadian historians involved in the project, Shotwell wrote: 'At a conference of the Canadian historians, held in Ottawa, the request was made that Judge Howay be invited to associate himself with Professor Sage in shaping up the projects in the Pacific area. Could you manage this? ... The conference seemed to put great importance upon our having Judge Howay associated with us.' James Shotwell to H.F. Angus, 5 January 1934, ibid., Box 284, file Can-American Relations, H.F. Angus

129 Chester Martin to James Shotwell, 20 April 1934, ibid.

130 Judge Howay thought little of academics in general ('the energetic amateur can beat them [academics] every time') and of W.N. Sage in particular (he once referred to a piece of 'SAGEAN research' as 'valueless'). Quotations in Chad Reimer, 'The Making of British Columbia History: Historical Writing and Institutions, 1784–1958,' PhD thesis, York University, 1995: 181.

131 James Shotwell to F.W. Howay, 30 July 1940, CUL, James Shotwell Papers, Box 286, file Can-American Relations, F.W. Howay – W.N. Sage

132 H.F. Angus to Chester Martin, 4 October 1940, ibid.

133 James Shotwell to Chester Martin, 24 June 1940, ibid.

134 'Memorandum on Howay-Sage Manuscript,' 12 June 1940, CUL, J. Bartlet Brebner Papers, Box 10, file Bartlet, John Brebner

135 Reimer, 'Making of British Columbia History,' 186

136 H.F. Angus to J. Bartlet Brebner, 7 October 1940, CUL, James Shotwell Papers, Box 286, file Can-American Relations, F.W. Howay – W.N. Sage

137 Reimer, 'Making of British Columbia History,' 187

138 'Howay-Sage-Angus MSS,' n.d., c. July 1941, CUL, J. Bartlet Brebner Papers, Box 10, file Brebner, John Bartlet

139 C.P. Stacey to James T. Shotwell, memorandum, 12 June 1934, UTA, Charles Stacey Papers, B90-0020, Box 42, file Carnegie Endowment for International Peace, 1934–46; 1971

140 J. Bartlet Brebner to C.P. Stacey, 21 February 1934, ibid.

141 C.P. Stacey to James Shotwell, 30 March 1939, ibid.

142 See Tim Cook, 'Clio's Soldiers: Charles Stacey and the Army Historical Section in the Second World War,' *Canadian Historical Review* 83, 1 (March 2002): 29–57

143 J. Bartlet Brebner to C.P. Stacey, 27 May 1941, UTA, Charles Stacey Papers, B90-0020, Box 42, file Carnegie Endowment for International Peace, 1934–46; 1971. Similarly, Shotwell changed the proposed title of Charles Tansill's volume. 'I am not wholly carried away by the title "Rival Partners,"' he told Brebner. 'It seems to me that it may be just a little too challenging in wartime. It is the "rival" part of it that bothers me. We historians have a ten-

dency to be too honest!' The volume in question was published as
Canadian-American Relations, 1875–1911. James Shotwell to J. Bartlet Breb-
ner, 8 September 1942, CUL, J. Bartlet Brebner Papers, Box 10, file Bartlet,
John Brebner

144 J. Bartlet Brebner to C.P. Stacey, 1 April 1946 and James Shotwell to C.P.
Stacey, 8 May 1946, UTA, Charles Stacey Papers, B90-0020, Box 42, file
Carnegie Endowment for International Peace, 1934–46; 1971

145 In his memoirs Stacey commented on the experience. Shotwell, he wrote,
never 'fully recovered from his experiences at the Peace Conference in
1919, when he was a member of the American "Inquiry."' For the remainder of his long life he harboured an exaggerated sense of self-importance.
Throughout the Canadian-American relations series, he 'thought he was
being an international statesman when he was in fact merely organizing a
respectable scholarly project which few except scholars would be interested
in and which certainly would have little influence on international events.'
C.P. Stacey, *A Date with History* (Ottawa: Deneau, 1982): 54

146 Leon Fraser, Eliot Wadsworth, and William Marshall Bullitt, Confidential
Report, 26 January 1942, CUL, CEIP, Box 33, item no. 4579

147 James Shotwell and Philip Jessup, 'Memorandum of the Work of the
Endowment,' 4 February 1942, ibid., item no. 4588

Chapter 7

1 Diary of Fred Landon, 24 May 1940, J.J. Talman Regional Collection, University of Western Ontario, Fred Landon Papers, Box 4210, file 48

2 Entitled 'Carry On!,' the editorial implored academics not to suspend their
activities: 'These learned societies, in keeping their memberships as intact as
possible, and in continuing their various investigations into Canadian affairs
of both the past and the present, will set a fine example for the rest of the cit-
izenry. We must all carry on, as best we can, to lessen the shock of war upon
our social whole.' *Winnipeg Free Press,* 22 May 1940, 15.

3 'Canadian Historical Association Annual Meeting, May 22–24, 1940,' *Canadian Historical Review* 21, 2 (June 1940): 238

4 'Historical Records and the Canadian War Effort,' *Canadian Historical Review*
21, 2 (June 1940): 239–41. See also Fred Landon, 'The Preservation of Wartime Material,' *Ontario Library Review* (November 1940): 401–2; and 'An
Appeal for the Preservation of Historical Material,' *Canadian Historical
Review* 24, 2 (June 1943): 336–7.

5 Arthur Lower was adamant on this point. As he told George Brown, 'Government is dependent upon its experts and for the expert these annual meet-

ings are valuable. Nor do I see that a line can be drawn between immediately available experts such as economists and the more removed, such as historians. More generally the cultural life must not be allowed to disintegrate, if our professed war objectives mean anything, and it is our responsibility to carry it on.' In a letter to Guy Stanton Ford of the American Historical Association, Lower explained that the travel of 'womenfolk moving around the country after their men' put more of a strain on the transportation systems 'than any demand our societies might make.' In an undated circular letter, the following agreed that it was more important to continue the annual meeting than it was to suspend it: Ralph Flenley, Donald Creighton, Noel Fieldhouse, and D.C. Masters. See Arthur Lower to George Brown, 2 October 1942; Arthur Lower to Guy Stanton Ford, 16 December 1942, Queen's University Archives (QUA), Arthur Lower Papers, Box 47, C 47; and n.a., n.d., ibid. In May 1943 the CHA Council decided to continue meeting throughout the war: 'it seemed to us that continuance of such meetings was necessary if the values of our civilization, for which we fight, are to be maintained.' Quotation in n.a., 'The Social Sciences and the War,' *Canadian Historical Review* 24, 4 (December 1943): 451

6 For a sustained analysis of what was really a larger phenomenon see Philip Massolin, *Canadian Intellectuals, the Tory Tradition, and the Challenge of Modernity, 1939–1970* (Toronto: University of Toronto Press, 2001).

7 According to Frank Abbott, university teachers' salaries 'were little, if at all, higher in 1950 than they had been a generation before, while the real income of all other occupational groups had risen an average of sixty per cent.' In this context, the Canadian Association of University Teachers (CAUT) was founded in 1951 with the intention of improving professors' salaries and pensions. Frank Abbott, 'Founding the Canadian Association of University Teachers, 1945–1951,' *Queen's Quarterly* 93, 3 (Autumn 1986): 509.

8 Arthur Lower noted that when he turned sixty-five in 1954, he continued to teach because he was in 'no position financially to retire.' He also conceded that in 1955 he accepted a four-month position as Visiting Professor of Commonwealth History at the University of Wisconsin over an eight-month position as Harold Innis Professor at the University of Toronto precisely because Wisconsin offered twice the salary and he had to provide for his old age. Arthur Lower, *My First Seventy-five Years* (Toronto: Macmillan, 1967): 357, 363

9 See Frank Abbott, 'The Crowe Affair: The Academic Profession and Academic Freedom,' *Queen's Quarterly* 98, 4 (Winter 1991): 818–39; Michiel Horn, *Academic Freedom in Canada: A History* (Toronto: University of Toronto Press, 1999); and Michiel Horn, 'Tenure and the Canadian Professoriate,' *Journal of Canadian Studies* 34, 3 (Fall 1999): 261–81.

10 Donald Creighton, 'Education for Government: What Can the Humanities Do for Government,' n.d., National Archives (NA), Donald Creighton Papers, MG 31 D 77, vol. 15. A deep liberal humanism underpinned both the submissions to and the 1951 final report of the Royal Commission on National Development in the Arts, Letters and Sciences. See Paul Litt, *The Muses, the Masses and the Massey Commission* (Toronto: University of Toronto Press, 1992).

11 J. Bartlet Brebner, 'Canadianism,' Canadian Historical Association, *Annual Report* (1940): 5–15

12 Arthur Lower to Chester New, 15 December 1936, QUA, Arthur Lower Papers, Box 1, file A 8

13 Arthur Lower to James Shotwell, 10 April 1938, ibid., Box 10, file A 10

14 Lower, *My First Seventy-five Years*, 239, 243

15 n.a., 'Muskoka, 1940 – Lower's Conference!' n.d., QUA, Arthur Lower Papers, Box 1, file A 14; and n.a., circular letter, 15 August 1940, QUA, Arthur Lower Papers, Box 13, file B 142

16 George Brown to Arthur Lower, 17 December 1940, ibid., Box 13, file B 142

17 Arthur Lower, 'The Social Sciences in the Post-War World,' *Canadian Historical Review* 22, 1 (March 1941): 1–13

18 'The Social Scientist in the Modern World,' Canadian Historical Association, *Annual Report* (1941): 83–6

19 Arthur Lower, 'The Social Sciences in Canada,' *Culture* 3, 4 (December 1942): 433–40

20 Ramsay Cook, 'An Interview with A.R.M. Lower,' in Eleanor Cook, ed., *The Craft of History* (Toronto: Canadian Broadcasting Corporation, 1973): 36. See also Lower, *My First Seventy-five Years*, 264–5.

21 Arthur Lower, *Colony to Nation*, 4th ed. (Don Mills, Ont.: Longmans, Green, 1964): 563–4. At least one future historian was moved by Lower's conclusion: 'The closing passages of Colony to Nation,' wrote Peter Waite, 'constitute the grandest and perhaps the most fervent plea for a Canadian spirit and unity that I have ever read. Your charged prose moved me deeply – once again, you cannot see this country from coast to coast and not feel the grandeur and loftier Canada, or be a more firmly rooted Canadian.' Peter Waite to Arthur Lower, August 1948, QUA, Arthur Lower Papers, Box 26, file B 691

22 Lower, *Colony to Nation*, 532, 5, xii

23 Quotation in Joseph Levitt, *A Vision beyond Reach: A Century of Images of Canadian Destiny* (Ottawa: Deneau, 1983): 88.

24 Arthur Lower, 'Foreword,' in W.H. Heick, ed., *History and Myth: Arthur Lower and the Making of Canadian Nationalism* (Vancouver: University of British Columbia Press, 1975): xiii

25 Arthur Lower, 'Time, Myth and Fact – The Historian's Commodities,' *Queen's Quarterly* 64, 2 (Summer 1957): 248–9

26 Frank Underhill to Noel Fieldhouse, 22 July 1941, University of Toronto Archives (UTA), Department of History, A70–0025, Box 7, file 15

27 Noel Fieldhouse to Frank Underhill, 1 August 1941, ibid.

28 Noel Fieldhouse, 'The Failure of Historians,' Canadian Historical Association, *Annual Report* (1942): 52–65. In an unpublished 1949 rumination on history, Fieldhouse stressed the autonomy of history 'against that positivism, so powerful in the nineteenth century, and still by no means dead, which raised the methods of natural science to the level of a universal method, and maintained that natural science was the only kind of knowledge.' Moreover, history was not a social science: 'Indeed, the attempt of the latter to formulate laws from the facts which it supposes the historian to discover produces eschatology, and not science.' In the end, history was a humanity: 'It aims ... to provide man with a knowledge of himself. It shows man what he is by showing him what he has done.' See 'Revised and Continued Interim Report of the General Committee of the Humanities Group,' Appendix on History, Authorized abstract of a statement by Dean Fieldhouse, 10 June 1949, McGill University Archives (MUA), Accession 256, Box 2-3, file Graduate Studies Misc.

29 'Discussion,' Canadian Historical Association, *Annual Report* (1942): 65–70. In 1946 Saunders stated: 'Too many of us are rootless. We have lost touch with the spiritual sources of our life. We do not know what we believe. We drift in a sea of chaos.' He therefore called for a return to the study of our values and our beliefs, a process, he believed, that was essential in the coming battle against our very way of life. The fundamental question was 'Are we to produce utilitarians or men of faith?' See Richard M. Saunders, 'Introduction,' in Saunders, ed., *Education for Tomorrow* (Toronto: University of Toronto Press, 1946): ix–xiii.

30 Reginald Trotter, 'Aims in the Study and Teaching of History in Canadian Universities Today,' Canadian Historical Association, *Annual Report* (1943): 50–60

31 Ibid.

32 'Discussion,' ibid., 60–2

33 University of Saskatchewan Archives (USA), President's Office Fonds, J.S. Thomson, RG1, Series 2, President's Report, 1937–1938, 7–8

34 Ibid., 1938–39, 9

35 Ibid., 1939–40, 9

36 George Simpson, Annual Report of College of Arts and Science, ibid., 1942–43, 16

37 USA, Annual Report, 1943–44, Department of History, RG 13 S.8, I. Departmental a) Annual Reports, 1939–40 – 1961–62

38 G.W. Simpson to Editor, *Canadian Historical Review,* 30 October 1944, UTA, University of Toronto Press, CHR Files, A86-0044, Box 5, file CHR, 25th Anniversary Letters, no. 2

39 George Wilson, 'Why Study History?' *Queen's Quarterly* 40, 3 (August 1933): 412–13. See Henry Roper, 'The Lifelong Pilgrimage of George E. Wilson, Teacher and Historian,' *Collections of the Royal Nova Scotia Historical Society* 42 (1986): 139–51.

40 George Wilson to President Mackenzie, Dalhousie University Archives (DUA), 2 August 1930, MS-1-3, President's Office Staff Files, no. 543

41 Donald Creighton to Frank Underhill, 29 September 1940, NA, Frank Underhill Papers, MG 30 D 204, vol. 3, file D.G. Creighton 1928–1956

42 George Wilson, 'Wider Horizons,' Canadian Historical Association, *Annual Report* (1951): 3

43 Edgar McInnis, 'The Contribution of the Social Sciences to the Importance of Living,' c. 1940s, York University Archives, Edgar McInnis Papers, 1973-004, Box 17

44 James F. Kenney, 'The War and the Historian,' Royal Society of Canada, *Proceedings and Transactions of the Royal Society of Canada,* 3rd series, 37 (1943): 121–9

45 A.B. McKillop, *Matters of Mind: The University in Ontario, 1791–1951* (Toronto: University of Toronto Press, 1994): 529; Wallace quotation, 531; 533

46 'Arts Courses in Wartime,' *Globe and Mail,* 24 December 1942, 6

47 Watson Kirkconnell, *A Slice of Canada: Memoirs* (Toronto: University of Toronto Press, 1967): 236

48 For a history of the CSSRC see Donald Fisher, *The Social Sciences in Canada: Fifty Years of National Activity by the Social Science Federation of Canada* (Waterloo, Ont.: Wilfrid Laurier University Press, 1991).

49 Arthur Lower to Harold Innis, 8 November 1942, QUA, Arthur Lower Papers, Box 48, C 73

50 See responses to Kirkconnell in Acadia University Archives (AUA), Watson Kirkconnell Papers, Box 45, P20/4-A

51 Watson Kirkconnell to Harold Innis, 10 December 1942, ibid.

52 Harold Innis to Watson Kirkconnell, 14 December 1942, ibid.

53 CSSRC, *Correspondence with the Prime Minister Concerning Liberal Arts Courses in Canadian Universities* (Ottawa, 1943): 10

54 Quotation in Kirkconnell, *A Slice of Canada,* 238

55 CCRSC, *Correspondence with the Prime Minister,* 11

56 RSC, *Proceedings and Transactions of the Royal Society of Canada*, series 3, vol. 37 (1943): 50

57 For a history of the HRCC see n.a., *Humanities Research Council of Canada / Canadian Federation of Humanities, 1943–1983: A Short History* (Ottawa: Canadian Federation of the Humanities, 1983).

58 Kirkconnell, *A Slice of Canada*, 240

59 Michael Gauvreau, 'Baptist Religion and the Social Science of Harold Innis,' *Canadian Historical Review* 76, 2 (June 1995): 195. Brian McKillop writes that Innis's work on 'nature and implications of communications' grew out of his nineteenth-century cultural inheritance, the moral project which 'sought to reconcile inquiry with affirmation.' See A.B. McKillop, *A Disciplined Intelligence: Critical Inquiry and Canadian Thought in the Victorian Era* (Montreal and Kingston: McGill-Queen's University Press, 1979, 2001): 230–1.

60 Harold Innis, *The Bias of Communication* (Toronto: University of Toronto Press, 1951): xvii. This question also appeared in his notes from 1948–9. See William Christian, ed., *The Idea File of Harold Adams Innis* (Toronto: University of Toronto Press, 1980): 17/21.

61 See Rick Salutin, 'Last Call from Harold Innis,' *Queen's Quarterly* 104, 2 (Summer 1997): 245–59; Judith Stamps, *Unthinking Modernity: Innis, McLuhan, and the Frankfurt School* (Montreal and Kingston: McGill-Queen's University Press, 1995); Graeme Patterson, *History and Communications: Harold Innis, Marshall McLuhan, the Interpretation of History* (Toronto: University of Toronto Press, 1990); John Watson, 'Marginal Man: Harold Innis' Communication Work in Context,' PhD thesis, University of Toronto, 1981.

62 Harold Innis, 'This Has Killed That,' *Journal of Canadian Studies* 12, 5 (Winter 1977): 5. This article is an edited version of an unpublished, undated address given by Innis sometime during the Second World War.

63 Harold Innis, 'A Plea for the University Tradition,' *Dalhousie Review* 24 (1944–45): 298–305. On Innis's determined defence of the university see Donald Creighton, *Harold Adams Innis: Portrait of a Scholar* (Toronto: University of Toronto Press, 1957): 106–16.

64 Harold Innis to John Marshall, 22 September 1947, UTA, Harold Innis Papers, B72-0025, Box 11, file 3

65 Harold Innis, 'A Plea for Time,' in Innis, *The Bias of Communication*, 61–91. This concern with the marginalization of philosophy and morality also found expression in a 1944 article in which Innis quotes a personal letter from his friend, E.J. Urwick. Urwick had written: 'The whole trend today is to exalt the rationalist scientific approach and to discard the philosophical. I am not thinking only of the worship of the physical and mechanical sciences,

but rather of the attempt to make ethics, philosophy, sociology, etc., conform in method and language to the physical sciences – with disastrous results. Specialization runs mad, and when it does so, *never* leads to understanding. Its natural result is strife and violent dogmatism.' Quotation in Harold Innis, 'Political Economy in the Modern State,' reprinted in Innis, *Political Economy in the Modern State* (Toronto: Ryerson Press, 1946): 144. For the original letter see E.J. Urwick to Harold Innis, 24 April 1944, UTA, Harold Innis Papers, B72-0025, Box 11, file 15

66 Gauvreau, 'Baptist Religion,' 199–200
67 'Notes on Values Discussion Group,' 5 April 1949, UTA, Harold Innis Papers, B72-0003, Box 30, file 5
68 Stamps, *Unthinking Modernity,* 45
69 Donald Creighton, 'Harold Adams Innis: A Special and Unique Brilliance,' in Donald Creighton, *The Passionate Observer: Selected Writings* (Toronto: McClelland and Stewart, 1980): 146. William Christian made the same observation. 'For Innis, without doubt, the most important moral fact was the value of the individual.' Christian, *The Idea File,* xv
70 Innis, *Political Economy in the Modern State,* xii
71 Hilda Neatby to George Brown, 6 November 1944, UTA, A86-0044, Box 5, file CHR, 25th Anniversary Letters, no. 1. For Neatby's defence of biography see also 'National History,' in *Royal Commission Studies: A Selection of Essays Prepared for the Royal Commission on National Development in the Arts, Letters and Sciences* (Ottawa: E. Cloutier, Printer to the King, 1951): 208–9.
72 Hilda Neatby, *So Little for the Mind* (Toronto: Clarke, Irwin, 1953): 18. See Kenneth C. Dewar, 'Hilda Neatby and the Ends of Education,' *Queen's Quarterly* 97, 1 (Spring 1990): 36–51.
73 Neatby, *So Little for the Mind,* 318, 324–5
74 Hilda Neatby, 'University Studies in a Christian Framework,' unpublished address, November 1955, Saskatchewan Archives Board, Saskatoon, Hilda Neatby Papers, A 139 VIII.202.6
75 Hilda Neatby, 'Christian Views of History: Toynbee and Butterfield,' *Proceedings and Transactions of the Royal Society of Canada,* 3rd series, 52 (June 1958): 34
76 Neatby, 'University Studies in a Christian Framework'
77 John Marshall, Interview with Anne Bezanson, Rockefeller Archives Center (RAC), Rockefeller Foundation (RF), RG 1.2, 427R, Box 14, file 128
78 Through his friendship with Henry Allen Moe of the John Simon Guggenheim Foundation, Innis secured Guggenheim Fellowships for Donald Creighton and Gerald Graham as well. See Creighton, 'Harold Adams Innis,' 152; and Paul T. Phillips, *Britain's Past in Canada: The Teaching and Writing of British History* (Vancouver: UBC Press, 1989): 130.

79 Frank Underhill to John Marshall, 7 April 1943, RAC, RF, RG 2, 427R, Box 256, file 1767
80 John Marshall, Memorandum, 15 April 1943, ibid.
81 John Marshall, Interview with F.H. Underhill, 20 April 1943, ibid. Underhill and Marshall also thought Abbé Maheux would be a suitable choice for French Canada. Although he expressed an interest, in the end Maheux was not funded.
82 John Marshall to Donald Creighton, 22 April 1943, RAC, RF, RG 1.2, 427R, Box 14, file 128
83 Donald Creighton to John Marshall, 10 May 1943, ibid.
84 Donald Creighton to John Marshall, 9 June 1943, ibid.
85 John Marshall to Donald Creighton, 11 June 1943, ibid.
86 Donald Creighton to John Marshall, 6 January 1943, ibid.
87 Donald Creighton to John Marshall, 5 January 1944, ibid.
88 John Marshall, Interview with Donald Creighton, 22 March 1944, ibid.
89 Carl Berger, *The Writing of Canadian History: Aspects of English-Canadian Historical Writing since 1900*, 2nd ed. (Toronto: University of Toronto Press, 1986): 127
90 Donald Creighton to John Marshall, 31 March 1944, RAC, RF, RG 1.2, 427R, Box 14, file 128
91 John Marshall to Donald Creighton, 4 April 1944, ibid.
92 Action Report, 19 May 1944, ibid. Nine years later the RF provided Creighton with a $2,000 grant to complete the archival research in England. Action Report, 14 January 1953, ibid.
93 Donald Creighton to John Marshall, 21 April 1944, ibid.
94 Donald Creighton, 'The Writing of Canadian History,' Founders' Day Address, University of New Brunswick, 19 February 1945, 16. Copy in University of New Brunswick Archives and Special Collections. Arthur Lower said much the same thing. 'When all the impersonal factors are set out, a large gap still remains, for history, after all, consists in the inter-action, not of blind forces, but of human beings. It is the role of individuals which is of ultimate significance.' Lower, *Colony to Nation*, 319–20.
95 Berger, *The Writing of Canadian History*, 220. For a similar argument about biography today see Sven Birkerts, 'Losing Ourselves in Biography,' *Harper's Magazine* (March 1995): 24–6.
96 Frank Underhill could not resist the temptation to score one off Creighton. It was an easy shot and he took it. Only 'Communists and a diehard remnant of Tories go about talking of "American Imperialism." Well, no, this isn't quite correct. There are also those academic intellectuals in our universities who are still thinking up nasty wisecracks about American imperialism

regardless of the fact that most of their own pet research projects are apt to be financed by money from Rockefeller or Carnegie or Guggenheim.' Frank Underhill, 'Concerning Mr. King,' *Canadian Forum* 30, 356 (September 1950): 122

97 Creighton, 'The Writing of Canadian History,' 16

98 Arthur Lower could not have agreed more. Historians, he said, have failed to reach a wider audience. They must strive to write for the 'general public' and to 'bind' Canadians together through their writing. 'That will probably be the chief task of the Canadian historian.' See 'Discussion,' Canadian Historical Association, *Annual Report* (1945): 13–14.

99 Transcript of CBC Interview with Paul Fox, 1959, NA, Frank Underhill Papers, MG 30 D 204, vol. 34, file 172. In a special study prepared for the Royal Commission on National Development in the Arts, Letters and Science, W.L. Morton made the same point. 'It might be,' he wrote, 'that such activities [the promotion of popular history] by the larger [historical] societies would help to soften the rigid professionalism of Canadian historians. The situation must not develop that the scholar will win most reputation and gain promotion most quickly by writing a book for other scholars. There are ought to be such books ... but if history is to play a role in Canadian culture, then some historical books must be written to be read by laymen, and must be written to please by their art and insight.' W.L. Morton, 'Historical Societies and Museums,' in *Royal Commission Studies*, 253. In 1950 the Canadian Historical Association created a Local History Section for the encouragement and improvement of local history. A year later, the CHA launched the Historical Booklets series in an attempt to reach high-school history teachers.

100 W.K. Ferguson, 'Some Problems of Historiography,' Canadian Historical Association, *Annual Report* (1961): 8–9

Conclusion

1 See A.B. McKillop, ed., *A Critical Spirit: The Thought of William Dawson LeSueur* (Toronto: McClelland and Stewart, 1977); and W.D. LeSueur, 'History: Its Nature and Methods,' *Proceedings and Transactions of the Royal Society of Canada*, 3rd Series, 7 (1913): Appendix A

2 See A.B. McKillop, *A Disciplined Intelligence: Critical Inquiry and Canadian Thought in the Victorian Era* (Montreal and Kingston: McGill-Queen's University Press, 1979, 2001).

3 Hilda Neatby, 'National History,' in *Royal Commission Studies: A Selection of*

Essays Prepared for the Royal Commission on National Development in the Arts, Letters and Sciences (Ottawa: E. Clatier, Printer to the King, 1951): 205–16

4 J.R. Miller, 'The Invisible Historian,' *Journal of the Canadian Historical Association* 8 (1997): 3–18

5 See W.S. Wallace, 'Some Vices of Clio,' *Canadian Historical Review* 7, 2 (June 1926): 197–203.

6 W.K. Ferguson, 'Some Problems of Historiography,' Canadian Historical Association, *Annual Report* (1961): 8

7 Arthur Lower in A.B. Corey, R.G. Trotter, and W.W. McLaren, eds, *Conference on Canadian-American Affairs, 1939: Proceedings* (Boston: Ginn, 1939): 153

8 George Wrong, 'The Historian and Society,' *Canadian Historical Review* 14, 1 (March 1933): 7

9 Eric Hobsbawm, *Age of Extremes: The Short Twentieth Century, 1914–1991* (London: Abacus, 1994): 3

Bibliography

This bibliography lists only primary sources. The secondary sources consulted can be found in the notes.

Archival Sources

Acadia University Archives (AUA)
Watson Kirkconnell Papers
Ronald Longley Papers

Archives of Ontario (AO)
William Canniff Papers
Lennox and Addington Historical Society Fonds
Lundy's Lane Historical Society Fonds
Niagara Historical Society Fonds
Ontario Historical Society Fonds
Women's Canadian Historical Society of Toronto Fonds

Brock University Special Collections
Women's Literary Club of St Catharines Fonds

Bytown Museum Archives, Ottawa
Women's Canadian Historical Society of Ottawa Fonds

Canadian Baptist Archives, McMaster University (CBA)
McMaster University Chancellor's Reports

Columbia University, Rare Book and Manuscript Library (CUL)
J. Bartlet Brebner Papers
Carnegie Endowment for International Peace (CEIP)
James Shotwell Rapers

Dalhousie University Archives (DUA)
President's Office Staff Files

J.J. Talman Regional Collection, University of Western Ontario (JJTRC-UWO)
J.H. Coyne Papers
Wallace K. Ferguson Papers
Fred Landon Papers
J.J. Talman Papers
University of Western Ontario Scrap Books

McCord Museum of Canadian History, Archives
McCord Family Papers

McGill University Archives (MUA)
E.R. Adair Papers
John Irwin Cooper Papers
Department of History

McGill University, Department of Rare Books and Special Collections (MURBSC)
W.D. Lighthall Papers

Mount Allison University Archives
Administrative Records, Subject Correspondence

National Archives (NA)
Robert Laird Borden Papers
A.L. Burt Papers
Canadian Historical Association (CHA) Fonds
Donald Creighton Papers
A.G. Doughty Papers
Norman Fee Papers
Eugene Forse Papers
W.L. Grant Papers
Gustave Lanctôt Papers
Historic Landmarks Association (HLA) Fonds

W.D. LeSueur Papers
W.D. Lighthall Papers
George Parkin Papers
L.B. Pearson Papers
Royal Commission on National Development in the Arts,
    Letters and Sciences Fonds
H.M. Tory Papers
Frank Underhill Papers
J.C. Webster Papers
William Wood Papers

New Brunswick Museum Archives (NBMA)
W.F. Ganong Papers
J.C. Webster Papers

Public Archives of Nova Scotia (PANS)
D.C. Harvey Papers

Queen's University Archives (QUA)
Arthur Lower Papers
Lorne Pierce Papers
Adam Shortt Papers
Reginald Trotter Papers

Rockefeller Archives Center (RAC)
Rockefeller Foundation (RF)
Social Sciences Research Council (SSRC)

Saskatchewan Archives Board, Saskatoon (SABS)
J.M. Hayden Papers
Hilda Neatby Papers

Stanstead Historical Society Archives
Colby Fonds

Thomas Fisher Rare Book Room, University of Toronto (TFRBR-UT)
George Wrong Papers
Chester Martin Papers
W.S. Wallace Papers

University of Alberta Archives (UAA)
Department of History and Classics
History Club
Lewis G. Thomas Papers
Lewis H. Thomas Papers

University of British Columbia Archives (UBCA)
S. Mack Eastman Papers
W.N. Sage Papers

Université du Québec à Montréal, Service des archives et de gestion des documents
Stanley Bréhaut Ryerson Fonds

University of Manitoba Archives (UMA)
Department of History, Annual Reports

University of New Brunswick Archives (UNBA)
A.G. Bailey Papers
W.S. MacNutt Papers

University of Saskatchewan Archives (USA)
J.M. Hayden Papers
A.S. Morton Papers
Jean Murray Papers
E.H. Oliver Papers
President's Office Fonds

University of Toronto Archives (UTA)
Robert Bothwell Papers
Jean Burnet, Oral History
Canadian Historical Association, Committee on Historical Broadcasting
J.M.S. Careless, Oral History
James Conacher, Oral History
Department of English
Department of History
Harold Innis Papers
Gerry Riddell Papers
R. Saunders, Oral History
Charles Stacey Papers
University Historian
University of Toronto Press, Canadian Historical Review

William Ready Division, Archives and Research Collections, McMaster University
Board of Governors, McMaster University
Macmillan Company of Canada Fonds
W.L. Morton Papers

York University Archives (YUA)
Edgar McInnis Papers

Interviews
Margaret Banks
J.M.S. Careless
Jill Ker Conway
W.J. Eccles
David Farr
James A. Gibson
Irene Spry
Sylvia Van Kirk
Peter Waite

Printed Sources

University Calendars
Acadia University
Dalhousie University
McGill University
McMaster University
Mount Allison University
Queen's University
University of Alberta
University of British Columbia
University Manitoba
University of Saskatchewan
University of Toronto
University of Western Ontario

Articles
Adair, E.R. 'Dollard des Ormeaux and the Fight at the Long Sault.' *Canadian Historical Review* 13, 2 (June 1932)
– 'The Military Reputation of Major-General James Wolfe.' Canadian Historical Association, *Annual Report* (1936)

- 'The Study of History at McGill University.' *Culture* 2, 1 (March 1941)
- 'The Canadian Contribution to Historical Science.' *Culture* 4, 1 (March 1943)
Brebner, John Bartlet. 'Canadianism.' Canadian Historical Association, *Annual Report* (1940)
- 'Uses and Abuses of History.' *Dalhousie Review* 24 (1944–5)
Burpee, Lawrence. 'Co-operation in Historical Research.' *University Magazine* 7, 3 (October 1908)
- 'Presidential Address.' Historic Landmarks Association of Canada, *Annual Report* (1921)
- 'Professor Morton and La Vérendrye.' *Canadian Historical Review* 10, 1 (March 1929)
Burt, A.L. 'On the Study of History.' 1927; reprinted in Lewis Thomas, *The Renaissance of Canadian History: A Biography of A.L. Burt.* Toronto: University of Toronto Press, 1975
- 'The Need for a Wider Study of Canadian History.' Department of Extension of the University of Alberta, *Press Bulletin* 9, 5 (23 November 1923)
Brown, George, and Donald Creighton. 'Canadian History in Retrospect and Prospect.' *Canadian Historical Review* 25, 4 (December 1944)
Burnet, Jean. 'Minorities I Have Belonged To.' *Canadian Ethnic Studies* 13, 1 (1981)
Carnochan, Janet. 'Some Mistakes in History.' *Ontario Historical Society: Papers and Records* 13 (1915)
Colby, Charles. 'History and Patriotism.' *Proceedings of the Canadian Club, 1904–1905.* Toronto, 1905
Creighton, Donald. 'Presidential Address.' Canadian Historical Association, *Annual Report* (1957)
- 'The Ogdensburg Agreement and F.H. Underhill.' In Carl Berger and Ramsay Cook, eds. *The West and the Nation: Essays in Honour of W.L. Morton.* Toronto: McClelland and Stewart, 1976
Cruikshank, E.A. 'The Study of History and the Interpretation of Documents.' *Proceedings and Transactions of the Royal Society of Canada,* 3rd series, 15 (1921)
Curzon, Sarah. 'Historical Societies.' *Journal and Transactions of the Wentworth Historical Society* 1 (1892)
Eccles, W.J. 'Forty Years Back' *William and Mary Quarterly* 41, 3 (July 1984)
Fieldhouse, Noel. 'The Failure of Historians.' Canadian Historical Association, *Annual Report* (1942)
Grant, W.L. 'The Study of History in Ontario.' *Canadian Magazine* 22, 5 (March 1904)
- 'The Teaching of Colonial History.' *Queen's Quarterly* 18, 3 (January 1911)

Harvey, D.C. 'The Importance of Local History in the Writing of General History.' *Canadian Historical Review* 13, 3 (September 1932)

Innis, Harold. 'The Role of Intelligence: Some Further Notes.' *Canadian Journal of Economics and Political Science* 1, 2 (May 1935)

– 'A Note on Universities and the Social Sciences.' *Canadian Journal of Economics and Political Science* 1, 2 (May 1935)

– 'Discussion in the Social Sciences.' *Dalhousie Review* 15 (January 1936)

– 'A Plea for the University Tradition.' *Dalhousie Review* 24 (1944–5)

Kenney, James F. 'The War and the Historian.' *Proceedings and Transactions of the Royal Society of Canada,* 3rd series, 37 (1943)

Lanctôt, Gustave. 'Was Dollard the Saviour of New France?' *Canadian Historical Review* 13, 2 (June 1932)

LeSueur, W.D. 'Science and Materialism.' 1877; reprinted in A.B. McKillop, ed., *A Critical Spirit: The Thought of William Dawson LeSueur.* Toronto: McClelland and Stewart, 1977

– 'The Scientific Spirit.' 1879; reprinted in A.B. McKillop, ed., *A Critical Spirit: The Thought of William Dawson LeSueur.* Toronto: McClelland and Stewart, 1977

– 'History: Its Nature and Methods.' *Proceedings and Transactions of the Royal Society of Canada,* 3rd series, 7 (1913)

Lighthall, W.D. 'A New Hochelagan Burying-Ground discovered at Westmount on the Western Spur of Mont Royal, Montreal, July–September 1898.' Montreal: n.p., 1898

Loudon, James. 'The Universities in Relation to Research.' *Proceedings and Transactions of the Royal Society of Canada,* 2nd series, 8 (1902)

Lower, Arthur. 'Some Neglected Aspects of Canadian History.' Canadian Historical Association, *Annual Report* (1929)

– 'The Social Sciences in the Post-War World.' *Canadian Historical Review* 22, 1 (March 1941)

– 'Time, Myth and Fact – The Historian's Commodities.' *Queen's Quarterly* 64, 2 (Summer 1957)

– 'Harold Innis as I Remember Him.' *Journal of Canadian Studies* 20, 4 (Winter 1985–6)

Martin, Chester. 'Fifty Years of Canadian History.' In *Royal Society of Canada: Fifty Years Retrospect.* Ottawa, 1932

McArthur, Duncan. 'The Teaching of Canadian History' Ontario Historical Society, *Papers and Records* 21 (1924)

Miller, J.R. 'The Invisible Historian.' *Journal of the Canadian Historical Association* 8 (1997)

Morison, J.L. 'Some Recent Historical Literature: European and British' *Queen's Quarterly* 19, 3 (January 1912)

Morton, A.S. 'La Vérendrye: Commandant, Fur-Trader, and Explorer.' *Canadian Historical Review* 9, 4 (December 1928)

Morton, W.L. 'Historical Societies and Museums.' In *Royal Commission Studies: A Selection of Essays Prepared for the Royal Commission on National Development in the Arts, Letters and Sciences.* Ottawa: E. Cloutier, Printer to the King, 1951

Neatby, Hilda. 'National History.' In *Royal Commission Studies: A Selection of Essays Prepared for the Royal Commission on National Development in the Arts, Letters and Sciences*, Ottawa: E. Cloutier, Printer to the King, 1951

– 'Christian Views of History: Toynbee and Butterfield.' *Proceedings and Transactions of the Royal Society of Canada,* 3rd series, 52 (June 1958)

Preston, Richard. 'Is Local History Really History?' *Saskatchewan History* 10, 3 (1957)

Shortt, Adam. 'Social Evolution, According to Mr. Kidd.' *Queen's Quarterly* 2, 4 (April 1895)

– 'The Aims of the Canadian Political Science Association.' *Proceedings, Canadian Political Science Association* (1913)

– 'The Significance for Canadian History of the Work of the Board of Historical Publications' *Proceedings and Transactions of the Royal Society of Canada.* 3rd series, 13 (1919)

Shotwell, James T. 'A Personal Note on the Theme of Canadian-American Relations' *Canadian Historical Review* 28, 1 (March 1947)

Smith, Pemberton. 'President's Address.' Historic Landmarks Association, *Annual Report* (1915)

Trotter, Reginald. 'Aims in the Study and Teaching of History in Canadian Universities Today,' Canadian Historical Association, *Annual Report* (1943)

Tweedsmuir, Lady. 'The Amateur Historian.' *Canadian Historical Review* 20, 1 (March 1939)

Underhill, Frank. 'Canadian and American History – And Historians.' *Canadian Forum* 8, 93 (June 1928)

– 'On Professors and Politics,' *Canadian Forum* 15, 182 (March 1934)

– 'The Conception of a National Interest' *Canadian Journal of Economics and Political Science* 1, 3 (August 1935)

Wallace, W.S. 'Some Vices of Clio.' *Canadian Historical Review* 7, 2 (June 1926)

Williams, R. Hodder. 'The Tutorial Experiment.' *University of Toronto Monthly* 15, 4 (February 1915)

Wilson, George. 'Why Teach History?' *Queen's Quarterly* 40, 3 (August 1933)

Wrong, George. 'History in Canadian Secondary Schools' American Historical Association, *Annual Report* (1898)

– 'A College for Women.' *University of Toronto Monthly* 10, 1 (November 1909)

- 'The Historian's Problem.' Canadian Historical Association, *Annual Report* (1927)
- 'The Historian and Society.' *Canadian Historical Review* 14, 1 (March 1933)
- 'What Has Befallen Us.' *University of Toronto Quarterly* 4, 1 (1934–5)
'The Beginnings of Historical Criticism in Canada: A Retrospect, 1896–1936.' *Canadian Historical Review* 17, 1 (March 1936)

Books

Bourinot, John G. *Canada under British Rule, 1760–1900*. Cambridge: Cambridge University Press, 1900
Colby, Charles, *Canadian Types of the Old Régime, 1608–1698*. New York: Henry Holt, 1908
Creighton, Donald. *British North America at Confederation*. Ottawa, 1939
- *The Passionate Observer: Selected Writings*. Toronto: McClelland and Stewart, 1980
Ferns, H.S. *Reading from Left to Right: One Man's Political History*. Toronto: University of Toronto Press, 1983
Innis, Harold. *The Bias of Communication*. Toronto: University of Toronto Press, 1951
Kirkconnell, Watson. *A Slice of Canada: Memoirs*. Toronto: University of Toronto Press, 1967
LeSueur, W.D. *William Lyon Mackenzie: A Reinterpretation*. Edited and with an introduction by A.B. McKillop. Toronto: Macmillan, 1979
Lighthall, W.D. *An Account of the Battle of Chateauguay*. Montreal: W. Drysdale, 1889
- *The Master of Life: A Romance of the Five Nations and of Prehistoric Montreal*. Toronto: Musson, 1908
- *The Young Seigneur, or Nation Making*. Montreal: Wm Drysdale, 1888
Lower, Arthur. *Colony to Nation: A History of Canada*. Toronto: Longmans, Green, 1946
- *My First Seventy-five Years*. Toronto: Macmillan, 1967
McNaught, Kenneth. *Conscience and History: A Memoir*. University of Toronto Press, 1999
Neatby, Hilda. *So Little for the Mind*. Toronto: Clarke, Irwin, 1953
Newman, Albert Henry. *A Manual of Church History*. Vol. 1. Philadelphia: American Baptist Society, 1900
Pearson, Lester B. *Mike: The Memoirs of the Right Honourable Lester B. Pearson*. Vol. 1: *1897–1948*. Toronto: University of Toronto Press, 1972
Saunders, Richard, ed. *Education for Tomorrow*. Toronto: University of Toronto Press, 1946

Shotwell, James T. *The Autobiography of James T. Shotwell.* New York: Bobbs-Merrill, 1961

Sirluck, Ernest. *First Generation: An Autobiography.* Toronto: University of Toronto Press, 1996

Smith, Goldwin. *Canada and the Canada Question.* 1891. Toronto: University of Toronto Press, 1971

Stacey, C.P. *A Date with History.* Ottawa: Deneau, 1982

Wallace, W.S. *The Story of Laura Secord: A Study in Historical Evidence.* Toronto: Macmillan, 1932

Waugh, W.T. *James Wolfe: Man and Soldier.* Montreal, New York: Louis Carrier, 1928

Wilson, George Earle. *All for Nothing?* 1972. A copy of this self-published memoir is located in the Dalhousie University Archives, MS-1-Ref.

Wrong, George. *Application and Testimonials of George M. Wrong, BA, for the post of Professor of History in the University of Toronto.* Toronto, 1894

– *Historical Study in the University: An Inaugural Lecture.* Toronto: Bryant Press, 1895

Index